MW01240968

The Official CompTIA DataSys+ Study Guide (Exam DS0-001)

Course Edition: 1.0

Acknowledgments

CompTIA.

Robin E. Hunt, ThinkData Solutions, Inc., Author

Daniel Bishop, ThinkData Solutions, Inc., Author

Todd Miranda, Author

Becky Mann, Senior Director, Product Development

James Chesterfield, Senior Manager, User Experience and Design

Alyssa Lincoln, Senior Manager, Product Development

Notices

Disclaimer

While CompTIA, Inc. takes care to ensure the accuracy and quality of these materials, we cannot guarantee their accuracy, and all materials are provided without any warranty whatsoever, including, but not limited to, the implied warranties of merchantability or fitness for a particular purpose. The use of screenshots, photographs of another entity's products, or another entity's product name or service in this book is for editorial purposes only. No such use should be construed to imply sponsorship or endorsement of the book by nor any affiliation of such entity with CompTIA. This courseware may contain links to sites on the Internet that are owned and operated by third parties (the "External Sites"). CompTIA is not responsible for the availability of, or the content located on or through, any External Site. Please contact CompTIA if you have any concerns regarding such links or External Sites.

Trademark Notice

CompTIA®, DataSys+®, and the CompTIA logo are registered trademarks of CompTIA, Inc., in the United States and other countries. All other product and service names used may be common law or registered trademarks of their respective proprietors.

Copyright Notice

Copyright © 2023 CompTIA, Inc. All rights reserved. Screenshots used for illustrative purposes are the property of the software proprietor. Except as permitted under the Copyright Act of 1976, no part of this publication may be reproduced or distributed in any form or by any means, or stored in a database or retrieval system, without the prior written permission of CompTIA, 3500 Lacey Road, Suite 100, Downers Grove, IL 60515-5439.

This book conveys no rights in the software or other products about which it was written; all use or licensing of such software or other products is the responsibility of the user according to terms and conditions of the owner. If you believe that this book, related materials, or any other CompTIA materials are being reproduced or transmitted without permission, please call 1-866-835-8020 or visit **https://help.comptia.org**.

Table of Contents

About This Course

CompTIA is a not-for-profit trade association with the purpose of advancing the interests of IT professionals and IT channel organizations. Its industry-leading IT certifications are an important part of that mission. CompTIA's DataSys+ certification is a foundation-level certification designed for professionals with two to three years of work experience as a database administrator or database manager.

> This exam will certify the successful candidate has the knowledge and skills required to deploy, manage, and maintain databases, including employing the fundamentals of scripting and programming in a database environment while using security and business continuity best practices.
>
> *CompTIA DataSys+ Exam Objectives*

Course Description

Course Objectives

This course can benefit you in two ways. If you intend to pass the CompTIA DataSys+ (Exam DS0-001) certification examination, this course can be a significant part of your preparation. But certification is not the only key to professional success in the field of database administration. Today's job market demands individuals with demonstrable skills, and the information and activities in this course can help you build your database administration skill set so that you can confidently perform your duties in any DBA role.

On course completion, you will be able to do the following:

- Understand database types and structures.

- Recognize standards and commands.

- Run scripts for data and data systems.

- Explain the impact of programming on database operations.

- Understand database planning and design.

- Implement, test, and deploy databases.

- Monitor and report on database performance.

- Understand common data maintenance processes.

- Understand governance and regulatory compliance.

- Secure data.

- Secure data access.

- Secure the database and server.

- Classify types of attacks.

- Plan for disaster recovery.

- Implement backup and restore best practices.

Target Student

The Official CompTIA DataSys+ (Exam DS0-001) is the primary course you will need to take if your job responsibilities include managing, maintaining, and securing data in one or more data systems, with consideration for data storage, organization, presentation, utilization, and analysis from a technical perspective. You can take this course to prepare for the CompTIA DataSys+ (Exam DS0-001) certification examination.

Prerequisites

To ensure your success in this course, you should have two to three years of hands-on experience working as a database administrator.

The prerequisites for this course might differ significantly from the prerequisites for the CompTIA certification exams. For the most up-to-date information about the exam prerequisites, complete the form on this page: www.comptia.org/training/resources/exam-objectives.

How to Use the Study Notes

The following notes will help you understand how the course structure and components are designed to support mastery of the competencies and tasks associated with the target job roles and will help you to prepare to take the certification exam.

As You Learn

At the top level, this course is divided into **lessons**, each representing an area of competency within the target job roles. Each lesson is composed of a number of topics. A **topic** contains subjects that are related to a discrete job task, mapped to objectives and content examples in the CompTIA exam objectives document. Rather than follow the exam domains and objectives sequence, lessons and topics are arranged in order of increasing proficiency. Each topic is intended to be studied within a short period (typically 30 minutes at most). Each topic is concluded by one or more activities that are designed to help you to apply your understanding of the study notes to practical scenarios and tasks.

Additional to the study content in the lessons, there is a glossary of the terms and concepts used throughout the course. There is also an index to assist in locating particular terminology, concepts, technologies, and tasks within the lesson and topic content.

In many electronic versions of the book, you can click links on key words in the topic content to move to the associated glossary definition, and on page references in the index to move to that term in the content. To return to the previous location in the document after clicking a link, use the appropriate functionality in your e-book viewing software.

Watch throughout the material for the following visual cues.

 A **Note** provides additional information, guidance, or hints about a topic or task.

 A **Caution** note makes you aware of places where you need to be particularly careful with your actions, settings, or decisions so that you can be sure to get the desired results of an activity or task.

As You Review

Any method of instruction is only as effective as the time and effort you, the student, are willing to invest in it. In addition, some of the information that you learn in class may not be important to you immediately, but it may become important later. For this reason, we encourage you to spend some time reviewing the content of the course after your time in the classroom.

Following the lesson content, you will find a table mapping the lessons and topics to the exam domains, objectives, and content examples. You can use this as a checklist as you prepare to take the exam and to review any content that you are uncertain about.

As a Reference

The organization and layout of this book make it an easy-to-use resource for future reference. Guidelines can be used during class and as after-class references when you're back on the job and need to refresh your understanding. Taking advantage of the glossary, index, and table of contents, you can use this book as a first source of definitions, background information, and summaries.

Lesson 1

Understanding Database Types and Structures

LESSON INTRODUCTION

Database administrators work with databases in many different ways. They maintain data, maintain databases, write queries, and analyze and report on data. In order to perform all these various actions, you must first understand the basic foundations of databases. It is important to have a solid understanding of what differentiates relational from non-relational databases. In this lesson, you will discover the different NoSQL options that support applications of many different types and will also learn about different data systems, like data warehouses and data lakes.

Lesson Objectives

In this lesson, you will do the following:

- Identify relational and non-relational databases.

- Understand different types of NoSQL databases and tools.

- Understand relational database design.

- Identify other data systems.

Topic 1A

Identify Relational and Non-Relational Databases

 EXAM OBJECTIVES COVERED
1.1 Compare and contrast database structure types.

Database administrators must be able to work within existing databases, creating objects like tables and views, as well as develop new databases. Familiarizing yourself with the design theory of databases will help you to understand and accurately interpret them. Here, we will cover the key characteristics of the two main types of databases: relational and non-relational.

Relational Databases

If you are already working in the data field, whether as a database administrator, data analyst, or even a data worker, then you have likely been exposed to relational databases and the software used to maintain them. If you haven't, we'll walk you through the basics. A **relational database** uses tables to store data that is captured. You might also note that this type of format is often referred to as tabular schema, due to the rows and columns it employs. Software that maintains relational databases is often referred to as a **relational database management system (RDBMS)**.

Tables are created with fields, often called field names, and each row is a record of data. Tables in a relational database have two main design components: the field name and the data type.

Department Table Design and Data in Microsoft SQL Server Management Studio
(Used with permission from Microsoft.)

In the screenshot above, you see the design in the top-left side that shows the column name, data type, and additional setting of whether to allow null values. In the results section, you see the data that is stored in this table based on the table design.

Tables are designed in a manner to efficiently store and display data, either for reporting purposes or for further use within an application.

There is often a great amount of time spent designing a relational database. Database architects must determine what data needs to be stored and how to relate the tables of data to each other through relationships.

Structured query language (SQL) is the language used to query and manage data in a relational database. SQL is a programming language for data; it's not a single software, which is important to remember. Just like any spoken language, there are different forms of SQL. For example, when using SQL in Microsoft, you are likely using T-SQL, which has additional coding elements that are specific to Microsoft software.

When you retrieve data from relational databases, there is usually some version of SQL involved in the process, whether you are coding it directly through SQL statements or using an interface that is coding it in the background for you.

Non-Relational Databases

A **non-relational database**, often referred to as NoSQL, is any alternative to a relational SQL database. This type of database addresses the need for web-based databases to handle large amounts of traffic and data, and is easier to scale for web applications.

A non-relational database does not use the same tabular schema (rows and columns) that you find in relational databases. Whereas a relational database contains tables with defined relationships, non-relational databases store their data in several different ways depending on the type of data required by a specific development. A non-relational database is more flexible than a relational database, and it is ideal for data that doesn't fit into the more rigid structure of a relational database.

The way we retrieve data from non-relational databases also differs from the way we do this for relational databases. While relational databases require traditional SQL-based queries, you will often use different programming languages to retrieve the data you need from a non-relational database.

There are four basic categories of NoSQL databases.

- **Document-oriented databases** store data in XML documents or JavaScript Object Notation (JSON). They are flexible in that they allow developers to reshape the data to meet the format needed for the application.

- **Key-value stores** store each value with a key value. This is similar to a table with just two columns: a field (key) and value.

- **Column-oriented databases** store data in columns rather than rows. This design can make for easier analysis in some cases, such as when counting the total number of orders.

- **Graph databases** store individual elements as nodes. This type of database is more complex and focuses on the relationships among data elements. In a graph database, the connections are first-class elements of the database and stored directly. You will often find that graph databases run side by side with a relational database.

When software developers create a new application, they must make many decisions, each carrying their own set of pros and cons. Arguably the most important decision they'll need to make (outside of software development process in general) is what type of database structure will work best for the data it will hold. NoSQL databases offer large volume, velocity, and a variety of data formats. They are often faster for scaling and can have better performance than the traditional relational data system.

However, they are not without their drawbacks; they often require everyone on the team (including database administrators and the developers themselves) to learn new languages, and are typically not as general purpose as a relational database. Relational databases are often designed with not only the data capture in mind, but also the reporting. However, they require thorough planning.

Key Differences Between Database Structure Types

As a database administrator, how a database is designed, and in particular how it stores data, determines how you will work with that database. This will also determine which tools you will use when doing so. There are a few key differences between the two types of databases that bear repeating in a direct comparison.

Relational Database	Non-Relational Database
Contains tables that store fields in columns, and rows of records that hold data	Store their data in several different ways depending on the type of data required by a specific development
Must be thoroughly designed and not as easy to scale	Can easily be built and scaled for web-based applications
Uses primary and foreign keys to establish relationships that control how certain data relates to data in other tables	Uses key value pairs designed to work for the data being stored
Leverages normalization techniques for optimal design	Does not require detailed planning and structure to build
Uses traditional SQL language to query and handle transactions within the database	Uses various programming languages to retrieve and handle transactions within the stored data
Expects data to fit within the tables that are designed for the database	Can store structured and unstructured data with more flexibility

Simplified Comparison of Relational vs. Non-Relational Databases

Review Activity:

Relational and Non-Relational Databases

Answer the following questions:

1. A relational database uses _____ to establish relationships that control how certain data relates to data in other tables.

2. A non-relational database is often referred to as what?

3. What are the four basic categories of non-relational databases?

4. Which category of non-relational database tends to run alongside a relational database?

5. What type of software maintains relational databases?

Topic 1B

Understand Different Types of NoSQL Databases and Tools

 EXAM OBJECTIVES COVERED
1.1 Compare and contrast database structure types.

Relational databases use tabular models to store data, meaning they have tables with defined fields and records. Just like NoSQL databases, relational databases can handle large amounts of transactions, but they are not always the best choice for massive data sets in real time with growing and ever-changing requirements. In this case, and in others, NoSQL is a good alternative to a relational SQL database. NoSQL databases address the need for web-based databases to handle large amounts of traffic and data, and are easier to scale for web applications. Each NoSQL type has different benefits, and there are also many tools available for the various types of NoSQL databases.

Document-Oriented Databases

Whereas a relational database stores data in table structures, a document-oriented database stores information in documents, hence making it non-relational. Documents will use field-value pairs stored in a document, but you can also store documents into collections.

Let's use a fictional toy company to walk through an example. In a document-oriented database, you might have a document that contains user information. For each user, the document stores their data in field-value pairs, or **key-value pairs**. (This is why a document-oriented database is known as a simple key-value store, or a key-value database.) The snippet of JSON code below defines a user record with an ID of 1, the person's name, their email, and their cell number.

```
{
    "_id": 1,
    "first_name": "Daniel",
    "last_name": "Bishop",
    "email": "daniel@thinkdatasolutions.com",
    "cell": "205-855-8555",
}
```

This is a very flexible model, because fields can be different for documents. For example, consider the next code sample below. You should note that while it includes all of the same information as the screenshot above, we can also see this user's preferences (toy trucks, block toys, and garden toys).

```
{
    "_id": 2,
    "first_name": "Robin",
    "last_name": "Hunt",
    "email": "robin@thinkdatasolutions.com",
    "cell": "205-555-5555",
    "prefers": [
        "toy trucks",
        "block toys",
        "garden toys"
    ]
}
```

As you can see from this example, a document-oriented database is more flexible in what information it can contain, unlike a relational database that has a rigid, defined table structure. And while relational databases store information in various tables, a document-oriented database stores different information in different documents (as the name suggests). A group of documents with content that would be considered similar in nature is known as a **collection**. Whereas a relational database will have a table of users, with records for each user, a document-oriented database may store all user documents in a collection called "Users."

Key-Value Stores

A **key-value store** is a set of key-value pairs. A key-value pair consists of two related data elements: a key, which is a constant that defines the data set, and a value, which is a variable that belongs to the set. You can consider a key-value pair to be a general form of an array, which charts the relationship between a key index and its values.

A key-value store uses the relationships between key-value pairs to store and analyze data. Programmers use key-value stores to store data quickly and provide ways to retrieve and update data within a database. Key-value stores are much more flexible than other database storage systems because they store data in an array, which can accommodate different data types and dimensions, as opposed to other databases that store data in tables.

A phone number directory is a good example of how key-value pairs can be used to store data. The key, in this case, is the name of a person or business, and the values are their phone numbers. The directory is easy to scan because the keys are in one row and the values are in another. You can scan the names, or the keys, in order to find the correct phone number or values.

Due to the simplicity of key-value pairs, it's easy to write to them and read from them. The quicker and easier it is to scan and process information, the more scalable the database is. Using key-value pairs in a database fosters scalability due to how easy it allows for the processing of data pairs. Further, key-value stores are easy to program and do not require the same design requirements as a relational database.

Whereas document-oriented databases store values in documents, key-value stores store the data in memory. It's important to note that when navigating a key-value store, you can't search for the values themselves, but you *can* search for the keys, to then gain the values. In our phone number example, we cannot search for a specific phone number, but we could search for the key value for the business phone number.

Column-Oriented Databases

Column-oriented databases store data in columns rather than rows. They may also be referred to as columnar databases or wide-column databases. Column-oriented databases are often used for complex analysis and queries, as they can make for easier analysis in some situations, such as when counting the total number of orders.

Product ID	Product Class	Product Type Name	Product Name	Total Order
1101	Accessory	Gloves	Active Outdoors Crochet Glove	36811.67
1106	Accessory	Gloves	Active Outdoors Lycra Glove	30365.41
101151	Bicycle	Competition	Descent	245137.83
103151	Bicycle	Competition	Endorphin	103390.50

Data Stored in Rows

A notable difference between a relational database (above) and a column-oriented database (below) is certainly the direction of the stored data. What this switch really means is that instead of each row being a record, as it is in a relational database, each column is a record in a column-oriented database.

Product ID	1101	1106	101151	103151
Product Class	Accessory	Accessory	Bicycle	Bicycle
Product Type Name	Gloves	Gloves	Competition	Competition
Product Name	Active Outdoors Crochet Glove	Active Outdoors Lycra Glove	Descent	Endorphin
Total Order	36811.67	30365.41	245137.83	103390.50

Data Stored in Columns

This database type is not ideal for all types of data. It works well for **online analytical processing (OLAP)**, such as complex queries and the analysis of big data, but would not be a good choice for **online transactional processing (OLTP)**, such as ATM transactions. This is due to how the data is retrieved from the data system.

A DBA would not typically pull an entire record for their needs; they would choose a subset of columns. When the data is stored in this manner, we can more efficiently pull the data. This is ideal when working with large data sets for reporting. Thus, you will find this type of database system aligns more with data warehouse technology, which is meant for reporting and analysis.

Graph Databases

A graph database directly stores individual elements as nodes, and also the connections between them. This type of database mainly focuses on the relationships among data elements. A NoSQL graph database is able to handle structured, unstructured, and semi-structured data. Although graph databases are great for big and complex data sets of all types, they are not meant for large-scale transactional data.

For example, consider a social media platform. This type of platform often uses graph databases for the purpose of linking objects together, like showing you the friends of your friends. The object (you), your friends, and your friends' friends are all related. This relationship is captured in a graph database, as opposed to being stored like a record in a table in a relational database.

Further, unlike a relational database, a graph database does not require a schema (tables and relationships) to be mapped out before data is added. It also doesn't have to be redesigned for any new type of data or information to be gathered. You will often find that graph databases run alongside relational databases.

In a graph database, data is represented by nodes that are connected to one or more other nodes. This type of database is just one example of a non-linear data structure. In non-linear data structures, the data is not arranged in any sequential or linear fashion. This is in contrast to linear structures, which organize data in a predefined order. Whether a structure is linear or non-linear is determined in part by how a computer processes stored information. Linear structures are ideal for data items that are ordered sequentially, while non-linear structures are well suited for big data structures and apps in constant flux. The decision of which type of data structure to use is often made during the process of software development and, in part, based on the size of the data system and what the application is intended to do. Non-linear data structures can scale faster, which makes them suitable for big data sets.

 You can explore the different types of linear and non-linear structures, and learn more about their various use cases, by visiting sites like https://www.dbvis.com/thetable/a-comprehensive-guide-to-data-structures-in-sql.

Non-Relational Data Systems

In many cases, NoSQL databases have enabled software developers to design and scale faster than when they were using traditional relational database models. As NoSQL databases became more ubiquitous, so too did many types of NoSQL technologies. These technologies were developed with the intention of overcoming challenges in application that occurred when using relational database models.

Let's again consider the example of a social media platform. Your profile is connected to that of a friend, and your friend's profile is connected to your other friends. Thus, all of your friends' other friends are in some way connected to your sibling, who is directly connected to your profile but not to theirs. Try to imagine how this data would be stored in a relational database. To capture every type of potential connection in a relational model, it would have to be full of many-to-many relationships, and to serve it, the database would require an immense amount of junction tables.

One of the primary benefits of noSQL databases is that they are built to easily scale for more users and more data. These options are also available in traditional databases, but they require you to increase storage capacity, ram, and processing speeds. Developers need the ability to develop these necessary data options without the downtime and technical overhead of a traditional client-based application. Database administrators will work with the systems through potentially different interfaces, depending on which technology is chosen for any application. If the database administrator at an organization manages the internal servers, but an application that is used for one of the applications is in a serverless environment (like Amazon Dynamo DB), they will just perform the necessary functions to support that application where its needed and inside the environment that they are provided.

Let's highlight a few of the most common NoSQL data systems and some basic use cases.

It's important to remember that what's considered "common" is relative to your situation. When it comes to NoSQL databases, what's major to your organization and what's major to the world at large might be different. These technology tools are meant to solve challenges regarding how to provide users with the data that is most relevant to them amidst the immense amount of data captured. A technology that is commonly used in one industry might not be very relevant for another.

Apache Cassandra

Cassandra is an **open source** column-oriented NoSQL database. It works with it's own language, Cassandra Query Language (CQL), which is similar to structured query language (SQL). Cassandra is ideal for big data, as it was designed to handle large amounts of data across many different servers; it was initially developed to support the inbox search feature of Facebook before releasing as open source in 2008.

MongoDB

MongoDB is an open source document-oriented NoSQL database that has it's own query editor and uses JSON. It was founded in 2007 in order to solve the challenges around serving ads at a very high volume that were associated with traditional relational databases.

Neo4j

Neo4j is an open source NoSQL graph database technology. The source and copyright are owned and maintained by Neo4j, although there are different licenses for commercial uses. Neo4j was founded in 2002 to address performance problems that were faced with relational databases.

In 2019, Neo4j AuraDB, a fully managed cloud application, launched. This subscription-based service enables people to build graph applications without the need for database administration.

Amazon DynamoDB

DynamoDB is a key-value store database system that is proprietary to Amazon, who owns and fully manages the system, and part of Amazon Web Services. It is serverless and meant to run at high performance at any scale. This allows companies to leverage server technology without having to host their own servers.

Azure Cosmos DB

Cosmos DB is a multi-model database service that is proprietary to Microsoft and part of the Microsoft Azure Platform. Being able to incorporate multiple models into a single database lets information technology (IT) teams and other users meet various application requirements without needing to deploy different database systems. It will integrate with many other NoSQL databases, like MongoDB. This technology is also meant to support application development; based on licenses, the service will handle most database administration for scale and performance across servers and datacenters.

Review Activity:

Different Types of NoSQL Databases and Tools

Answer the following questions:

1. **In a document-oriented database, what is a group of documents with content that would be considered similar in nature called?**

2. **Where is data stored in key-value stores?**

3. **When navigating a key-value store, what challenge will you likely encounter, and how is it resolved?**

4. **What type of data is not compatible with column-oriented databases?**

5. **In graph databases, data is stored in what form?**

Topic 1C
Understand Relational Database Design

EXAM OBJECTIVES COVERED
2.1 Compare and contrast aspects of database planning and design.
3.4 Given a scenario, implement data management tasks.

You do not have to be a database designer to be an effective database administrator. However, understanding the way databases are designed can help you support the database you either are implementing or have inherited. If you understand the fundamentals of how tables are designed conceptually, and how they transition into physical objects in the database, then you can more easily interpret the design of other databases. When planning for a database, understanding the design of the system, knowing the schema, and leveraging diagrams that show all the tables and their relationships can help you to communicate the data structure to leadership.

Normalization

While there are many different definitions across the industry for **database schema**, when we discuss it here, we are referring to the structure and design of a database. Imagine the schema as a blueprint of the database, containing the tables, data types, constraints, and properties. Schema can be expressed in documentation through a database model diagram or a data dictionary, as we will discover in later parts of this lesson.

When a database schema is designed, the data is structured for optimal storage and use within the program. That means the data is **normalized data**. Have you heard the saying "everything has a place, and everything in its place"? That is, in a nutshell, what the process of normalizing data means. Normalizing data is a form of organization, and it supports the design by optimizing storage. Normalization of data also adds flexibility in working with the data to support the design of front-end interfaces.

For example, an organization is unlikely to store all of its customer and salesperson data in the same table. Customer information goes in a customer table, and salesperson data goes in a salesperson table.

As a database administrator, you hope to work with databases that have followed proper design theory and the principles of the normal forms. Most database designers will at least attempt to get data to the third normal form. Breaking the data down into these normal forms allows you to easily see what primary keys are formed and foreign keys are established in the design.

- **First Normal Form (1NF):** This form eliminates redundant information in individual tables. Each set of related data will be stored in a dedicated table. Each table of related information will have a primary key assigned.

- **Second Normal Form (2NF):** In this form, related information that is applicable to multiple tables will have its own table and will be associated through the use of a foreign key.

- **Third Normal Form (3NF):** This form eliminates fields that do not depend on a key. You will likely find that while some designs go to the 3NF, most do not.

The less practical fourth and fifth normal forms are rarely used, so we won't go into them here, but you should know they exist.

The following table shows inventory data that is not normalized. The table has a column for every delivery day, and each row contains a supplier and a quantity delivered for that day. This design is not very functional, as it requires every delivery ever made to have a field name.

Delivery Date	1/1/2022	1/2/2022	1/3/2022	1/4/2022
Supplier 1	100	50	75	25
Supplier 2	200	150	50	50
Supplier 3	50	75	25	200

Not Normalized Delivery and Supplier Data

Instead, we would normalize the inventory data to the 1NF by creating a single student record in a table meant to hold each different type of information (e.g., a table for suppliers, a table for delivery dates). In order to store that related data in separate tables, we must first break it down. Let's start with the table for supplier data, which should include all data related to the supplier, including the address and name. We then give that information a SupplierID, so we can uniquely identify each supplier with a single ID.

DeliveryID	SupplierID	Delivery Date	Payment Amount	Quantity Received
1	1	1/1/2022	$87.32	100
2	1	1/2/2022	$56.78	50
3	1	1/3/2022	$43.21	75
4	1	1/4/2022	$92.46	25
5	2	1/1/2022	$73.59	150
6	2	1/2/2022	$35.79	50
7	2	1/3/2022	$35.79	50
8	2	1/4/2022	$67.89	100
9	3	1/1/2022	$50.12	50
10	3	1/2/2022	$84.36	75
11	3	1/3/2022	$95.47	25
12	3	1/4/2022	$28.60	200

Normalized Delivery and Supplier Information

This table shows how we would normalize the delivery data to the 1NF. Note that we now use a dedicated DeliveryID, rather than repeating the dates as field headings. By creating a table to hold the delivery date, we eliminate having to add a new field for each date. We can now have a single field named Delivery Date, and add a record for each delivery for that supplier. Further, the SupplierID is how we identify the supplier in the delivery table, making it the primary key. Once data has been normalized, relationships among the data can then be established.

Relationships and Key Fields

A relational database is "relational" because relationships are formed between keys in the tables. This design allows a unique identifier to be assigned to a record of data in the table, which distinguishes that record from every other record in that table. A key used to identify a record is referred to as a **primary key**. When a primary key is used in another table to refer to your record, it's known as a **foreign key**.

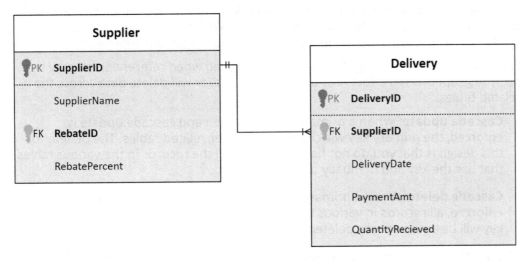

Entity Relationship Depiction of Supplier and Delivery in Microsoft Visio (Used with permission from Microsoft.)

Notice in this image that the Supplier table has the "PK" or Primary Key designation. This denotes that the Supplier in this table will be assigned a key before it can be used in a record in the Delivery table.

At our toy company, new suppliers are brought on as the company decides to offer new products for sale. Because we want to design our database to efficiently store data, we make sure that when a supplier comes on board, they are given a supplier ID that follows them through the system.

Previously, we designed supplier and delivery tables for inventory management. We then ensured each new supplier went into the Supplier table and got their defined key. Now, we can use that key to identify the supplier in other tables, like our Delivery table. The SupplierID, which is primary in the Suppliers table, can be linked to SupplierID, which is a foreign key in the Delivery table. We also know that each delivery gets its own unique record ID, which allows us to retain a delivery history.

Normalization also offers a productivity benefit—it saves you from having to retype the same information about the supplier in every place where we need to reference that supplier information. If the data was not normalized, and we did have to reenter that data in multiple places, we would have redundant data. When redundant data exists, and a change needs to be made, that information would need to be manually updated in many different places. In a design with relationships and keys, any updates are automatically available for anyone who needs the information to query.

Referential Integrity

A database design that uses primary and foreign keys to set relationships between records must also establish **referential integrity**, which ensures that a foreign key definitively has a primary key in the related table.

Referential integrity helps to prevent the occurrence of bad or missing data in any of the tables in the design. In short, it ensures that database users are not allowed to add records when a related record doesn't exist. Let's return to our toy company example. If the database did not have referential integrity, someone could add a delivery record for a supplier that does not exist. With referential integrity, you would not be allowed to add a delivery record for an unknown supplier.

There are additional settings that can be established when referential integrity is set. These options will affect how data updates and/or will delete data across the related tables.

- **Cascade update:** When a primary key is changed and cascade update is enforced, the primary key will change in all other related tables. The benefit to this design is that you do not have to identify all the records in the various tables that use the key and manually update them.

- **Cascade delete:** When a primary key record is deleted and cascade delete is enforced, all records in various tables that are related to the record through that key will be automatically deleted.

When referential integrity has a cascade update setting when the key changes, the update will cascade to all other tables and records where that key is used. Although it's rare to really change keys, it does happen. Let's say that a Supplier ID was entered incorrectly and needed to be updated to the corrected ID. Then cascade update would recognize that the key was changed, and it would make sure that everywhere that key is used is updated to reflect the corrected value.

Cascade delete, if enabled, when a supplier record is deleted, the cascade delete setting can ensure that all records relating to the supplier are deleted when the key is deleted. Due to the permanent nature of cascade delete, you will likely find that it is not set on many relationships. In our example, the enforcement of cascade delete could mean we lose all the historical records of a supplier's deliveries. So, while this option may be set on some relationships, it is used less frequently than the more convenient cascade update setting.

Entity Relationship Diagrams

As you can imagine, an organization typically utilizes many different databases to perform the operations and production of the organization.

An **entity relationship diagram (ERD)** is the pictorial representation of a database schema that shows how entities (like people or objects) relate to each other through the data.

As a part of an organization's overall data governance strategy, entity relationship models are used to identify each database schema and show the relationships between the data held in the various databases. These diagrams, when available, help the organization and other professionals (like the data analyst) to easily visualize the database design. It also can display how data is related to each other, which assists you in creating queries and joins, and boosts your overall knowledge about the database schema.

There are three types of entity relationship models you should be familiar with:

- **Conceptual data model:** This is the conceptual view of what should exist in a data system and how it could be related.

- **Logical data model:** This is a more detailed view of the conceptual model that includes data fields and the relationships between them.

- **Physical data model:** This is the actual data system with tables, relationships, fields, and attributes.

All of these models are meant to visualize the database schema.

Conceptual Model

The conceptual data model is exactly as it sounds— a concept model that will represent the starting point. It will list all the tables that can be determined up front and their potential relationships. Simple design models like this can really help the designer lay out a lot of different tables without getting into the deeper details of a single table at this stage.

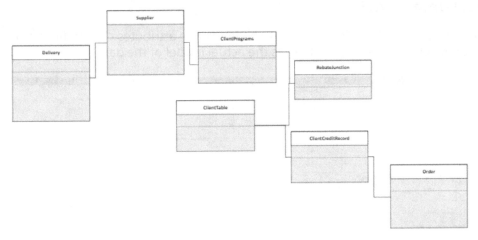

ERD Displaying the Conceptual Data Model in Microsoft Visio (Used with permission from Microsoft.)

As you can see in the above example, an ERD displaying the conceptual model is just blocks of tables, with no real detail on each individual table, although it might sometimes include limited detail about fields.

Logical Model

The logical model goes further into the design, and will list not only the tables, but also fields and relationships with their cardinality. We can use a diagramming software that allows us to create entity relationship diagrams to look at an example. Below is a logical diagram of a few of the tables in the toy company inventory management system. It displays the tables, the fields, and the relationships between tables.

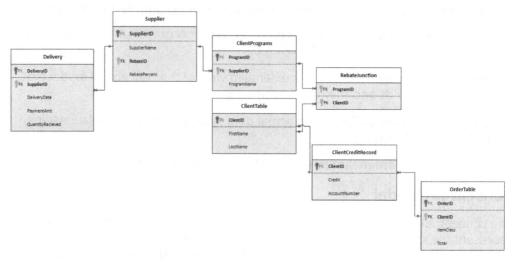

ERD Displaying the Logical Data Model in Microsoft Visio (Used with permission from Microsoft.)

Physical Data Model

A physical data model includes the tables, the fields, the attributes of each field, and the relationships between each table. It's the actual model of the data system.

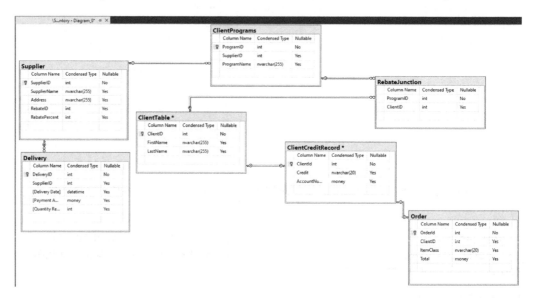

ERD Displaying the Physical Data Model in SQL Server Management Studio (Used with permission from Microsoft.)

The diagram above is displayed using the diagram option in Microsoft SQL Server Management Studio. These are the actual database tables and the attributes that were assigned to these fields.

Types of Relationships

Database tables that use primary and foreign keys to create relationships have varying levels of **cardinality**, which describes how many possible occurrences of one entity (record in a table) can be associated with the number of occurrences in another (records in another table).

One-to-One Relationship

A **one-to-one relationship** means that one record in a table will be associated with only one record in the other table. In a one-to-one relationship, the primary key in the first table is often the primary key in the other table as well. Let's walk through an example. A client record is created when a new client is onboarded to our system. The client gets one record, and they are uniquely identified by the key, ClientID, that is created in the ClientTable. The unique ClientID is also present in another client table, ClientCreditRecord, and it's the primary key for this table as well. It holds only one record for each client, which shows the values related to their credit with the company.

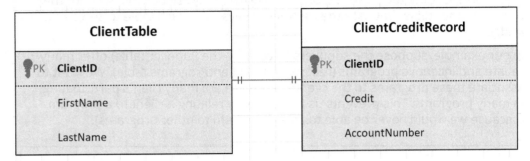

ERD Displaying Client Table Related to Client Record in Microsoft Visio (Used with permission from Microsoft.)

The symbols on the relationship line indicate the type of relationship that exists between these two tables. There can be only one record per client in ClientTable and only one record per client for credit in the ClientCreditRecord. Thus, the relationship, and the cardinality of the two tables, is a one-to-one relationship. This relationship results when you join a primary key to a primary key, and you enforce referential integrity. It will not allow a client credit record to exist if there is not an actual client record establishing the key for the client. This is a great way for designers to ensure accurate order of entry into the system.

One-to-Many Relationship

In a **one-to-many relationship**, a primary key is joined to a foreign key, meaning there is one record (in the table in which the key is primary) associated with multiple records in other tables (in which the key is foreign). In our example, the ClientID is the primary key in the ClientTable. In the OrderTable, OrderID is the primary key, and ClientID is the foreign key.

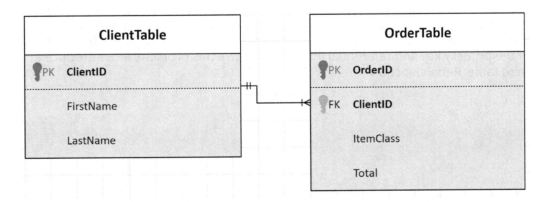

ERD Displaying Client Table Related to Order Table in Microsoft Visio (Used with permission from Microsoft.)

The symbols on the relationship line again represent the cardinality. There can only be one record in ClientTable for a client, but an infinite number can exist for that same client in OrderTable; thus, this is a one-to-many relationship. When a client is entered into the system, they can start to create orders. These orders produce records in the orders table. The client is only entered in by the key, and through the relationship we can associate any order to all the client details. You will see this type of relationship a lot within databases.

Many-to-Many Relationship

A **many-to-many relationship** means that many records are associated with many other records. Data tools can't resolve a many-to-many relationship without the use of another table that uses the associated keys from each table to serve as a bridge.

In our example, suppose the suppliers (records in the Supplier table) offer many rebate and incentive programs (records in the ClientPrograms table). We want to associate these programs to the clients, but there are many clients participating in many programs. This prevents us from directly relating a client to a program (because we would never be able to associate them to other programs).

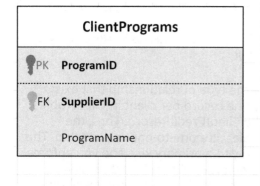
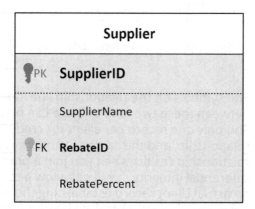

ERD Displaying Not Related Supplier and ClientPrograms Tables (Used with permission from Microsoft.)

When you are designing, it's important to use sample data to test your design, so you can determine if it will work. In our records, SupplierID = 345, which is Truck Supply Company. Truck Supply Company offers a 15% rebate on all toys that have been in stock for five years or longer. ClientID = 245 orders from Truck Supply Company, so that field value will be set to 345, which is the SupplierID. Once we have set this value in our current design, we can't really add another program for the client. This is because we only have space for one key. Further, if we had a second client, we would need to repeat the ProgramID, which isn't possible because of the primary key and referential integrity. To solve this problem, let's introduce a third table: RebateJunction.

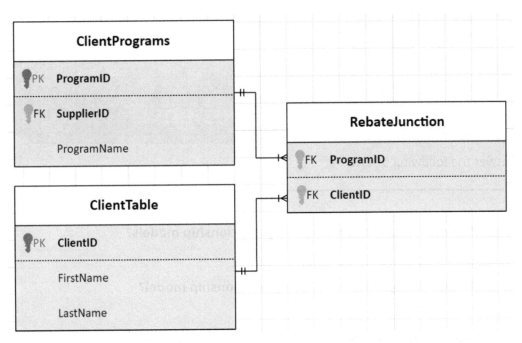

ERD Displaying the Many-to-Many Relationship in Microsoft Visio (Used with permission from Microsoft.)

This table allows us to associate a ClientID to a ProgramID by bridging the gap caused by a many-to-many relationship. This table will contain ClientID and ProgramID, both of which are foreign to this table and establish the one-to-many relationship when linked to the other tables.

Review Activity:

Relational Database Design

Answer the following questions:

1. **What are the three types of entity relationship models?**

2. **What is the objective of an entity relationship model?**

3. **What are the two types of key fields used to join tables?**

4. **What must be set in a database design in order to establish relationships between records?**

5. **When dealing with a many-to-many relationship, what serves as a bridge?**

Topic 1D

Identify Other Data Systems

 EXAM OBJECTIVES COVERED
1.1 Compare and contrast database structure types.

Previous topics have covered the various types of relational databases and NoSQL databases. These are not the only types of data systems you will encounter or admin in your role. In an organization where data is being captured all the time, you may find that it is captured through various databases or other types of systems. In this section, we will explore data warehouses, data marts, and data lakes. As a DBA, you may find that you administer permissions or build queries to either supply data to these other systems, or pull data from them for others in the organization. These types of data systems are not unlike other data systems, in that they store data, but they are made up of data from many databases.

Data Warehouses

A **data warehouse** is a technology that is dedicated to the storage of company data from a wide range of sources for reporting and decision-making purposes. Data warehouses unify and hold the data from multiple source systems. Different data from different systems can be queried together without impacting the performance of the separate source systems. The advent of data warehousing gives us a reporting model that overcomes the gap in reporting when data is stored in different systems.

Consider our fictional toy company. Suppose the different departments within the company have different databases that capture data from various processes and software, and there is no single system that captures every part of the process. The company uses a custom ordering system and is currently building a custom inventory system. The company has separate tools for accounting and other functions. Even though these data sets are not directly related, we can use a system like a data warehouse to bring all these data sets together. This means we can capture data in separate source systems where it makes sense, but still have a single place for most organizational reporting.

 To learn more about the valuable concepts of data warehousing, you can explore Dimensional Modeling Techniques from The Data Warehouse Toolkit, Third Edition *by Ralph Kimball. https://www.kimballgroup.com/data-warehouse-business-intelligence-resources/kimball-techniques/dimensional-modeling-techniques/*

Data warehouses provide a single source of truth, meaning the data in the warehouse is trustworthy, as there's a lot of rigor involved in confirming what data should go into the warehouse, determining where that data comes from, and effectively relating the data for the use of reporting.

Data warehouses can also leverage online analytical processing (OLAP) technology, making data processing more effective. For example, OLAP can summarize thousands of records far faster than traditional tools like Excel. The "heavy lifting" of the data work, such as grouping data by month and then totaling that data, can be done through the use of OLAP cubes.

These three-dimensional cubes provide data that is already grouped by different dimensions. Thus, when analysts access the data, they can further analyze it without having to group and total it first.

When an organization's data warehousing professionals know the types of reports that are routinely run, they can use this knowledge to design cubes that support business intelligence requirements within the organization.

Data Marts

A **data mart** is a subset of the data warehouse that is dedicated to a specific department or group. Data marts ensure that the data needed by a defined group of users is available to them. Data marts also ensure that data is secure and only available to the users who should have access to that data.

Imagine it this way: The data warehouse is like an airport terminal—full of different types of stores and restaurants that everyone has access to. While you can walk up to any gate once you are past security, you can't just board any plane you like. You need a ticket to get past gate security. This is the data mart; you must have permission to access it. The data mart has been specifically designed for you and/or your department, and your access is controlled based on what data you need.

Data warehouses and data marts are structured, and that structure allows other data professionals like business analysts, data analysts, and leadership to report on or build visualizations from data without requiring access to every single source system. Without a data warehouse, we would have to integrate all of the data from different source systems ourselves.

Data Lakes

Data Lake

In the world of data and within an organization, we really only analyze a percentage of all the data that we collect. Organizations make a significant investment in software, storage, and reporting capabilities. However, they need a place to hold data of all types when it doesn't follow the same rigid structure that is used by databases and data warehouses. When data has been collected, but is not yet ready for cleaning or analysis, it can be stored in what is called a **data lake**. Data lakes hold both structured and unstructured types of information, allowing an organization to store large amounts of all types of data in their original formats. Data lakes serve as a kind of "catchall" for data.

Data warehouses, although extremely powerful, require diligence in determining what goes in and where it comes from, and preparing that information for analysis. Data lakes capture large amounts of data in holding, while waiting for those processes to be conducted.

The biggest drawback of data lakes is that, unlike a data warehouse, there is less rigorous oversight of and control over how data is entered. That's not to say that there is no data governance, but a data lake isn't acknowledged as the single source of truth in the way that a data warehouse is.

Data Lakehouse

Because the world of data is constantly evolving, new innovations can change the way we store and access data. The **data lakehouse** is a data management system that combines the best of the data warehouse and the data lake. Data lakehouses provide flexibility, like a data lake, and yet are often more cost effective than a data warehouse. Data lakehouses serve up information not only for data analysts, but also data scientists and data engineers. Data lakehouses support business intelligence and analytics projects in addition to machine learning and data science.

Review Activity:

Other Data Systems

Answer the following questions:

1. **Data warehouses can leverage which technology to make data processing more effective?**

2. **What characteristic of both data warehouses and data marts allows reporting without requiring access to every single source system?**

3. **True or false: A data lake is a subset of a data warehouse.**

4. **Which data system stores data that has been collected but is not yet ready for cleaning or analysis?**

Lesson 1

Summary

After this lesson, you should be able to identify the differences between relational databases and non-relational databases. You should be able to explain the purpose of benefits of different types of noSQL databases. You should also understand how relational databases are designed for optimal storage and how relationships between tables are set. Finally, you should be aware of other types of data systems, like data warehouses and data marts.

Guidelines for Understanding Database Types and Structures

Consider these best practices and guidelines when you are working with the various databases and systems at your organization.

1. **Identify whether the database is relational or non-relational.**

2. **Ensure you have a clear understanding of the application or function the database serves to the organization.**

3. **For non-relational databases, you must be able to recognize what type of database it is and what technology it uses and what languages.**

4. **For relational databases, you will need to understand how data is normalized and how that impacts the storage.**

5. **In the systems you support, it is crucial to know how the tables are related in the systems you support, what the key fields are, and what types of relationships exist.**

6. **Be familiar with reading entity relationship diagrams to understand the schema (design) of the data system.**

7. **Be aware of any other data systems your organization uses, such as data warehouses and data marts.**

Lesson 2

Recognizing Standards and Commands

LESSON INTRODUCTION

As you enter the world of data systems, you will discover the vast differences that exist between the systems and designs, as well as the way we can choose to interact with them. Due to this, as technology has grown, the need for standards has grown with it. As you can imagine, when different people with different skills are using different commands and languages, if there are no standards to follow, then the systems they develop can be difficult to adopt and integrate into the technical landscape of any organization. Once you are familiar with the varying standards that you must follow, you will discover the different ways we use tools and languages to interact with operating systems, and the many types of administrative commands you will likely perform.

Lesson Objectives

In this lesson, you will do the following:

- Understand standards and principles.

- Examine operating systems and command line scripting.

Topic 2A

Understand Standards and Principles

EXAM OBJECTIVES COVERED
1.2 Given a scenario, develop, modify, and run SQL code.

Imagine if there existed no standards for how major systems are created. In this world, every person could create whatever they'd like, and every organization that adopted the system that person created would need to conform to their way of doing things. This would be not only inefficient, but confusing and unreliable. Thus, just like relational databases have design principles that are best followed, the data systems themselves—and everything around them—also have standards to be followed. In this section, we'll discuss the two popular organizing bodies that support standardization, as well as cover principles for ensuring complete records.

ANSI and ISO Standards

There are two major organizations you should be familiar with that provide guidance and publish standards for many types of organizations and processes, including data systems.

American National Standards Institute (ANSI)

Founded in 1918, the **American National Standards Institute (ANSI)** is a private, non-profit organization that administers and coordinates the U.S. voluntary standards and conformity assessment system. ANSI works closely with both the government and various industries to identify and develop standards and conformance-based solutions.

ANSI does not develop the standards itself, but rather provides a framework in which standards can be developed. It serves as a neutral party across industry, private, and public sectors.

It's worth mentioning that the ANSI framework applies to more than just database systems. You can visit https://www.ansi.org to learn more about the institute and the framework it provides.

International Organization for Standardization (ISO)

The **International Organization for Standardization (ISO)** works to develop and publish standards internationally. So while ANSI is focused on the United States, ISO concerns itself with the entire world. It's important to understand that ISO covers a large range of activities, from manufacturing, sales, trade associations, regulators, and even customers. The standards that ISO publishes are standards that companies attempt to achieve in order to demonstrate that the processes they manage and decisions they make follow an internationally recognized standard.

ISO proposes that we think of their standards like formulas that describe the best way to do something. You can learn more about ISO and their standards on their website: https://www.iso.org/home.html.

We can all agree that it is important for SQL code to follow a standard that can be used across relational database systems. According to ANSI, SQL was standardized in ANSI X3.135 in 1986, and, within a few months, it was adopted by ISO as ISO 9075-1987.

There are two standards that you should familiarize yourself with that help support the development of SQL databases: the Federal Information Processing Standards (FIPS) and ANSI SQL-92.

A data system that is ANSI-compliant conforms to the ANSI standard for the SQL language. Companies that have achieved ISO standard recognition have met the requirements of that ISO standard, and thus have received that compliance designation.

ACID Principles

The **Atomicity, Consistency, Isolation, Durability (ACID)** principles exist to guide us in developing data systems that create complete transactions and reject partial transactions from being recorded. When a data system is designed in accordance with these principles, data is validated to ensure completeness. The four principles that make up ACID are as follows:

- **Atomicity:** Atomicity guarantees an "all or nothing" approach to transactions, meaning either all of the transaction succeeds or none of it does. A data system following this principle will not create partial records or transactions, so if one part of the transaction fails, the whole transaction fails. An example of this would be that if all fields have been set to required, the system will require information before the transaction is committed.

- **Consistency:** Consistency ensures that all data within a data system is just that—consistent. When this principle is followed, we can be sure that the data will be valid based on all the defined rules for that data. If a field has properties with rules, the transaction will not save until it matches those specified rules.

- **Isolation:** Isolation means that all transactions occur isolated from other transactions. In a system following this principle, one transaction can't be impacted by another, meaning a transaction can't read data from any other transaction that isn't completed.

- **Durability:** Durability confirms that once a transaction is committed, it will remain in the system. Even if a record is submitted right before a crash occurs, that record will successfully be in the system.

When suggesting a database for your company, you will definitely want to consider whether or not it follows ACID principles, but it's important to know that this doesn't have to be a deal breaker for an organization. While most major systems are ACID compliant, not every database is programmed with care and consideration to these principles.

Review Activity:

Standards and Principles

Answer the following questions:

1. When a data system is an ANSI-compliant database, this means that it conforms to what standard for the SQL language?

2. Which organization publishes standards for an international audience?

3. Which principles exist to guide us in developing data systems that create complete transactions?

4. Which principle takes the "all or nothing" approach to records being entered into a data system.

5. What are some benefits of the ACID principles?

Topic 2B

Examine Operating Systems and Command Line Scripting

EXAM OBJECTIVES COVERED
1.3 Compare and contrast scripting methods and scripting environments.

As a data administrator, you will encounter different utilities that will impact the way you work with operating systems and database servers. Some commands are built into the operating system, while others are cross-platform and can exist in different environments (like Windows and Linux). In this section, you will discover how to use scripts and languages to interact with your operating system and explore the tools involved.

Command Line Scripting

While there are many different operating systems out there, Windows and Linux are the two most commonly found in the corporate environment. As you likely know, an operating system controls the computer, the software, and the types of languages we can use.

There are many different tools that allow you to interface with your database and its settings. Depending on your job role, you may use one tool more than another. However, if you enjoy coding, you will likely be inclined to interact with your database by writing command line scripts.

Command Line Scripting for Windows

One of the main tools used to conduct command line scripting in Windows is **command prompt**. This tool will likely already be installed on your machine when you start your role, as it's part of the installation and setup of Windows. Command prompt accepts the commands you write and interacts with the **shell**, which is actually running the program.

If you are interested in hardware and networking, you might explore the technical way that the hardware and software interact elsewhere. However, as a DBA, you do not need to have a deep knowledge of why these tools work—just how to work with them.

You must first connect to the database server, and then you will be able to access the database, or databases, within that server (as long as you have permission to do so). You can then use various commands to perform actions such as opening tables, creating tables, listing all databases in the server, and grabbing the last backup date. Commands are a quick and easy way to gain insight into your database (and the data within).

In order to use command prompt with SQL, you will use SQLCMD, a shell utility, to interact with command line and the database (or databases). In the screenshot below, we use SQLCMD -S to connect to the local database server, which is where you can perform test scripts and learn more about the company's data.

The SQLCMD -S allows you to connect to the database server, and the backward slash tells the command to look at the local machine and the default SQL Server instance (which we will discuss in more detail in a later lesson).

```
SQLCMD -S <NameoftheComputer>\SQLServerInstanceName>
```

```
C:. Administrator: Command Prompt - sqlcmd -S DESKTOP-          \SQLEXPRESS - SQLCMD

Microsoft Windows [Version 10.0.19045.2486]
(c) Microsoft Corporation. All rights reserved.

C:\WINDOWS\system32>sqlcmd -S DESKTOP-          \SQLEXPRESS
1> use AdventureWorks2019
2> go
Changed database context to 'AdventureWorks2019'.
1>
```

Using Command Prompt in Microsoft Windows to Connect to AdventureWorks (Used with permission from Microsoft.)

If you work with multiple SQL servers and databases, you can specify the database server name and the instance when you run the command. This will allow you to type single line commands to interact with the operating system and database server. In command prompt, you will type each command on an individual line and execute them one by one, line by line.

 Most DBAs no longer use command prompt, because it only executes a single line command, and we are often running more than one step. But the command line is available by default, whereas other tools may require additional installations. In the past, DBAs would create a .dat file, and then run the .dat file from command prompt, in order to perform multiple actions at one time. However, newer tools (such as PowerShell) have overtaken command prompt in popularity, as they allow you to script and execute multiple commands at once. We'll learn more about PowerShell in the next section.

Command Line Scripting for Linux

SQLCMD is cross-platform, which means that although it is native to Windows, you can install it as a separate utility on a Linux machine. When you install SQL Server in your Linux environment (starting with the 2019 version), this utility is also installed by default. The commands are consistent across both environments.

The Linux counterpart to command prompt is terminal, which serves to interact between command lines and the operating system.

PowerShell

PowerShell is a tool that facilitates the same interaction as command prompt and terminal, but goes one step further by allowing you to script multiple commands. This ability can help you administer your database and facilitates the performance of other functions, like data creation, and other maintenance tasks, like backups. There is a large community of users, and while PowerShell is a Windows-based tool, it can be installed and used in Linux environments. In Windows, you can launch PowerShell by simply searching for it in the start menu.

PowerShell is used for more than just database administration; it's also popular with system and network administrators, who use it to perform commands needed for the technology they support. Remember that PowerShell allows us to interact with the operating system and everything contained within. PowerShell has gained popularity for use in the Azure administration, as well as Microsoft 365 and even SharePoint.

The screenshot below shows a side-by-side comparison of command prompt and PowerShell. The interfaces of the tools are similar, as they are both meant for scripting. The key difference is that PowerShell lets you script multiple commands versus the one-by-one execution model of command prompt.

Windows Command Prompt (Left) and PowerShell (Right) (Used with permission from Microsoft.)

The two commands above are both performing the same function. In command prompt, we are using the .bat file to remove age information from a file that contains key value pairs with name and age. It does this by replacing the age numeric data with empty strings. This requires a few steps, so we've coded in a text file saved as a .bat, because otherwise in command prompt you'd have to execute each step individually. The same code in PowerShell is much simpler and can be accomplished in a single line.

As mentioned earlier, you can install and use PowerShell on a Linux machine. However, you might instead use Bash scripts, which is the Linux equivalent to PowerShell. While the PowerShell community has grown quite tremendously, and has put out a lot of extensions for the tool, Bash has been around for a longer period of time. There are Bash libraries out there to do just about anything you can think of.

Other Languages

Python

Python is a programming and scripting language that has been gaining popularity in the tech industry, known for the fact that its syntax is easier to learn and read than other programming languages. It can be used for many different types of applications, such as software development, querying, and interfacing with databases in a wide range of environments. Python is incredibly powerful and useful for automating processes.

Python is an interpreted language like JavaScript, and it has been around a long time, so interpreters have been written for a lot of the existing operating systems, which convert the language to the commands of the operating system the interpreter was created for. If you have a Python interpreter installed on your OS, you can write and execute Python code that will interact with your database.

Python has different frameworks, software, and libraries that allow people to utilize it when working with varying solutions, applications, and data systems. Pandas is a popular data analysis and manipulation tool that is built upon Python. As a DBA, you might use Python toolkits and database interbases, like SQLAlchemy or pymssql. There are literally hundreds of packages that you can discover with Python, serving a broad range of purposes, from managing content on a website to connecting and querying big data sets.

You may find that using libraries like pymssql to connect with your Microsoft SQL Server can be a great place to start. This sort of tool provides you a simple user interface to the database, not unlike what Microsoft SQL Server Management Studio provides in a Microsoft environment.

There really is no connection or similarity between Python and PowerShell, or Python and command prompt. Python is simply a programming language. But as a DBA, having a good knowledge of all these languages allows you to select what tools you will use and when.

Structured Query Language (SQL)

The most comprehensive language is SQL, as this language provides syntax that is dedicated to working with data. One of the primary skills of a database administrator is the ability to script statements and query data.

SQL statements provide information to databases (such as SQL databases, or even data warehouses) and thereby allow data professionals to retrieve data from tables stored in the database. SQL statements not only query data, but also allow you to perform actions on the data. How extensively you use SQL depends on your particular job role within the organization where you work. For most DBAs, knowing how to create and run a basic SQL statement is an important first step.

SQL has a required syntax, but it is also important to understand that different versions of SQL do exist depending on the system you are using. For example, T-SQL, which stands for Transact – SQL, is used in software developed by Microsoft. Oracle also uses SQL, but it uses PL/SQL, or Procedural Language/SQL. When searching for syntax examples, it is helpful to look for the version of SQL that your particular software uses.

Review Activity:

Operating Systems and Command Line Scripting

Answer the following questions:

1. Which two operating systems are most commonly used?

2. What program layer executes the commands that you input?

3. Which command program allows for multiple commands to be executed at once?

4. Which program is the Linux equivalent to PowerShell?

5. Which popular programming language has packages that allow DBAs to use the language to interact with their data systems?

6. What language is used to create scripts and statements that allow you to query and retrieve data from databases?

Lesson 2

Summary

After this lesson, you should understand how the standardization of SQL through ANSI standards supports database design. You should also be able to explain the purpose of the ACID principles. You have discovered how you can use command line scripts to interact with your data systems in operating systems like Windows and Linux, and how programming languages like Python can also be used to interact with data systems. Finally, you should have an understanding of SQL as the primary language of data.

Guidelines for Recognizing Standards and Commands

Consider these best practices and guidelines when engaging with data systems and considering standards and ACID principles.

1. **Identify whether your database is following the SQL standards compiled by ANSI and whether your organization has achieved an ISO designation (or if they are pursuing it).**

2. **Familiarize yourself with each one of the ACID principles and how they impact the quality of data when they are applied.**

3. **Understand that there is risk involved when using a data system that does not follow ACID principles.**

4. **You should be able to explain the different options for interacting with your data systems based on your operating system.**

5. **Be prepared to interact with your database using command line prompts.**

6. **Be able to explain the differences between command prompt and PowerShell.**

7. **Familiarize yourself with the programming languages and tools that are appropriate for the organization and their data systems.**

8. **Understand that SQL is the primary language of data and used in many systems.**

Lesson 3

Running Scripts for Data and Data Systems

LESSON INTRODUCTION

In this lesson, we will highlight the types of scripts you will use as a DBA to create objects, maintain data, update data, and delete objects or data. We will also cover the scripts you use for data management tasks, like defining indexes and sharing data. All of these scripts are valuable when you need them. Although we will not cover the complete list of scripts you will ever use, we will go over common scripts that you will most certainly use or find in use at many organizations.

Lesson Objectives

In this lesson, you will do the following:

- Create and alter objects using data definition language.

- Manipulate data using data manipulation language.

- Work with transactions.

- Perform data management tasks.

Topic 3A

Create and Alter Objects Using Data Definition Language

 EXAM OBJECTIVES COVERED
1.2 Given a scenario, develop, modify, and run SQL code.
3.4 Given a scenario, implement data management tasks.

In your day-to-day life as a DBA, you will find yourself creating various objects, one such object being tables. You may enjoy scripting that creation process using SQL commands that are designed to help build the structure of a database. You will discover how to create and alter the design of database objects, using commands like CREATE and ALTER. You will also learn how to delete objects using the DROP command.

Data Definition Language (DDL)

Through SQL scripts, we can use **data definition language (DDL)** to define objects. The database itself would be an object, and inside that database you would find other objects, like tables and views. DDL is not a separate language from SQL, but rather the statements used to create and modify objects or the structure of the database. There are many reasons why you might use several of these in the life of a database you manage. For example, if the system is a growing software that has been internally built within the company, you might find yourself using these commands frequently to create tables and views. Some of the most common commands you will utilize when supporting databases that use SQL are as follows:

- CREATE (create objects, like databases, tables, and views)

- ALTER (modify objects, like fields, tables, views, and properties)

- RENAME (rename objects, like fields, tables, views, and databases)

- DROP (remove objects, like fields, tables, views, and databases)

- TRUNCATE (remove all records from a table)

Creating and Altering Databases

Let's walk through the creation of a database, named SampleScripts, using the CREATE statement. This sample database can be used as a test database, providing you a safe place to run your scripts prior to implementing them into a **production database**. When the script below is executed, it will create a database using all the default settings.

```
CREATE DATABASE SampleScipts
```

This script is the most basic method for creating a new database, but we can accomplish the exact same goal in tools like SQL Server Management Studio (SSMS) by right-clicking the database and selecting New Database. The benefit of using a software tool like SSMS is that as you learn to script more options, you will be able to review a visual display of the potential options and choose other options before you select OK.

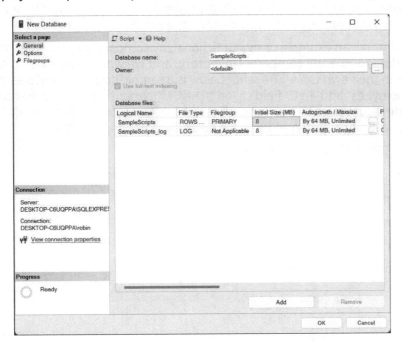

New Database in Microsoft SQL Server Management Studio (Used with permission from Microsoft.)

You can use other scripting commands to change the database properties, and when you execute it would adjust the defaults.

 It is important to remember that there are different ways to execute similar actions, and there are many commands in SQL to choose from. Further, the various tools that you can use also allow you to perform some of the same functions by using the tool interface. SQL Server Management Studio is one such tool.

After you've created your database, you may find you need to change it in some way. To do so, we use the `ALTER` statement. The sample script below shows one way a DBA might alter a database. In this example, the script would alter the database named "SampleScripts" and set the ANSI_NULL_DEFAULT property setting to "off" in the database.

```
ALTER DATABASE [SampleScripts] SET
ANSI_NULL_DEFAULT OFF

GO

ALTER DATABASE [SampleScripts] SET ANSI_NULLS
OFF

GO
```

There are many settings you will learn as a DBA, and they can all be adjusted to fulfill the requirements the data system must meet.

Creating Tables

Tables serve as valuable storage in your databases, and effective table design can be the key to getting the most from any of the data that is stored within. When it comes to designing the tables, the DBA might work as part of a team, or they might work alone to design the tables and then implement that design. Regardless of which path you take, as a DBA you will likely need to add tables to databases. When you create tables from scripts, you will use the DDL command `CREATE TABLE` to create a table and add the fields and their properties into that table. Once you have it scripted, to build out the table you execute the script.

Let's work through an example using our fictional toy company. Suppose our database holds the data for the toy company's inventory, and we want to add the company's employees to their own table. The script below is a sample script that will create a table called "Employees" and an ID field called "ID-NUM" containing a value that counts up and provides a unique number for each new record entered. This script also creates first name, last name, and middle name fields, with varying lengths.

```
CREATE TABLE Employees
(
 id_num int IDENTITY(1,1),
 fname varchar (20),
 mi char(1),
 lname varchar(30)
);
```

 When you create a table using a script, you need to include at least one field and the field data type, which controls what type of information can be stored in that field. There are several different core data types: numbers, text, and dates represent most of the data that we work with.

If we view this table design via a tool, like SSMS, then we can easily see what the script has just created: the table and the field names (labeled "Column Name"), the data type, and whether it will allow null values. In the screenshot below, the fields and their properties were all set by the above script. For all other properties, the default settings will be used unless specified otherwise in your script.

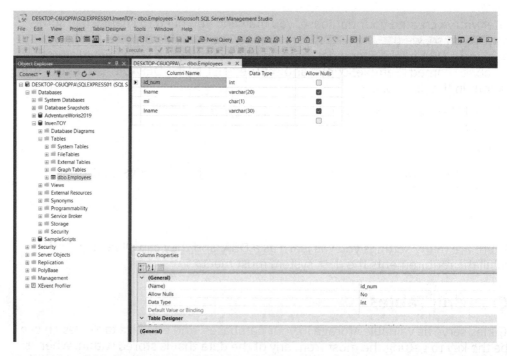

Design View of the dbo.Employee Table in Microsoft SQL Server Management Studio (Used with permission from Microsoft.)

Altering Tables

When you need to modify an object, there are two commands you will typically use:
`ALTER` and `RENAME`.

ALTER

There are many reasons you might use the `ALTER` clause, depending on why you
need to change the object. When data systems are being developed, there will be
changes made to the tables, such as adding fields, renaming objects, and removing
them. The **ALTER** statement will allow you to alter the objects within the database,
and the properties of those different objects, as you specify.

Recall that in our recent design of a table for the toy company's employees, we
did not include a field for their job title. We can use the `ALTER` clause on the
"Employees" table to have it add that title.

```
ALTER TABLE Employees
Add Jtitle varchar(75)
```

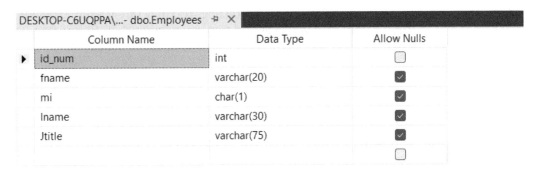

*Table Design View of Employees in SQL Server Management Studio (Used with permission
from Microsoft.)*

In the table layout above, we can see that the script, when executed, adds the field
name "JTitle" and sets its data type and size. You can also add and remove columns
using the `ALTER TABLE` statement. When you execute the statement, the design
of the specified table will change in structure. This script will add the field "Jtitle" and
assign the data type as varchar with a 75 character max length.

RENAME

There will be occasions where you will need to rename an object due to either
a misspelling or requirements change. We use `RENAME` alongside the `ALTER`
statement. The code below, when executed, will rename the "Jtitle" field to
"JobTitle"

```
ALTER TABLE Employees
RENAME COLUMN Jtitle TO JobTitle;
```

The exact syntax you use might vary depending on the system you are working
with.

 *There are also stored procedures in Microsoft SQL Server Management Studio, like
`sp_rename`, that can be used to rename objects.*

Deleting Fields and Tables

We are not always adding to structure; sometimes we also need to remove objects from our database or fields from our tables. There are several commands we can use to do this.

DROP Fields

We use DROP to remove unnecessary fields. Let's look at an example. Suppose we have imported a list of products into a table and need to remove several of the unnecessary columns. We might write something like the script below.

```
ALTER TABLE Employees
DROP COLUMN Jtitle;
```

Here, we combine ALTER with DROP COLUMN to modify the table and delete the column (which we have titled "Jtitle").

DROP Tables

Deleting tables can be a function of cleanup or of testing. You may rarely need to delete tables from a production database, if you ever find that you need to at all. Before you delete any table that is in use, you should carefully plan and consider the deletion.

 Deleting tables can create breaks in the programs that use those tables, so always handle with care.

In practicing your script writing for creating tables, you have created tables that should be deleted. You can right-click each table and remove them manually in a tool like SQL Server Management Studio, but this is one area where scripting is faster. When deleting tables, we use the DROP command to remove the table entirely from the database and from memory. To delete the "Employees" table we just created, we script the DROP TABLE command and list the table we want removed, as shown in the script below.

```
DROP TABLE Employees
```

Once this script executes, it will remove all of the information and the table itself from the database. This cannot be undone. This is why having proper plans and database backups is critical.

 The process of deleting a table entirely is not to be confused with deleting specific records from a table; we will discuss that type of delete in a later section.

TRUNCATE Command

TRUNCATE is another command used to delete all records in a table. It is a "delete all records" command, meaning there are no filters in place. Because it can only function as a way to delete all records, it is often used for testing and clearing a table of all data. An example of script for TRUNCATE is as follows.

```
TRUNCATE TABLE ProductDetails;
```

 As you will learn, some commands can be "undone" with other commands. However, it's important to understand that TRUNCATE is a permanent change, and you should be sure you have appropriate backups in place before executing.

Review Activity:

Data Definition Language

Answer the following questions:

1. **True or False: DDL is a separate language from SQL.**

2. **A database and its contents are referred to as what?**

3. **When creating a table, what must be paired with the column name?**

4. **Which clause would be used to change columns in a table:** `ALTER` **or** `TRUNCATE`**?**

5. **What clause is used to remove a table entirely?**

Topic 3B

Manipulate Data Using Data Manipulation Language

 EXAM OBJECTIVES COVERED
1.2 Given a scenario, develop, modify, and run SQL code.
3.4 Given a scenario, implement data management tasks.

SQL commands can be used to do more than create and alter objects in a database; they can also be used to manipulate the data itself. You might use these types of commands to select and update values, insert data from one table into another, or even remove bad data or test data. In this lesson, we will cover some of the basic commands that allow you to manipulate the data.

Data Manipulation Language (DML)

Data manipulation language (DML) includes the clauses and commands that allow us to select and manipulate data. We first use the SELECT command to state which fields we want to retrieve from any set of tables, and then follow up with commands that allow us to update or delete data. Like DDL, DML are commands within the SQL language used for manipulating our database.

You will likely find yourself using the following commands while supporting databases that use SQL:

*   SELECT (select fields from table(s) to view or use)

*   UPDATE (update field data)

*   INSERT (insert values from other tables)

*   DELETE (delete records based on criteria)

DML can be used alongside other languages, such as **transaction control language (TCL)**, to ensure that the script performs the correct changes before they are fully made available to everyone.

Selecting Data

We select data for so many reasons: to analyze it, correct it, verify it, move it, and use it. Using the SELECT statement will become second nature to anyone who regularly works with databases and queries, as we use SELECT anytime we have been prompted to review the data, for any number of reasons.

Let's return to our example of the toy company. Suppose you have been tasked with updating the pricing of a specific group of products within the database. Your first step would be to select the fields that would be subject to updating with the new pricing. If we want to update a specific product, we include the WHERE clause to filter to just that product.

Remember that SELECT *is a major component of almost all SQL scripts. You may discover spirited debate over it being included in DML, as it does not actually manipulate data but merely selects it.*

For example, the script below will return the name and price for all the products in our table, ToyProducts, where the name of the product is Toy Soldiers.

```
SELECT ProductName, ProductPrice
FROM ToyProducts
WHERE ProductName = 'Toy Soldiers'
```

When this script is executed, the only information that will display is the product that is named Toy Soldiers. This allows us to confirm that we have the accurate results—or in this case, product—before we update the field value.

Updating Data

The ability to update through a query is powerful, especially when those updates are going to impact hundreds of records. When running an update script, you must tell the system what data is being updated, and what it is being updated to. Let's walk through an example.

As covered previously, the first step is to use a SELECT statement to find the information that needs to be updated. Suppose that your organization's sales team has asked you to update the cost and price of a product with a ProductID of 25. These fields are both currently set to 0.00. Since the data we want to update lives in the "Production.Product" table, we can query this single table. The script below is a simple SELECT that pulls the ID, cost, and list price for this product only. Because we do not want to update all products, we set the WHERE filter to the appropriate ProductID.

```
SELECT ProductID, ProductCost, ProductListPrice
FROM ToyProducts
WHERE ProductID = 25
```

Now that we have the product filtered, we can change the two data values using the UPDATE command. We add the SET command to update the existing values to the new values (each field separated by a comma).

```
UPDATE  ToyProducts
SET  ProductCost = 5, ProductListPrice = 7
WHERE (ProductID = 25)
```

Once this script is executed, it commits the change to that product record. The execution message may vary depending on the program used, but regardless will likely include the number of rows impacted.

🖥 Messages

```
(1 rows affected)

Completion time: 2023-01-26T13:18:54.0511535-06:00
```

Execution Message in Microsoft SQL Server Management Studio (Used with permission from Microsoft.)

This information is important to note, even just mentally, because you want to confirm that the message matches what you selected. If you selected one record of data to be updated, the rows affected should be equal to one as well.

You can now run your original query, where you selected the product 25, and confirm that it does in fact show the update was completed.

Selecting Data from Multiple Tables

In an earlier lesson, we talked about relationships and cardinality. When you are selecting data from more than one table, your SELECT statement will then also include the join between the tables and their key fields. **Joins** are where we link tables together to associate the information. This is typically done through the use of a key field. Not all databases contain relationships between the tables, but they may have primary keys to use for joins. When two tables are listed in a query, the join controls what data is returned.

There are multiple join types that you can use when querying data, and it can be hard to know which would be best in any given situation. The decision about which join type to use should be based on what results you need from your data set.

- **Cross join/Cartesian join:** Data doesn't have a direct join on a key field.

- **Inner join:** Data is joined so that only records that exist in both tables appear in the result.

- **Left outer join:** The left table displays all results of the left table, while only matching records in the other (right) table appear in the result.

- **Right outer join:** The right table displays all results of the right table, while only matching records in the other (left) table appear in the result.

- **Full outer join:** Data is joined so that all records, matched or unmatched, show in the results.

Any data role that works with queries in this manner needs to understand the join types in order to gain the required data from the tables.

In our database, there is a single product record for each toy, and every time a toy is ordered, a related survey is generated via the marketing department. This data ultimately comes back into the inventory, and will provide the most current product rating from the buyers. The data is created and controlled by the marketing group, and they supply it to the DBA so that it can be updated in the database.

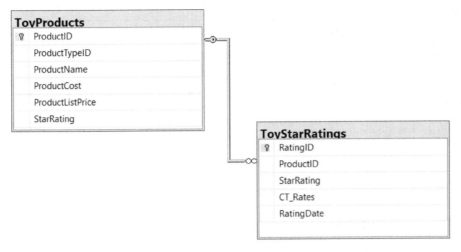

ERD of Tables in Inventory Showing the Physical Design of the Tables in Microsoft SQL Server Management Studio (Used with permission from Microsoft.)

In the screenshot above, we can explore the relationships that have been established. Being able to easily see how data is related will help us know how to design our query.

The SQL script below uses SELECT to pull the necessary fields from each table, and FROM will contain the tables and join type. For our purposes, we are only rating products that have a rating record provided by marketing. Since we are rating single products with a single rating from the ToyStarRatings table, an inner join is appropriate. If we wanted to produce a list of products that both had ratings or not, for reporting purposes, we might use a left outer join.

```
SELECT   ToyProducts.ProductID, ToyProducts.
StarRating, ToyProducts.ProductName,
ToyStarRatings.StarRating AS NewStarRating

FROM     ToyStarRatings INNER JOIN

   ToyProducts ON ToyStarRatings.ProductID =
ToyProducts.ProductID
```

It is important to both use the correct join type and join on the correct field for the objective of your script and the outcomes expected. If you want to see only records with matches in both tables, you use an inner join. If you want to see all records from one of the tables, then you use an outer join. It's important to understand that what each join type will return in the data sets is based on the join type itself.

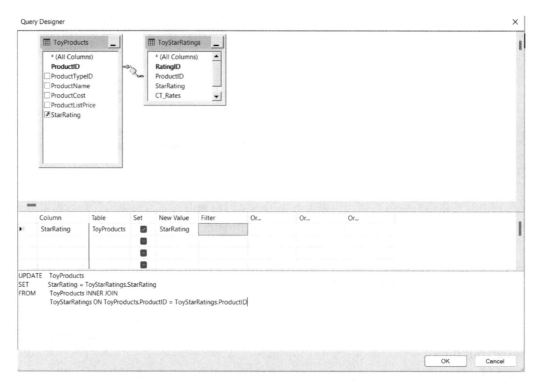

Update Query for StarRating in Query Designer in Microsoft SQL Server Management Studio (Used with permission from Microsoft.)

In order to effectively update the star rating, which is contained in the ToyStarRatings table, it must be included in the query. We can then run the update to use the StarRating field from the ToyStarRatings table to update the StarRating field in the ToyProducts table.

Inserting Data

There are several scenarios where database administrators might need to insert data into tables. You might be moving data that has been captured outside of the database into a database, or you could be moving data from one database to another. When you prepare to insert records from one table to another, it's important to first identify where you are getting the data from, so you can ensure you are capturing the correct data to be inserted into the table.

Suppose the toy company marketing team sends a customer survey to each customer upon their purchase of a product. Customers are asked to rate the product(s) they purchased, and that product rating is submitted back to the company. This data is used to create the star rating for the product and is imported into the StarRatingImport table each month. The data must then also be inserted into the ToyStarRatings table for the historical rating data.

We use a script to insert the raw ratings data into the ToyStarRatings table, with the `INSERT` clause.

```
INSERT INTO ToyStarRatings
     (ProductID, StarRating, CT_Rates,
RatingDate)

SELECT   ProductID, Star_Rating, Number_of_Ra-
tings, Rating_Date

FROM     StarRatingImport
```

When the script is executed, this data is then moved to ToyStarRatings, which allows it to be used for additional analysis by the marketing department.

Deleting Data

There are many reasons why you might be tasked with deleting data. It could be that you have identified bad data that needs to be removed, or maybe you need to remove test data from your newly defined database tables before the system goes live. You may even need to remove the records of an individual who has requested that their information be removed.

DELETE Command

When deleting data, it's important to understand that you are deleting records as a whole. You aren't just changing values in a field (like updating data values to blank), but rather fully deleting these records. Thus, using the `DELETE` command is not something you want to do haphazardly. It is simple to script deletes, so you must be cautious with your intent. Best practice would be to first run a `SELECT` statement to confirm you are returning the correct products before executing the deletion.

Consider the toy company's product data. In moving it from the existing system to a new one, we loaded all the products. Suppose that, upon review, we realize some of our legacy products made it through, but these product records do not need to be in the new system. Let's run a select statement to isolate product 26, which is a legacy product that is not needed in the new system.

```
SELECT * FROM ToyProducts WHERE PRODUCTID = 26
```

Once we have executed the query, it will show only the expected product to be removed from our records. Now that we've selected the product, we will want to delete all the associated product records. To do this, we change our script to execute a `DELETE` command. Unlike `TRUNCATE`, which can only delete all records, we use the `WHERE` clause alongside the `DELETE` command to specify which record we want to delete. This script, when executed, will delete this product record entirely from the Products table.

```
DELETE FROM ToyProducts
WHERE    ProductID = 26
```

There are two key traits that differentiate `DELETE` from `TRUNCATE`:

1. `TRUNCATE` can't be undone with other commands, whereas `DELETE` can.

2. You cannot use a `WHERE` statement with `TRUNCATE` to filter records for deletion, whereas `DELETE` will allow you to specify the records for deletion with `WHERE`.

Grouping and Aggregating Data

Sometimes we need to provide data to others in the organization that is not in its natural record format, like all of the raw data. We use the command `GROUP BY` to create groups of information, as well as provide aggregate functions. This can sometimes be considered a way to mask data, as we are providing the aggregated data versus all the records.

Aggregate Functions

There are functions that we write on a row-by-row basis, like an `IF` function or date conversion. In contrast, **aggregate functions** are written for all or a group of records, not just for a single record. Aggregate functions work with a column of data. For example, to calculate the total of all orders, you would use the SUM function. To obtain the total number of orders placed by a region, you could group the records by region and then use an aggregate function like COUNT to count them.

Here are some common examples of aggregate functions:

- SUM will add all the records together to produce a total. You will see this function used for amounts and quantities.

- COUNT will count all the records as individual lines to produce a record count.

- DISTINCT COUNT will count all the records in that column, but will only count the field one time, even if it appears multiple times.

- AVERAGE will total all the values in that column and then divide them by the count of values.

- MAX will give the largest value in that column.

- MIN will give the smallest value in that column.

When designing applications to capture data for a process, we want to capture down to a very granular level—as far as we can go. For example, when capturing data for a product rating, we wouldn't just capture the most recent rating: we would capture each rating for that period of time, or for all of time, based on the rating rules. We can then use aggregate functions to develop an average rating, or establish a total count of the number of ratings supplied. This level of detail in our capturing allows us to use these values for reporting, and when we do report on these values, the granular records get rolled up into groups and aggregate functions are applied.

GROUP BY

The GROUP BY clause will organize data into groups that can then have aggregated values calculated when you execute the statement. Because we need the average rating organized by Product ID, we would group the orders by the Product ID in order to calculate the average using the rating record.

```
SELECT    ProductID, AVG(StarRating) AS [Avg
Rating], COUNT(CT_Rates) AS [Total Count]
FROM  ToyStarRatings
GROUP BY ProductID
```

In the script above, we use the SELECT statement to select all the fields needed for the rating data from our ToyStarRatings table. We then use the GROUP BY statement to return the group and aggregated fields for that information.

If we want to exclude a certain set of values from the statement, using the GROUP BY clause, we use the HAVING statement as a filter. (In this way, HAVING functions similarly as WHERE does when using a SELECT statement, but HAVING is the proper filter clause to use for a GROUP BY statement.)

```
SELECT    ProductID, AVG(StarRating) AS [Avg
Rating], COUNT(CT_Rates) AS [Total Count]
FROM  ToyStarRatings
GROUP BY ProductID
HAVING  (ProductID = 15)
```

In the script above, the `HAVING` clause displays only the results where the ProductID is equal to 15.

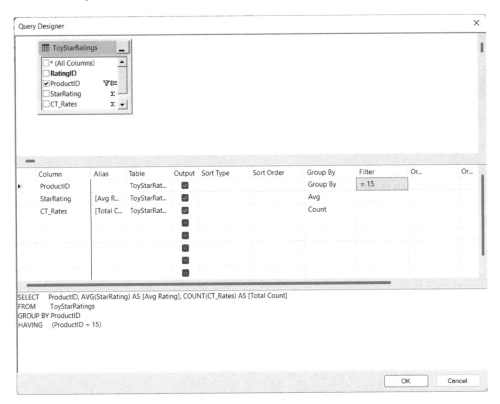

Microsoft SQL Server Management Studio Query Designer Showing GROUP BY *and* HAVING
Statements (Used with permission from Microsoft.)

The use of `HAVING` and `GROUP BY` allows SQL to pull the list of fields from the table and filter out the needed information before moving on to the grouping and aggregation.

Review Activity:

Data Manipulation Language

Answer the following questions:

1. **Which clause is most commonly used to query data?**

2. **When adding new records into a new table with the values of the original table, which clause should be used?**

3. **A business rule has been set that all fields containing a price of 5.00 be changed from 5.00 to 7.00. Which clauses should be used to change the values from 5.00 to 7.00?**

4. **To remove a specific value from a table or view, what three clauses are needed?**

5. **What clause is used when working with aggregate functions?**

6. **When working with** GROUP BY**, which clause is used when data needs to be filtered?**

Topic 3C

Work with Transactions

EXAM OBJECTIVES COVERED
1.2 Given a scenario, develop, modify, and run SQL code.

Databases store records of information that have been entered or captured from many different types of software. This can include off-the-shelf systems that integrate with SQL Server or applications that have been built internally within an organization. Most people participating in this process are just going about their everyday life, but for the DBA, a transaction represents something being done to the records, and a group of processes being applied. There are SQL commands dedicated to transactions that not only have the ability to start a valuable change process, but that can also protect against bad processes or incorrect data changes. In this lesson, we will learn more about transactions, the associated commands, and commits and rollbacks.

Transaction Control Language (TCL)

As a DBA, you will use **database transactions** to insert, update, or change records. Any action, such as updating a record to have a new value for price, or entering a new product, can begin a transaction. When you perform these commands, they are auto committed, meaning you cannot "undo" them. They are immediately made available to the database—unless you use them alongside **Transaction Control Language (TCL)**. TCL allows you to control the transactions that are generated from DML inserts, updates, and deletes. Opening the script with BEGIN TRANSACTION starts the process in SQL.

As a DBA, you will likely use scripts to make administrative or design changes to a database. When you are updating data, you are generating a transaction that is thereby updating that record. If you make a mistake, it's important for you to have the capability to then correct that mistake. TCL allows you to isolate a group of transactional changes and have more control over them. Here are a few TCL clauses you should know:

- COMMIT: Commits a transaction and makes changes available in the database.

- ROLLBACK: Rolls back to the last committed set of changes.

- SAVEPOINT: Creates a point in the transaction that you can roll back to if needed.

You'll learn about these clauses in more depth in the following sections.

You must complete any transaction process that you start. When you have open transactions on records, a lock will be created that will not allow others to edit.

Committing Data

You can imagine that when you have hundreds of users in a system, and they are all relying on the data to be accurate, changes must be handled with care—especially when you have to make intricate changes, such as updating the pricing structure of products.

If you fail to use TCL when making DML commands, you could easily make a mistake that is not easily undone. But, when you use the language of COMMIT, it commits that data to the users who are actively using the database, while also letting you create other queries to validate the data before it's saved to the database.

 When you do not type BEGIN TRANSACTION *in your SQL statement, it will perform what is considered an* AUTOCOMMIT. *This means that your changes are instantly available; if you make a mistake, you cannot "undo."*

Let's walk through an example using the toy company's inventory. We start with BEGIN TRANSACTION, because the settings of our database require this to be explicitly stated. This opens the transaction. Then we use UPDATE to correct the spelling of the Toy Soldier product name and COMMIT to commit the changes.

```
--Start the transaction because the settings of
the database require this to be explicitly stated
BEGIN TRANSACTION
--This is the update that is being performed
UPDATE  ToyProducts
SET  ProductName = N'Toy Soldier'
WHERE (ProductName = 'Toy Soldeir')
COMMIT
```

We could further add a SELECT statement, which would allow us to verify that all the ProductName updates were performed as expected.

```
--Start the transaction because the settings of
the database require this to be explicitly stated
BEGIN TRANSACTION
--This is the update that is being performed
UPDATE  ToyProducts
SET  ProductName = N'Toy Soldier'
WHERE (ProductName = 'Toy Soldeir')
--Test to confirm change is as expected
SELECT ProductName
FROM Products
WHERE ProductName = N'Toy Soldier'
COMMIT
```

If you ran this statement by statement, you could do even more query validation before you run COMMIT.

Rolling Back Data

When you are not working with transactions, any changes that you have committed are permanent. If you made a mistake, and needed to revert back to the previous version of the data, you would have to create another transaction. This would be another query that pulls back all the records you changed, so you could correct your mistake in the data and then change it again. While this sounds tedious enough, imagine how awful it would be if you can't even find the exact data that you changed but need to revert back. Luckily, when working with `BEGIN TRANSACTION`, you can leverage the `ROLLBACK` TCL command. This command performs an "undo" that allows you to reverse your most recent changes (because they have not yet been committed). It's important to note that this command will only undo changes you've made since the last `COMMIT`—and not anything before. So if you've made and committed four changes, but realize while performing a fifth command that you need to use `ROLLBACK`, the four committed changes would stay intact; only the fifth, uncommitted change, would undo.

This statement is designed to run in parts, not to be executed all at once. `ROLLBACK` lets us confirm the changes we are going to make. It allows us to confirmed they are made, and then if they are accurate, we can commit them. If they are inaccurate, we can roll them back. The screenshot below shows our use of `ROLLBACK` when updating the toy company database.

```
--Change the accidental mispelling of a product that made its way to our system

Select * From ToyProducts
WHere ProductName = 'Toy Soldeir'


--Start the transaction because the settings of the database require this to be explicity stated
Begin Transaction

--This is the update that is being performed
UPDATE      ToyProducts
SET             ProductName = N'Toy Soldier'
WHERE      (ProductName = 'Toy Soldeir')

--This query can confirm if the update was performed as expected
Select * From ToyProducts
WHere ProductName = 'Toy Soldier'

--If In Correct
ROLLBACK

--If Correct

COMMIT
```

TCL with DML Changes to Include `ROLLBACK` and Data Validation in Microsoft SQL Server Management Studio (Used with permission from Microsoft.)

Let's step through the code in this screenshot. The first `SELECT` pulls all the fields from ToyProducts that have a product name of "Toy Soldeir." This product name was initially misspelled, and we need to correct it. The query will show us the record that needs to be fixed. We then begin the process with `BEGIN TRANSACTION`, and we use the `UPDATE` statement to update the product name with the corrected spelling of Toy Soldier (when we execute the statement). While we are still in the transaction, we can query again to confirm the correction is made. If it's correct, we run `COMMIT`. Had it not been correct, we could have undone the change with `ROLLBACK`.

SAVEPOINT

Have you ever saved a file so you could return to that point in the event that something went wrong? That is exactly what a SAVEPOINT will allow you to do. A SAVEPOINT can be coupled with a ROLLBACK. This allows you to ROLLBACK to the SAVEPOINT without rolling back the entire transaction. We should note that you may not always have a SAVEPOINT in your transaction; whether you do or not will depend greatly on what you are trying to accomplish with the script and process you are working with.

Review Activity:

Transactions

Answer the following questions:

1. **When a user has a transaction open, what limitation is applied to other users?**

2. **Which command can set the data to the previous set of changes?**

3. **Which command is used to open a transaction?**

4. **Which command is used to mark the end of a transaction?**

5. **When you are not opening transactions to perform changes, but instead using DML to perform and execute changes, what type of commit is this?**

Topic 3D

Perform Data Management Tasks

EXAM OBJECTIVES COVERED
3.4 Given a scenario, implement data management tasks.

As a DBA, you will encounter varying scenarios that will require different data management techniques. Not every database administrator creates a database; while some will, most are working with designs that have already been created. Something as simple as a different data type existing between systems can require us to convert field data types. We also often receive data from other data systems, which is where an understanding of how to append data is important. You might even be involved in performance enhancements, working with indexes, and exporting from the database for sharing purposes. This is in no way a comprehensive list, but a few places you can start.

Converting Data Types

As you know, field data types are controlled by the database's design, and thus their usefulness hinges on the database designer recognizing the varying data types and understanding the importance of being intentional with the choice of each field data type.

When data fails to meet the specifications for your database or database project, you may need to change or convert data types. For example, if you need to calculate numbers, then your data type must be a number. The same goes for dates—if you need date-specific calculations, then you must work with data that is set to a date data type.

As a DBA, you have options. If you are designing the database, you can control the data type at the field level in the table you design. If you must have a field with a data type stored differently than how it will be used, you can convert it using functions in your scripts.

As you discovered earlier, when you design the table and add the fields, you also assign the data types. No single data software is identical in its methods for using functions to convert data types, but all data software will have this capability. Business analysis tools such as Power Query and Tableau allow you to adjust the data types without having to write a separate calculation.

You can write functions that will allow you to perform any type of conversion needed to meet the requirements. In SQL, you can use the CAST function to change the data type of any field in a query. It will *not* change the underlying data; it will simply convert the field for that data set generated by the script. The CAST syntax is simple, as you can see below.

```
CAST(ColumnName AS datatype(length))
```

If you have the ability to modify the data in the table, you may want to use the ALTER clause to adjust the data type in the table design. It's important to note that you can lose data if you are not careful when using `ALTER`. For example, if you are changing text to numbers, then it will drop the text and leave the field blank.

```
ALTER TABLE TableName
ALTER COLUMN ColumnName NVARCHAR(200)
```

Appending Data

Suppose that as your database has grown and processes have changed, you have been asked to add more fields to existing tables and update the values.

When you need to combine data from one data set with another data set, you will append the data. Which query you use will depend on the tool you are utilizing. Regardless, this action generates a single data set from multiple tables.

In SQL, we use `UNION`, which is an intermediate append. The use of an intermediate append creates a single set of records while still retaining the individual objects (like tables or queries). Many business analysis tools allow users to append data sets through the tool interface. For example, in PowerBI analysts can use the `APPEND` query, which will provide the same end result as what we achieve when using SQL.

It is important to understand when using unions that the two tables being combined must have the same number of columns and the exact same data types, in the same order. It's also worth noting that some tools will even require the heading names to be exactly matched.

The script below allows us to combine the contact information from the tables "ToyContacts" and "ToyBuyers."

```
SELECT FirstName, LastName, MI, ContactID as 'ID'
FROM ToyContacts
UNION ALL
SELECT FirstName, LastName, MI, BuyerID as 'ID'
FROM ToyBuyers
```

Because the two fields contain the same information but have different ID names (ContactID and BuyerID), we must change one (or both) to have the same name, so the resulting set will just show one set of IDs. Once we make this change, the end result will be a single data set that is the combined records from both tables.

Creating New and Temporary Tables

In addition to combining data using `APPEND` or `UNION`, you may also create new tables to maintain the original data set. You can use a `CREATE` script for this purpose, and if your data is in csv format, you can leverage imports to populate the data in your new table.

A **temporary table** is a table that is stored on the database server until a user disconnects from the server. Similar to a permanent table, temporary tables provide records, but they are for temporary use only.

```
SELECT *
INTO #ContactsToBeUpdated
FROM ToyContacts
WHERE City = 'Birmingham'
```

This code creates a temporary table that is only available when we are connected to our database and run the script. In this case, it would create a temporary table called ContactsToBeUpdated that would include all of the fields from ToyContacts that are located in the city of Birmingham.

Temporary tables can improve processing speeds for queries simply because they typically contain a smaller number of records than the permanent table.

Creating Indexes

Fields that will be commonly sorted, queried, or filtered will likely be indexed. **Indexing** is a field property setting that tells the database that a field needs to be used to create an index. It's an internal process that controls how much data must be looked at when processing the data for queries. When fields are indexed, it makes data processing faster and ultimately speeds up the performance of the query. There are some fields that are automatically indexed when they are created, like key fields.

You can define any field as an index, but understand that they are meant to enhance performance because they are sorting data, making it faster for searches and querying. If you make everything an index, this can negatively affect performance.

In the script below, we are creating an index on the status field in ToyStarRatings.

```
CREATE INDEX ToyStarRatings ON ToyStarRatings
(Status);
```

If you have access to the back-end database, you can confirm whether a field is indexed or not. However, you will need edit permissions for the database to change the properties. The screenshot below shows how to access the index in SQL Server Management Studio.

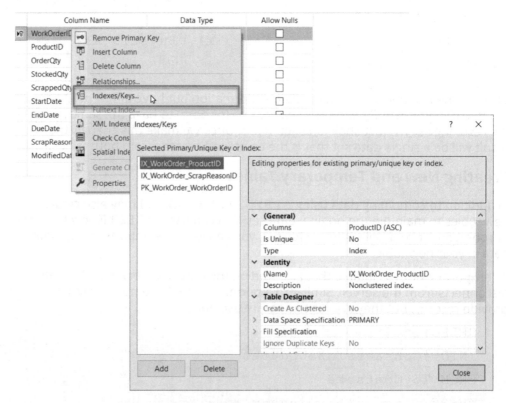

Indexes/Keys Screen via SQL Server Management Studio (Used with permission from Microsoft.)

This type of index is a non-clustered index, which doesn't sort the physical data inside the table. In fact, a non-clustered index is stored in one place, and table data is stored in another place. This is similar to a textbook, where the book content is located in one place, and the index is located in another. This setup allows for more than one non-clustered index per table.

When an index is created from a primary key setting, thus indexed by default, it establishes what is called a clustered index. A clustered index defines the order in which data is physically stored in a table. Table data can be sorted in only one way; therefore, there can be only one clustered index per table.

As we will cover in a later lesson, the DBA will also be responsible for reviewing the creation (and sometimes removal) of indexes to increase performance.

Sharing Data Exports

Many users will not have access to an organization's database, and even if they do, they won't have the ability to query the tables like the DBA would. For this reason, you will be responsible for sharing data exports.

There are several methods for working with data to export and provide it to others. If you are using a tool like SSMS, you can export via the interface. You can also directly connect to your data with popular spreadsheet tools like Microsoft Excel. In our example, in SSMS, you can share data by using Tasks to Export Data, as shown in the screenshot below. The export wizard will walk you through each step of the export.

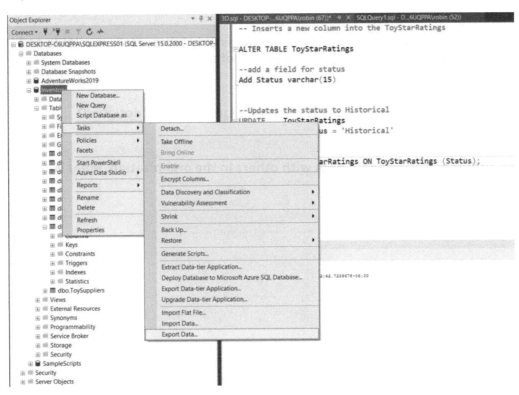

Export Command in Microsoft SQL Server Management Studio (Used with permission from Microsoft.)

 Remember that you will sometimes be sharing data with people outside your organization. You should always make sure you have a full understanding of who will receive the data, and what they are allowed to access, whether you're sharing with internal or external users.

Review Activity:

Data Management Tasks

Answer the following questions:

1. When a data type is designed as text or string but you need it for calculation like sum or average in your query, what do you do to prepare it for calculation?

2. Where are data types for fields designed for the database?

3. What SQL clause do you use to append tables/queries into a single data set?

4. What type of table can you design that is only temporarily available and can be used to create a smaller subset of data for use?

5. Which type of fields are automatically indexed when designed?

6. DBAs will often share data with others in the organization. What is the primary reason for this?

Lesson 3
Summary

After this lesson, you should have a better understanding of how we write scripts to create objects, maintain data, update data, and delete objects or data. You should be comfortable using the SQL commands that are designed to help build the structure of a database and the scripts used to manipulate the data itself. You should also understand the importance of using transactions in validating data before committing it and rolling back changes when mistakes have been made. Finally, you should be familiar with common data maintenance techniques, such as converting data types, appending data, indexing fields, and sharing data with others.

Guidelines for Running Scripts

Consider these best practices and guidelines when running scripts to create objects, select data, and perform data maintenance.

1. **Use DDL commands lik**e CREATE **and** ALTER **to create and modify various objects in a database.**

2. **Use DML commands like** SELECT, UPDATE, **and** INSERT **to modify the data within the database.**

3. **Make sure you have backups before using** TRUNCATE **to delete all records, as it is a permanent change.**

4. **Use** WHERE **to filter data for a basic SQL statement and** HAVING **when you need to filter data for a** GROUP BY **statement.**

5. **Use** BEGIN TRANSACTION **to create a safe place where you can test your scripts before they are committed to the database**.

6. **Perform a** ROLLBACK **if you see an error in your scripts or logic.**

7. **Use** UNION **to combine data from multiple tables in SQL, but be aware this function is served by** APPEND **in other systems.**

8. **Create and review indexes to enhance the performance of your database, and be aware of where indexes are already established.**

Lesson 4

Explaining the Impact of Programming on Database Operations

LESSON INTRODUCTION

In this lesson, we will highlight the impact of programming on a data system. You will be informed on the differences between views and snapshots, and how they can be used for data reporting and management tasks. You will discover how systems that have a front end and back end in different technologies communicate through object-relational mapping (ORM). You will learn how to leverage triggers to automate data and gain an understanding of how we benefit from set-based logic. You will also discover common functions used for data management and reporting.

Lesson Objectives

In this lesson, you will do the following:

- Work with views.

- Understand object-relational mapping.

- Program with SQL.

- Write functions.

Topic 4A

Work with Views

 EXAM OBJECTIVES COVERED
1.2 Given a scenario, develop, modify, and run SQL code.
3.4 Given a scenario, implement data management tasks.

Views are common to databases, as they allow us to store scripts that can be used for reporting. These views provide valuable joins and information for other users without requiring them to know how to join, or even what tables to add to the query. When we script, we are simply creating statements that we can open and execute. When we establish views or snapshots, we are creating more functionality for use. Views do not store data, but they do store the statements making the views/scripts available to other users. Snapshots are data stored at the time of the snapshot.

Creating Views

When we write SQL statements with different fields and filters, and then execute those scripts, we are given a list of data results at that specific moment. However, if other people need to be able to see this data, at times convenient to them, then it is the DBA's responsibility to provide them access to an object called a view.

To create a view using a script, we start with a SELECT statement, then add the CREATE VIEW command. This creates an object that gives other people access to some data, without giving them access to all the fields of data stored in the tables of the view.

It's always a good idea to first test that your SELECT statement is returning the results you want for the view. Once you know the statement is valid, you can easily execute the code to create the view. The script below shows how to create a basic view with the script. The CREATE VIEW statement will create the object as a view, and the SELECT statement is the query that will bring in the fields listed to the view.

```
CREATE VIEW ProductsAndRatings AS

SELECT   ToyProducts.ProductID, ToyProducts.
ProductName, ToyProducts.ProductListPrice,
ToyStarRatings.StarRating, ToyStarRatings.CT_Rates

FROM     ToyProducts INNER JOIN

         ToyStarRatings ON ToyProducts.ProductID =
ToyStarRatings.ProductID
```

This script will create the ProductAndRatings view when you execute it, which will be stored in the Views of the database.

Tools like SSMS have Query Editors that serve as a GUI for writing queries. These types of tools will generate the script for adding fields, WHERE clauses, and more based on your point-and-click interaction with an interface. The script is displayed while you select your options, so any adjustments you make will be reflected in the code. The interface in these types of tools can also be extremely helpful as you learn to write join statements between tables, because it describes the join types and what they will do for the data results.

You can also use existing views to create new views. If you have already created a view that has most of the information you need, you can script that view to allow you to modify and create a new view from it.

In the screenshot below, we use the tools of SSMS to script the ProductsAndRatings view in the Inventory database as a CREATE script. This takes us to the new query. We can then use this script to create other views with this data.

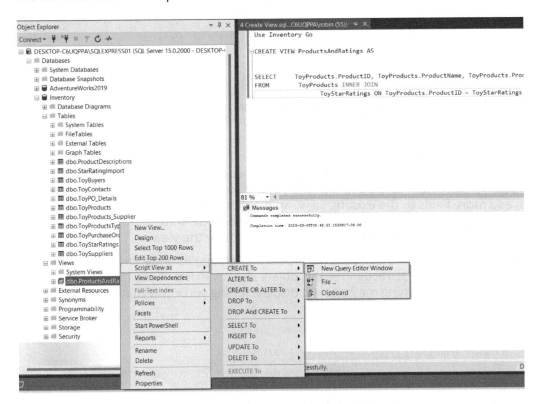

Script to Build a View in Microsoft SQL Server Management Studio
(Used with permission from Microsoft.)

In the following screenshot, you can see where SSMS is adding different items into the script; for example, the USE and GO commands at the top of the script will ensure that this script runs against this database.

```
SQLQuery1.sql - D...6UQPPA\robin (62))*  + X
    USE [Inventory]
    GO

    /****** Object:  View [dbo].[ProductsAndRatings]    Script Date: 3/10/2023 6:54:28 AM ******/
    SET ANSI_NULLS ON
    GO

    SET QUOTED_IDENTIFIER ON
    GO

⊟CREATE VIEW [dbo].[ProductsAndRatings] AS


    SELECT   ToyProducts.ProductID, ToyProducts.ProductName, ToyProducts.ProductListPrice,
             ToyStarRatings.StarRating, ToyStarRatings.CT_Rates
    FROM     ToyProducts INNER JOIN
             ToyStarRatings ON ToyProducts.ProductID = ToyStarRatings.ProductID
    GO
```

*Microsoft SSMS Generated Script using the Create to New Query on an Existing View
(Used with permission from Microsoft.)*

If we want to use an existing view to create a similar view—for example, one that filters to include only toys priced at $4.99—we would change the name, modify the SELECT statement to include this filter, and then execute the script. If we wanted to add more fields to the existing view, we would use the ALTER command. If you need to re-create the view, you could add the DROP statement to remove the existing view, and then execute the script to re-create the view.

You might also notice that "[dbo].[ProductsAndRatings]" is underlined in red. This line indicates that SQL recognizes this object already exists. If you hover over the red-lined text, a warning message will display, letting you know that the database sees the object.

```
⊟CREATE VIEW [dbo].[ProductsAndRatings] AS

                    There is already an object named 'ProductsAndRatings' in the database.
```

*Microsoft SSMS Default Message Error Text for an Existing Object (Used with permission
from Microsoft.)*

Every time you execute this view, it will query the table and show all requested data in the results. It's important to note that when we save these scripts, the data itself is not saved. So when we save views, we are not saving data, but rather enabling others to use the view, as it's now available as an object in the database. In the screenshot below, we can see the view ProductsAndRatings, which anyone with permissions can use.

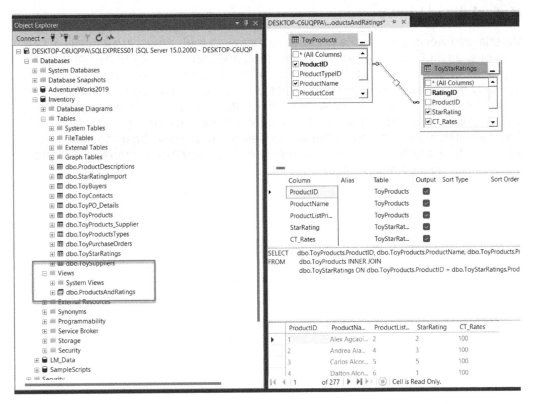

Views in Inventory Database in Microsoft SQL Server Management Studio
(Used with permission from Microsoft.)

Saving a view is simply saving the script so that it can be available anytime someone needs to see that data result. Views are a popular way to share data, so that any data modeling can be done prior to the reporting and visualization process.

Snapshots

Some database systems support the concept of a table **snapshot**. Like a view, a snapshot is created from an SQL `SELECT` statement, returning columns from one or more existing tables. Unlike a view, a snapshot is created as a read-only copy of the data that was queried in order to create the snapshot.

Snapshots are typically used for a few different purposes.

- Snapshots can be used as a way to recover data from the point in time that the snapshot was created.

- If the data does not change often, snapshots can be used to increase performance. By taking a complex query and saving that queried data as a snapshot, we are then able to query the snapshot instead of constantly using the complex query to retrieve the live data.

- In some cases, a snapshot's creation will be scheduled so that an updated version is created on a periodic basis.

Not all databases support natively creating snapshots. In those cases, a snapshot is often simulated by creating a table and copying data into the table. Read permissions are then given to the table to make it behave similarly to a snapshot table. This table can either be updated on a periodic basis, or new tables can be created using a naming pattern each time a snapshot is required.

Materialized Views

Materialized views, despite the presence of "view" in their name, are actually a form of snapshot. Typically, materialized views are used as a way to de-normalize data in a database. A materialized view is created as a way to store data that would normally be retrieved from multiple tables using joins, in a single row of a table, in order to make retrieving that data more efficient. Materialized views are typically updated when any source data used to create the materialized view changes. This means that the data in a materialized view should always be up to date, although there might be a small delay between the source data changing and the materialized view being updated.

Review Activity:

Views

Answer the following questions:

1. A read-only query of data at a specific point in time is known as what?

2. A read-only query that typically updates with the source data is known as what?

3. When a data set is needed by multiple people who may not know how to query data, you can save the script as what type of object?

4. What are some of the benefits of creating views?

Topic 4B

Understand Object-Relational Mapping

EXAM OBJECTIVES COVERED
1.4 Explain the impact of programming on database operations.

You have learned about the objects of a database, like tables and fields. Applications that are designed also have objects. No matter what we're doing with data, if there is data in one place that needs to be integrated with another, we will perform some form of mapping. In software development, we use object-relational mapping (ORM) to map objects from the application and database.

Mapping Objects

When working with data, DBAs work with tables, rows, and columns. But developers prefer to work with objects, collections, and properties. **Object-relational mapping (ORM)** software allows developers to work with data using objects, without focusing on the underlying database tables and columns where the data is stored. ORM is how we map application objects to the appropriate objects in a relational database. Using software like Entity Framework, developers can work at a higher level of abstraction when they deal with data, and they can create and maintain data-oriented applications with less code. For example, the suppliers for our toy company fill out their forms online in a web-based application. We use an ORM application to put the supplier information that is provided in the application into the correct table and fields in the database.

ORM Serves as a Bridge for Applications and Databases

Tables are designed to maximize storage and efficiently provide data. But tables are designed one way, and the way programmers design objects is by creating classes. ORM makes sure those classes are mapped to the appropriate table. Remember that developing an application is a totally separate object than the database. ORM allows these two to interface, essentially connecting, with ORM acting as a bridge.

Performing Database Operations Using Frameworks

When we need to connect applications that have been designed in other technologies to our databases, we use frameworks that are designed to support the application's ability to "write" back to the database. These frameworks enable different types of technology to integrate with our data systems, essentially allowing a front-end application and a back-end data system to communicate.

If you are working with an application that was built using a Microsoft tool (such as SQL Server, Visual Studio, or .NET), you will use Entity Framework, which is the open source ORM available for those tools. Hibernate and ebean are similar open source ORM frameworks that are used for applications written in the Java programming language. Hibernate is actually a suite of open source Java projects focused around domain models. One of the most recognized projects in the Hibernate suite is Hibernate ORM. Hibernate ORM allows the mapping of Java classes/data types to SQL tables/data types. Hibernate has an object-oriented version of SQL (HQL) that creates SQL-like queries to run against its data objects. Ebean is another open source Java ORM tool that has specific SQL features to increase ease of use. Both of these Java ORM frameworks have their strengths and weaknesses, but ultimately they accomplish the same goals.

As an example, suppose we want to build a query that will return all employees with the last name "Smith" from the toy inventory "Employees" table. The query would look like the below.

```
SELECT * FROM Employees WHERE lname='Smith'
```

If a .NET application developer wanted to retrieve the same data using an ORM framework (like Entity Framework), the same query would look different, but in a way that would be more familiar to a developer.

```
var dbContext = new InventoryContext();
var smithEmployees = dbContext.Employees.Where(emp
=> emp.lname == "Smith").ToList();
```

Likewise, if a Java application developer wanted to retrieve the same data using an ORM framework, like Hibernate, the same query would look different as well.

```
String hql = "FROM Employees E WHERE E.lname =
Smith";
Query query = session.createQuery(hql);
List results = query.list();
```

Although the specific queries you will use depend on which framework is being utilized, the end goal is the same—all ORM software allows applications and data systems to communicate. There are so many developments, and so many different technologies, out there. It's more important to understand that frameworks create the ability for these different technologies to communicate and less important to worry over what the syntax is across systems. As a DBA, you will become familiar with the syntax used for the framework that your organization requires.

Impact of Programming On Database Operations

When using ORM, there are no impacts to security, as it is secured the same way as any other device or person through secured accounts. The network configuration is also not affected, because the program itself will connect just as a user connects to the data system.

However, we can feel the impact of programming in queries, because the query is technically being rendered, or written, by the ORM. A developer who does not have a good grasp on how their ORM generates queries based on their programming can cause an inefficient query, which will impact the application as well as the database. For this reason, many DBAs do not like ORMs. The problem, however, is not the tool but rather how it is used.

A DBA who also plays the role of database developer will want to understand how the ORM generates the query so they can provide assistance and guidance to developers on how to most efficiently use the ORM to query the database.

Review Activity:

Object-Relational Mapping

Answer the following questions:

1. **A company website has a java front end and an SQL back end. What should we use to enable communication between these two different applications/systems?**

2. **Which type of ORM is used with .NET?**

3. **What is the point of ORM?**

Topic 4C

Program with SQL

EXAM OBJECTIVES COVERED
1.2 Given a scenario, develop, modify, and run SQL code.
2.2 Explain database implementation, testing, and deployment phases.

When working with the programmatic features of SQL, you will discover that you can gain immediate value with SQL's set-based logic. You will find that having access to pre-built, stored procedures can provide you valuable access for completing certain tasks, and even discovering information within your database. You will also find that you can automate routine tasks by leveraging triggers and even creating your own stored procedures.

Set-Based Logic

Without **set-based logic**, we would need to take a procedural approach, which can be time consuming. For example, if we wanted to create a calculation that performed a total on all the records in a table, we would literally have to write the procedure to loop through each row in that table, gather the value, and add it to the next value. We'd likely declare a variable to capture that value through each row and a variable that would add it to the last calculated value. As you can imagine, this could become cumbersome over time to code and to run.

Luckily, we enjoy the use of set-based logic when working with SQL. It doesn't require us to code every type of example, and even though we might not see the interworkings of how it works, we still reap the benefits. A great example is when you use GROUP BY. This command does exactly what we expressed in the procedural example above, but without us having to code it.

Joins are another example of the benefits of set-based logic. We simply create the join, and SQL knows how to actually join the data together using the technology built to serve that join type.

Existing Stored Procedures

As SQL has been around for more than 30 years, we have the value of plenty of **stored procedures**. These are just as they sound—procedures that are stored and can be reused. In tools like SSMS, stored procedures are located in the database, as well as in the MSDB database on the database engine. These stored procedures are preprogrammed or code statements that perform actions.

In the screenshot below, we are exploring the stored procedures in the MSDB database, which impact and are available to all the databases in this connection.

Stored Procedure `sp_addlogin` *in Microsoft SQL Server Management Studio
(Used with permission from Microsoft.)*

This stored procedure will create a new SQL Server login that allows a user to connect to an instance of SQL Server using authentication.

> *This is just one of many system stored procedures that will be deprecated and removed in a future version of SQL Server. In this particular case, it is recommended to use* `CREATE LOGIN`.

Database Engine Stored Procedures

There are hundreds of stored procedures to explore that will provide value in different situations. It can be challenging to list them all, or even specify the ones you might use, but the following three stored procedures are ones you're certainly likely to use in relation to the database.

- `sp_rename` – Changes the name of a user-created object, like a table, index, or column.

- `sp_executesql` -- Executes a Transact-SQL statement that has been built dynamically.

- `sp_helpdb` – Reports information about a specific database or all databases.

Although this list is certainly not comprehensive, it does give you an understanding of the types of stored procedures that you might use as a DBA.

Creating Stored Procedures

When you find yourself writing the same query over and over again, you would likely benefit from creating your own stored procedure. Any time you have a set of steps that need to occur in a certain order and at a certain time or event, you can create your own stored procedure to more effectively run this procedure. We can easily create a stored procedure in the "Inventory" database by using the template shown in the below screenshot.

*Template for Creating a Stored Procedure in Microsoft SQL Server Management Studio
(Used with permission from Microsoft.)*

For example, suppose every night we have a set of data checks that make sure inventory counts are accurate. We need to ensure that toy sales from both the physical store and online shop are reflected in our stock tables. We can create a stored procedure that we can execute to perform all the necessary steps. This code might look like the following.

```
UPDATE
    Inventory
SET
    QTY = inv.QTY - orderinfo.OrderQty
FROM
    Inventory inv
INNER JOIN
    (SELECT ProductID, SUM(Quantity_Ordered) AS OrderQty
        FROM OrderHeader
        WHERE OrderDate >=
DATEADD(d,0,DATEDIFF(d,0,GETDATE()))
        AND OrderDate <= GETDATE()
        GROUP BY ProductID) orderinfo
ON
    inv.ProductID = orderinfo.ProductID;
```

Once we have created a stored procedure, we can call on it or query with it any time we need to use the procedure. We can also schedule it to run at certain times during the day, or call it using triggers within the data system.

Types of Triggers

We have thus far created tables, scripted SELECT statements, and discussed views, so we should also discuss a special type of stored procedure called a **trigger**. These stored procedures will "fire" off based on certain events that can trigger an action to occur, and they can help you to automate certain processes.

Triggers will automatically run on DML commands, like INSERT, UPDATE, or even DELETE. They can also run with DDL commands, like CREATE, ALTER, and DROP.

Triggers can be of immense value to us, because they provide automation at the time of the event. Here are six different types of triggers that we will commonly use.

1. AFTER INSERT: after data is inserted into the table

2. AFTER UPDATE: after data in the table is modified

3. AFTER DELETE: after data is deleted/removed from the table

4. BEFORE INSERT: before data is inserted into the table

5. BEFORE UPDATE: before data in the table is modified

6. BEFORE DELETE: before data is deleted/removed from the table

When automating with triggers, you want to be sure you choose the appropriate trigger type for what you are trying to accomplish. For example, if we update a toy star rating in the product table, we might want a trigger to populate the field once the Toy Star Import routine has updated the data in the ToyStarRatings table. This type of trigger would need to be set for AFTER UPDATE, so as soon as the record is updated, it would trigger that process to run and make that update.

As another example, suppose we want to make sure before a record is deleted that an archived copy of that rating is inserted into another table for historical purposes. In this instance, we would use the BEFORE DELETE type of trigger.

Setting Triggers

To set a trigger, we first expand the table that requires the trigger and then create a new trigger statement, which is as simple as a right-click in tools like SQL Server Management Studio.

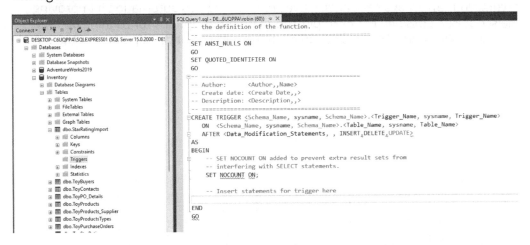

Template Code Provided by Microsoft SQL Server Management Studio When Creating a New Trigger on a Table (Used with permission from Microsoft.)

In our ToyStarRatingImport table, as soon as that data is up to date, we can add the following code to create the trigger. It's important to understand that the server will see this trigger and automatically execute the code as soon as the trigger activates.

```
USE INVENTORY
GO
SET ANSI_NULLS ON
GO
SET QUOTED_IDENTIFIER ON
GO
CREATE TRIGGER [dbo].[UpdateStarRatingsHistory]
ON [dbo].[StarRatingImport]
AFTER INSERT
AS
INSERT INTO ToyStarRatings(ProductID, StarRating,
CT_Rates, RatingDate)
SELECT ProductID, Star_Rating, Number_of_Ratings,
Rating_Date
FROM INSERTED;
GO
ALTER TABLE [dbo].[StarRatingImport] ENABLE
TRIGGER [UpdateStarRatingsHistory]
GO
```

The value of this automation is that we don't have to manually execute this query ourselves; we can set it to run automatically.

As with anything we do in our scripting and coding, creating triggers can impact the performance of the database. In some cases, you may find that a trial-and-error approach will be an everyday part of your life when you automate. If you build an automation that slows the entire server down when you run it, and then you apply it to a trigger that runs it automatically, there can be a negative impact. When this occurs, you can always seek alternatives for running this automation if improving the script isn't possible. For example, there are other options for running on timers, like using SQL Server Agent to set up a job that will run at certain times of the day.

Review Activity:

Program with SQL

Answer the following questions:

1. Using the `GROUP BY` command in an SQL query performs the grouping and provides a total. What type of logic is this an example of?

2. Unlike a view, a _____ can be used for steps that regularly need to occur and in a certain order.

3. A discount table has a date field for expiration and a Boolean field for active or inactive status. When the date passes on the discount, and we want to make the status "inactive," what function would be helpful?

4. What consideration should be made for using a trigger that runs automatically?

Topic 4D

Write Functions

EXAM OBJECTIVES COVERED
1.2 Given a scenario, develop, modify, and run SQL code.

The most common reason for using **functions** is the need to create data that doesn't exist in your database, or at least doesn't exist in the way you might require it for a data project. Databases are already large, so storing every single calculation that you would ever use (or maybe never use) does not make sense. The data that is stored can provide you with valuable information that can be used to create new data. You can also use functions to manipulate data, such as conversion-related or format-related functions.

Types of Functions

When databases are designed, they will often include the data we need, but for storage reasons we don't build a field to hold every type of calculation. One of the main reasons we use functions is to be able to provide the data from the calculations in views. Following are several different types of functions that we can use to do so.

System Functions

You likely are already familiar with the fact that there are hundreds of built-in functions we can leverage with our data. These pre-built functions can offer us convenience when building views and populating them with data.

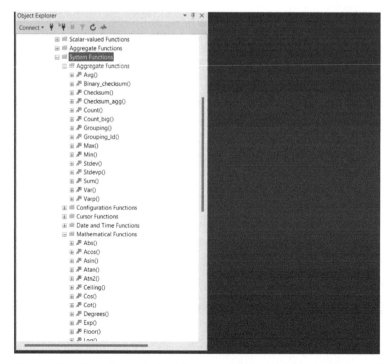

Systems Functions Expanded in Microsoft SQL Server Management Studio
(Used with permission from Microsoft.)

The screenshot above shows just a sampling of the many functions that are pre-built into the system functions palette. This selection of pre-built functions for common calculations saves us the time of designing them manually. For example, to produce the average manually, we'd have to write a calculation that totaled all the values, counted them, and then divided them. But we can instead just run the `AVG()` function. You can imagine the amount of coding that would be required to create calculations if so many of these pre-built functions didn't exist.

User-Defined Functions

Even with such a large selection of built-in functions, there are still times when you will need something more customized. User-defined functions allow the SQL developer to create routines that accept parameters, perform an action (such as a complex calculation), and return the result of that action as a value. User-defined functions have a few benefits over just writing Transact-SQL queries.

- **Modularity:** User-defined functions allow for the creation of the function once, storing it in the database, and calling it any number of times in your program. This reduces having to repeat that same code multiple times in different SQL programs.

- **Execution:** Similar to stored procedures, user-defined functions reduce the compilation cost of the code by caching the plans and reusing them for future executions. This eliminates the need for the user-defined function to be parsed and optimized every time it is executed.

Scalar Functions

One common subtype of the user-defined function is the scalar function. Scalar functions accept a single or multiple parameters and return only a single value as output. Scalar functions are often used to perform complex calculations on the input values or perform some special formatting on the returned value. But scalar functions can also be used to simplify code and reduce the amount of code that would need to be replicated in multiple queries. The returned single value can be of any data type. Scalar functions can be used as elements of a `SELECT` statement or as criteria in a `WHERE` clause.

For example, if you were retrieving sales data from the SalesOrderHeader table and needed to display the order date as a formatted month and year, you could create a function to perform that date manipulation.

```
CREATE FUNCTION FormatDateForSales (@FullDate
[DATE])

RETURNS varchar(10) AS

BEGIN

RETURN CONVERT(VARCHAR(2), MONTH(@FullDate))
+ ' | ' + CONVERT(VARCHAR(4), YEAR(@FullDate))

END
```

This function would then be called in a query.

```
SELECT TOP 100 OrderDate,
dbo.FormatDateForSales(OrderDate) FROM
Sales.SalesOrderHeader
```

Text Functions

There are several types of built-in functions that you will frequently use. You will likely see text functions in all tools designed to work with data. Some common functions you will find helpful when working with text are as follows.

- `=TRIM()` – Removes leading and trailing spaces.

- `=LEFT()` – Returns a number of characters from the left side of the field.

- `=RIGHT()` – Returns a number of characters from the right side of the field.

- `=LEN()` – Produces a number that tells you how many countable characters are in that field.

- `=CONCATWS()` – Produces a combined set of fields with a delimiter.

Let's look at a code sample of the `TRIM` command, which we will use here to remove the leading and trailing spaces in the product description field.

```
SELECT ToyProducts.ProductID,
ToyProducts. ProductName, ToyProducts.ProductCost,
ToyProducts.StarRating,

--the trim command removes leading and trailing
spaces

TRIM(ProductDescriptions.ProductDescription) as

ProductDescription

FROM  ToyProducts INNER JOIN
    ProductDescriptions ON
ToyProducts.ProductID =
ProductDescriptions.ProductID
```

Date Functions

When we know when something occurred, but need more data around that date, we use date functions. Here are some of the most common date functions and their purposes.

- `NOW()` – Uses the computer system time to tell the current date and time of a calculation. When you use `NOW()` and another date, like ShipDate, in a function together, it can tell you how many days have elapsed from the time it was shipped or how many days are left until it should be shipped.

- `DATEDIFF()` – Used to calculate the amount of days between two dates: a start date and an end point. `NOW()` or `TODAY()` is the start or end point for the `DATEDIFF()`.

- `DATEADD()` – Allows you to add a specified number of days, months, or years to a date.

Suppose we are creating a query for a business analyst who needs to know the timeline for follow-up after issuing a purchase order. We can use the `Now( )` function to capture the date and time when we run this query, as well as the 30-day follow-up required when a PO is issued.

```
SELECT
ToyPO_Details.PO_ID, ToyPurchaseOrders.PO_Date,
ToyPO_Details.ProductID, ToyProducts.ProductCost,
ToyPO_Details.QTY,
---Functions added after this line
{ fn NOW() } AS DataDate,
DATEADD (dd,30,PO_Date) as FollowUpDate
FROM   ToyPO_Details INNER JOIN
       ToyProducts ON ToyPO_Details.ProductID =
ToyProducts.ProductID INNER JOIN
       ToyPurchaseOrders ON ToyPO_Details.PO_ID =
ToyPurchaseOrders.PO_ID
```

Logical Functions

Logical functions work with data that is either true or false, checking if a condition is met and returning a result based on the outcome. Logic is a powerful tool for ensuring data meets business rules. There are several types of logical functions, but a few of the most common examples are listed below.

- `IIF` – Allows you to perform a logical test that will return only true or false and then lets you specify values for the true and false part of the test.

- `ISNULL` – Returns true if a field value is null (empty) and false if it's not.

- `CASE` – Allows you to have muliple cases and results. It is similar to an IIF but with multiple logical tests.

In the script below, we are displaying product ratings information but also including a case statement that will return the various "*" for our data set. This is similar to an `IF` or `IIF` function but with multiple outcomes for each star rating.

```
SELECT [ProductID], [ProductName],
[ProductListPrice],[StarRating], [CT_Rates],
    CASE
WHEN [StarRating] = 1 THEN '**'
WHEN [StarRating] = 2 THEN '**'
WHEN [StarRating] = 3 THEN '***'
WHEN [StarRating] = 4 THEN '****'
WHEN [StarRating] = 5 THEN '*****'
    END as Stars
FROM [Inventory].[dbo].[ProductsAndRatings]
```

If you look at the Stars column in our results screenshot, you will see a varying number of asterisks based on the actual star rating number for each product.

⊞ Results ▦ Messages

	ProductID	ProductName	ProductListPrice	StarRating	CT_Rates	Stars
1	1	Alex Agcaoili action figure	2	2	100	**
2	2	Andrea Alameda action figure	4	3	100	***
3	3	Carlos Alcorn action figure	5	5	100	*****
4	4	Dalton Alonso action figure	6	1	100	**
5	5	Evan Alvaro action figure	7	4	100	****
6	6	Gabrielle Ansman-Wolfe action figure	9	2	100	**
7	7	Isabella Beanston action figure	10	3	100	***
8	8	James Becker action figure	11	5	100	*****
9	9	Julia Benson action figure	12	1	100	**
10	10	Kevin Berge action figure	2	4	100	****
11	11	Richard Blythe action figure	4	2	100	**
12	12	Sean Boseman action figure	5	3	100	***
13	13	Xavier Bready action figure	6	5	100	*****
14	14	Alisha Bright action figure	7	1	100	**
15	15	Meghan Brumfield action figure	9	4	100	****
16	16	Milton Bruno action figure	10	2	100	**
17	17	Alexandria Burkhardt action figure	11	3	100	***

✔ Query executed successfully.

Results of the Case Statement in Microsoft SQL Server Management Studio
(Used with permission from Microsoft.)

Aggregate Functions

Aggregate functions perform some calculation on a set of values to return a single value. You will use these types of functions regularly when working with GROUP BY to create the appropriate aggregated data set. Some common examples of aggregate functions are as follows.

- SUM – Adds all records together to produce a total; often used for amounts and quantities.

- COUNT – Counts all the records as individual lines to produce a record count.

- DISTINCT COUNT – Counts all the records in a column, but will only count the field one time, even if it appears multiple times.

- AVERAGE – Totals all the values in a column and then divides them by the count of values.

- MAX – Gives the largest value in a column.

- MIN – Gives the smallest value in a column.

In the script below, the code will count all the records from the ToyBuyers table and display a count with a field label of "Total Buyer Record." This is an easy script that is frequently used to obtain record counts.

```
SELECT Count (*) as 'Total Buyer Records'
    FROM [ToyBuyers]
```

Review Activity:

Functions

Answer the following questions:

1. **When you need to use a function that is not already available as a system function, what type of function would you build?**

2. **Which type of user-defined function is often used to perform complex calculations on the input values or perform some special formatting on the returned value?**

3. **Pre-built functions are also know as what?**

4. **What type of function would you use to calculate the total number of days between when an order was shipped and when it was delivered?**

5. `CASE WHEN Color = 1 THEN 'RED' ELSE 'Gray'` **is an example of a(n) _____ function.**

Lesson 4

Summary

After this lesson, you should have a better understanding of how we build views for data that people will use often, including snapshots, which can store valuable data. You will understand more about how ORM applications and frameworks allow systems that have a front end and back end in different technologies to communicate. You should understand how triggers, stored procedures, and set-based logic can help automate and streamline some of the data management tasks you will perform as a DBA. You should also be familiar with the types of functions you will use for queries, data management, and reporting.

Guidelines for Supporting Data Systems Through Programming

Consider these best practices and guidelines when working with the programming aspects of data systems.

1. **Use views to create repeatable queries that can be shared with others, so they can use the data without having to build their own scripts.**

2. **Determine what programming languages are at use in the systems you support and what ORM technology is used to support the mapping.**

3. **Find the existing stored procedures at your organization and determine which procedures are commonly used.**

4. **Explore the use of triggers to automate some of the scripts you might run routinely.**

5. **Explore built-in functions to determine if a function you need already exists.**

Lesson 5

Understanding Database Planning and Design

LESSON INTRODUCTION

There are many considerations when planning and designing data systems, from understanding architecture, like hosting servers on-site, to leveraging cloud-based environments. No matter the infrastructure, there are some common planning steps that must be undertaken, such as gathering requirements for users and size, identifying the use case for the application, and understanding the different database designs. You must also be familiar with all the documented requirements that will affect your design.

Lesson Objectives

In this lesson, you will do the following:

- Understand types of architecture.

- Gather requirements.

- Review documentation requirements.

Topic 5A

Understand Types of Architecture

EXAM OBJECTIVES COVERED
2.1 Compare and contrast aspects of database planning and design.

In the not-so-distant past, businesses stored all of their data on-premise. Nowadays, there are some modern companies that have never hosted their own servers, or even paid for datacenter space. Most organizations fall somewhere in between, storing their information both in an on-premise location and on the cloud. The number of cloud solutions is continually growing, and so is the use of cloud computing environments. When planning your database, you must understand the types of architecture used by your organization.

Cloud vs. On-Premise

No matter the size of an organization, there is one question that will always present itself: Where should company information be stored? As a database administrator, the answer to this question can affect your role. There are two major types of storage locations.

An **on-premise database** is a database hosted on an organization's server. That server could be located physically on-site, in the company's server room, or off-site at a datacenter—sometimes even in a closet! In the past, organizations hosted their own environments and also had total control over the total architecture. As a database administrator, if your organization uses an on-premise database, you will be more involved in and responsible for performance monitoring, deployment, and the database's availability to the application.

A **cloud database** is a database hosted by a cloud computing vendor who installs, configures, and manages server and system infrastructure for the chosen database platform. Cloud databases make data storage more accessible, and their flexibility has become critical as organizations hire increasing numbers of remote workers. If your organization uses a cloud database, you will focus on optimizing the database and monitoring cost and performance, since the responsibility of database deployment and installation is shifted to the cloud platform.

Ultimately, a DBA should be aware of how their responsibilities may shift with the change from on-premise to cloud. When working with on-premise servers and infrastructure, you might be responsible for installing the database, setting the necessary properties, and preparing it for end users to use. In a cloud-based setup, you might be communicating with others who are responsible for the install and properties. You will likely find that you are doing some of the same things regardless of environment, like performance tuning on queries. The differences might be where you are performing the change and what software you are using.

Platform as a Service (PaaS)

Platform as a service (PaaS) is a cloud computing solution where the service provider handles the creation and maintenance of the infrastructure, in addition to performing other tasks associated with supporting application development. PaaS is broad and can include many different types of network and server infrastructure that a client can purchase, along with the required platform and support.

A cloud database solution is becoming the standard for many organizations, but there are still situations where an organization might utilize a hybrid solution, such as when a third-party cloud database software is installed on a company's own server.

Another type of PaaS leverages **database as a service (DBaaS)**. This solution might include a service package that provides coverage for tasks that an internal DBA might typically perform, such as backups and routine maintenance.

As a database administrator, this may sound like the loss of your daily tasks, and for the most part it does remove a few of the more basic responsibilities. This ultimately frees up time for you to focus more on performance tuning, monitoring, and securing your database, especially if it holds sensitive data. Typically, organizations utilize PaaS when they require an infrastructure for various types of technical projects. PaaS is also used for the following:

- **Application Development:** The use of PaaS provides a complete development and deployment environment that is ready for the building of applications.

- **Business Intelligence (BI) Development:** Tools like Power BI and Tableau work on the enterprise level and provide a platform for people to distribute and share data and visualization.

- **Internet of Things (IoT):** A platform of services that works with the technology allows you to benefit from information and hardware that isn't built internally from the ground up.

Some of the more common providers for PaaS that you will come across include the following:

- Microsoft Azure

- Amazon Web Services (AWS)

- Oracle Cloud

- Google App Engine

- SAP Cloud

Software as a Service (SaaS)

When an organization does not have the programming resources or data management team in place to support ever-changing business requirements, it will often leverage **software as a service (SaaS)**. SaaS shifts more of the responsibility away from the organization, which allows for a quicker path to delivery and implementation with users. When using a SaaS solution, the provider of the solution handles all of its development. The end users, which will be the technical team and the organization's staff, will use the system by logging into the SaaS solution, such as via a web browser.

The DBA will likely admin the users, but they will use the system that has been provided to add users and maintain users. For example, if the organization has tools for single sign-on (SSO), the DBA will work with the SaaS provider to establish the access this way. If the organization does not have SSO, then the DBA may enter the users and modify them as needed inside the provided system.

SaaS is a very well-known service offering, even outside of the DBA role. SaaS is consumed not only by IT users, but also the public. For example, SaaS is used for streaming services, online shopping websites, and IoT applications. You will see this term used often when it comes to technology, because anytime software does something—like conducting a process or providing information—it might be labeled as SaaS. When you log into an accounting software account to manage your finances, or sign into a streaming service to watch a popular TV show, you are using software as a service.

SaaS offerings range in complexity. It could be as simple as integrating a few users of an accounting system with an organization's database server, or as complex as customer relationship software that also manages inventory and shipping. The provider of the SaaS solution handles the software and integration to the database, but the DBA handles the daily maintenance of the database. Although a SaaS database will be fully managed by the provider, the DBA will be responsible for ensuring scalability and utilization, which in return increases the value of the SaaS.

For example, a DBA may be asked to manage a data cube for a specific department or work with building scripts to provide data to other databases the DBA manages. DBAs should further be aware of the responsibilities they will have on a new SaaS implementation. They may work with a third-party team to implement the solution at their organization, or they may work with an internal technical team to deploy the solution with the third party.

 SaaS can provide a lot of different capabilities for an organization that are not being built by the internal team. The ability to provide off-the-shelf software is a massive time saver for an organization. This doesn't mean that these types of solutions aren't customizable; many are, and the DBA may be involved in customizing the SaaS solutions that are adopted at the organization.

These types of decisions and responsibilities will be defined by the team that is responsible for this software at the organization. The type of work you may or may not do will vary depending on the type of SaaS offering and the project. Below are a few SaaS offerings you will likely recognize:

- Salesforce
- Microsoft Office 365
- Google Sheets
- Netflix

Infrastructure as a Service (IaaS)

Similar to PaaS, **infrastructure as a service (IaaS)** is a cloud computing solution where the service provider hosts the servers, storage, and hardware that you would typically find in a physical datacenter. This gives an organization the most flexibility and control over their infrastructure, but also requires them to manage more internal resources. Because of that, you will most often find IaaS implemented in medium to large organizations. As a database administrator, you are likely to be a part of a team gathering requirements. The DBA is typically responsible for gathering technical requirements and assessing the infrastructure needs, as a part of the overall plan. Gathering accurate requirements is critical with IaaS because of its pricing; accurate requirements can mean a potential cost savings, whereas a lack of planning can mean increased costs.

As the DBA working with IaaS, your main responsibilities would be managing data and backup and recovery. However, you would also likely be responsible for evaluating the processing power necessary for your database systems.

Review Activity:

Types of Architecture

Answer the following questions:

1. **A database hosted on-site is known as what?**

2. **What are the three database storage solutions?**

3. **An organization will typically utilize a _____ solution when they require an infrastructure for various types of technical projects.**

4. **True or False: Software as a service (SaaS) is only consumed by IT users.**

5. **What main responsibilities exist for a DBA using an infrastructure as a service (IaaS) solution?**

Topic 5B

Gather Data System Requirements

 EXAM OBJECTIVES COVERED
2.1 Compare and contrast aspects of database planning and design.

One of the worst-case scenarios for a developer is to develop a system without putting time and effort into gathering all the requirements. For example, imagine that you spend a lot of time developing a complex data system that can be used by anyone within a large organization. However, after you've put all the work in, you discover that the organization only needs 25 users from a single department to access the system, and only for a single purpose. Knowing the requirements up front saves you from spending too much time developing something that's not needed, and also from developing something that does not meet the organization's needs.

Requirements dictate how the data will be used, and for what purpose. This means getting into the details of how many users will be accessing the system and using it as designed. It will also include how often the system will be used and what type of process and data it controls. You must also decide how much space will be needed, what type of scale is expected, and what data sources could be used. Then you will consider all these requirements to determine what you have and what you will need to change.

Understanding the Objective of the Database

The first critical step when gathering requirements is to determine the objective of the database. Having a clear understanding of the objective will clarify why the data is important and what process(es) it will be involved in. For example, the database for a private toy company will have different processes than a database of healthcare information (which would have different compliance requirements than toy transactions).

Database Objective for the Organization

If you are on a project from its beginning, you might be involved in the development of the database's overall objective, but if you are assigned to a project after the objective has been set, you will want to quickly familiarize yourself with it. This type of database objective is the objective of the data system as it pertains to the organization.

When organizations don't do a good job of documenting projects, it can be challenging to figure out the objective for the organization.

Database Objective for the Data System

When considering the objective not of the organization, but of the data system itself, the type of system can give you clues. For example, the objective of a customer relationship management (CRM) system is to manage customer relationships. But other systems might not be so obvious. If the database system is a legacy system, and it was built internally over years, it might have many processes covering a lot of different areas of an organization. It does not have a single objective like CRM, making it more difficult to know exactly what the system is meant to do.

You can and should ask for documentation on the processes, as well as documentation on the database. If this is an off-the-shelf system, like a CRM, you can find supporting materials on the vendor site, which will also help to determine the objective of the system and identify how it is meant to support an organization.

Let's talk again about relational vs. non-relational databases. The objective of a relational database is to provide a system that has structured tables and relationships designed for storage and reporting purposes. The objective of a non-relational system is to gather and store data, specifically a certain type of data that is best suited for the system. For example, social media data is mostly unstructured, as videos and images are unstructured by nature. Thus, the objective of non-relational systems is to make the process of designing and scaling much more simplified, without the overhead of designing relational systems.

In short, there is an objective at every level of a data project—from the internal goal and objective for the organization, to the data system itself, and finally to the technology it uses.

Identifying User-Related Information

As a part of the requirements gathering, when working with a new system (or even just trying to understand existing systems within an organization), it is important to learn who is using the database and which departments they belong to. You might ask what they do with the system and what function(s) it helps them to perform. A great deal of thought needs to be put into understanding who will ultimately be using the data and what they will be doing with the information.

Let's imagine a manager has asked you to design a vendor incentives database in SQL Server in order to support a system that helps with vendors. You can start by asking some simple questions to begin identifying the users for the new vendor incentive system, such as who this system is intended for. The manager might answer that it's for vendors and only vendors. But if they say it's for vendors, clients, and internal employees, then this presents three different user groups (and likely three different types of permissions).

Next, you need to understand who the users are in each group. How many of them exist, and what types of permissions will they need? Would this group only need to read the data (meaning they can't edit it)? It is helpful to begin gathering this type of information at the start of any project. You also need to determine what user information the system expects and requires. For example, does it need a user's first name, last name, middle initial, valid phone number, and email address? In order to add users to the SQL database, you might first need to create a list of users with all the required fields.

Gathering Storage and Size Requirements

When implementing a data system that has a database, reporting capabilities, and applications associated with it, you must also consider size and storage. First, there are requirements in regard to actual data storage. Suppose your data has to be maintained for seven years. This means you must have storage available for that data for at least seven years, or at least a strategy for storing it that long. Then, there are actual storage requirements based on the need of the data system itself. If you are installing a large database, then you must have enough space to hold it. The reverse is also true; a smaller database will not be the same size as a large database, and it will require the appropriate amount of storage for its size. There are also storage requirements to consider regarding the growth of the data and scale. We will dig more into managing growth and scale at a later point. For now, just note how much data is anticipated and how much it will grow over time when gathering requirements.

In addition to requirements for actual storage, it is also important to know what type of data is being stored, so that the correct type of system is selected. Relational databases are meant to hold structured data and will have various storage settings. Non-relational data systems are designed to be more flexible and are commonly used for gathering data on other items, like images on posts and videos. Think about the early days of social media. There were maybe only one or two social media platforms, with not nearly as many users as there are now. Imagine the amount of change the various data systems that provide us our social media platforms have undergone—not only in features, but also in size. The storage requirements continuously change and grow throughout the life of the service, and in some cases even overnight.

In addition to size requirements, you will also encounter speed requirements. We will discuss this further in later chapters, but processing speed will always be a factor to consider when gathering requirements. Data systems will have a minimum requirement for starting up, and this requirement can grow and scale over time and with use. You will want to make sure you identify the minimum requirements for storage and speed when planning for a new data system.

Gathering Data Sources

Data systems can be brought into an organization to either support a new process or to change the software for an existing process. In either case, you and others involved in the project will need to gather data sources. Consider software that will be used for inventory management. This software will use an SQL backend, and users will work with an application that has been designed to manage inventory.

It's likely that the company already has most of the data that is needed to populate this new system in some form, whether that form is databases, spreadsheets, or other web-based applications, to name a few. In this scenario, the old inventory data system will not automatically populate the new inventory system. The DBA will need to identify all the data that is needed from the older system, and note that there will be some manual intervention. The supporting system accounting tools were likely also considered when the system was purchased. Identifying the appropriate tools allows us to identify what accounting data is needed and how that data will pass through the system.

 Keeping great notes and documentation during this discovering and gathering stage can be invaluable. You should note each data source, where it is from, and why it matters to the new data system.

Review Activity:

Data System Requirements

Answer the following questions:

1. **What is the first critical step when gathering requirements?**

2. **If an employee database is being developed, what additional user-related information might be needed?**

3. **Two companies are merging, and a new database is being created to accommodate historical data. The objective, users, and data sources have been outlined. What other consideration must be taken?**

4. **When moving a legacy system to a new system, which requirement is critical for populating the data?**

Topic 5C

Review Documentation Requirements

EXAM OBJECTIVES COVERED
2.1 Compare and contrast aspects of database planning and design.
3.3 Given a scenario, produce documentation and use relevant tools.

The last time you purchased a type of machine, or some tech gadget, it likely came packaged with a set of instructions—maybe even multiple booklets. This accompany material can contain anything from standard operating procedures to exact technical specifications to instructions for modification. Data systems are no different; each system may have its own type of nuances, and there may seem to be no shortage of information you have to comb through before you can use it. You might even be tasked with creating documentation for others. Here, we will cover the main pieces of data systems documentation that you need to be familiar with as a database administrator.

Standard Operating Procedures

Standard operating procedures (SOPs) are used to document a process that operates within an organization. It's how employees know how to perform some action, including what steps need to be taken when following said process. The implementation of SOPs provide consistency, ensuring that all people are performing the process in the same way. Whether a department has five members or 500, the process will be done exactly the same, as intended and outlined by the SOP.

It's important to note that SOPs are not a one-size-fits-all solution. While different organizations may use SOPs for common procedures throughout their industry, each organization's SOPs will be defined by how that company operates and be framed around their mission.

For example, consider the onboarding procedure for when an employee is hired to the organization. This procedure likely includes assigning the new employee their computer login, and because they are a part of a department, it will include or will also note what permissions they should have in the organization's data systems.

Depending on how the organization handles permissions, this could be an automated process, where the employee immediately gains the needed permissions when they are assigned to a group. However, in other situations, the database administrator might be notified of the new hire by their manager, requesting that this person be granted access to certain data. So while the varying organizations will each have SOPs for onboarding the employee, the actual content of the SOP will vary.

Organizations that are regulated are often required to maintain compliance documentation, which will most certainly include standard operating procedures.

Organizational compliance documentation exists in addition to SOPs. Third-party compliance documentation is another requirement for organizational compliance. This documentation ensures that vendors, suppliers, and partners also comply with the rules and regulations an organization must adhere to. For example, when an organization that must comply with HIPAA purchases software, that software is also required to fall under HIPAA compliance measures.

No matter what organization you work for, one of the very first types of documentation you should ask for is the standard operating procedures at your company.

Data Dictionary

The **data dictionary** is a critical part of data management and a valuable resource for the organization (and all its data professionals). This resource document serves as the truest authority on all definitions that have been agreed upon for the database.

The data dictionary may contain all the information related to a table design, relationships, views, and other data properties. It will likely contain data elements and their definitions and field attributes, along with the relationships and structure of the data.

The data dictionary should be a living tool—as definitions change or new data systems are added to the organization, the definitions will be updated and new data will need to be added to the data dictionary.

Having a complete data dictionary helps to increase your ability to find the appropriate fields and tables and to understand the relationships needed to build their required data sets. This is great information for a new database administrator to have access to when adding a new database to their projects or workload.

Data dictionaries can be created by hand or generated by tools that work with databases. The simplest form of a data dictionary can still be a powerful asset. Even tools intended for lightweight databases, like Microsoft Access, often have the ability to generate basic data dictionary-type information.

The script provides information on the columns of a particular table (or all tables and various properties). This is information that you might find in a data dictionary.

```
SELECT * FROM AdventureWorks2019.INFORMATION_SCHEMA.
COLUMNS
```

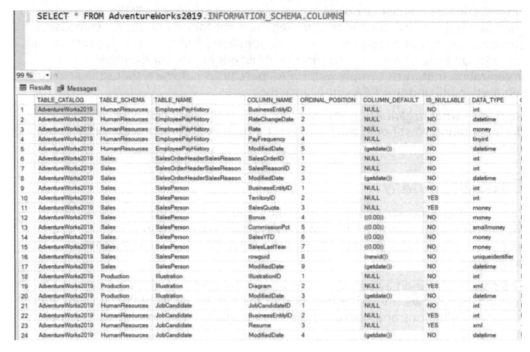

Information Schema Script for Columns in Microsoft SQL Server Management Studio
(Used with permission from Microsoft.)

Although you won't see all of the columns in the screenshot, you can see that this simple script pulls a lot of detailed information about the tables and fields, and their attributes. This can be a big time-saver when searching for information or writing scripts to impact data.

System Specifications and Requirements

Specifications describe the intended use of a software program or database. This documentation can also include **system requirements**, which are the "specs" needed to run a software, database, or application. For example, you can't load a software program that requires 16 gigs of memory onto a machine that only has 4 gigs.

Before installing any program, you will want to first review the system requirements for the environment to ensure it can properly run. If the environment does not meet the needed specification, you will need to ensure it is brought up to the minimum system requirements before any implementation can occur. This process is known as an inventory and **gap analysis**, and it involves identifying the current system specs and determining what needs to be added in order to properly run the program. You will perform this type of inventory and gap analysis throughout the process of implementing a database.

Let's consider an example. Imagine that someone from your organization's business unit found an amazing software program that they believe can provide a lot of the data needed to measure and create value for the organization. They have spending rights up to $10,000 and have used this money to purchase the software, which was then brought to the technology department for implementation. The first thing that the tech department will do is verify the system requirements. The key question to ask is: Can this software properly run on the existing environment? Suppose you discover the server you wanted to place this software on requires 500 gigs of space, and your environment only has 250 gigs. This means you have a gap to overcome. You might contact the network admins or server admins to increase your space and see if that will incur more costs.

System requirements are also important when considering any existing software, database, or application used by the company. You already know that the system meets the requirements for existing programs, but upon reviewing the requirements, you may find that your environment exceeds them. If the environment's specs are higher than needed, the organization is paying unnecessarily for more space or power.

Software programs typically provide tools to test your environment, to see if your machine meets the minimum specifications and suggest solutions if it does not.

Maintenance Documentation

Maintenance documentation is intended to help you maintain the data system you have in place. Database maintenance is a set of steps or procedures followed to maintain your database's health. Think of it like the maintenance we do for our cars. We must change the oil in the car every so many miles to keep it running effectively. Similarly, databases must be maintained because when they fail to perform, we know something is not happening in the organization that should be.

Let's imagine that something goes wrong, and all of an organization's salespeople can no longer enter sales into the database. This has a ripple effect that can be damaging to the company. Failures do happen, but the DBA's goal is to prevent them from happening, especially when we can control certain routine actions.

An example of a type of database maintenance is maintaining a backup of the database. There are steps that you perform to create the backup, and there may even be time points. Suppose your organization automates backups of the data. In that case, you might perform less of this type of maintenance, but you would still need to confirm that the necessary steps for conducting backups are included as intended.

Leveraging Tools for Documentation

As a database administrator, you will not only find yourself reading documentation related to your data systems, but you will also create documentation.

It's important to remember that because you are supporting a data system, you will have more access to the data than others, and these other users will often need documentation on the system and the structure of the database. In some cases, you can provide the standard documentation that comes with a data system (like a new CRM). However, if you're working with an internal system, you may find you must create many different types of documentation. For example, the new data analyst asks you how certain tables are joined so they can start working on a set of reports for their department. You might provide them documentation that shows those relationships, or you might even create it for them.

You will typically review and create documentation using the **Unified Modeling Language (UML)**, which is a general development and modeling language in software and database engineering. You can use diagram programs to diagram data systems and relationships; tools like Visio, Lucid, and more have built-in features to make this an easier process. These diagrams can be beneficial not only for the DBA in the process of designing, but also for others who will build queries that support reports. For example, suppose you have been asked to give a business analyst who's supporting the production department's reporting effort access to one or more tables in the database. They have reached out and asked you if you have any insight into how to join the data together. You can easily give them a quick diagram that can help display this.

Word processing tools like Google Docs or Microsoft Word are used to write requirements, or procedures. Microsoft Word is a robust document editor with useful features like headings, bullets, and even an automatic table of contents.

In addition to diagram and word processing tools, you will find that spreadsheets are useful when working with data for meetings or even displaying data as tables for presentations. The features in a spreadsheet tool, such as Microsoft Excel, allow you to not only share information but also to verify and validate information. Some programs even offer tools for pivots and charting to more easily make sense of the data.

Review Activity:

Documentation Requirements

Answer the following questions:

1. **What type of documentation ensures consistency in the execution of processes by those across an organization?**

2. **What information might be contained within a data dictionary?**

3. **What process is used to ensure minimum system requirements are met before implementation can occur?**

4. **What is Unified Modeling Language (UML)?**

Lesson 5

Summary

After this lesson, you should be able to identify the different types of database architecture that your organization uses and understand how it affects your role when designing a database. You should be familiar with the requirements that must be gathered during the planning and designing stage, as well as the documentation you will need to keep and/or refer to. You should be able to fully plan the design of a database so that you can move onto implementation.

Guidelines for Understanding Database Planning and Design

Consider these best practices and guidelines when planning and designing data systems or when being a part of the design team.

1. **If your organization uses an on-premise data system, you will be expected to manage systems based in an internal network.**

2. **If your organization uses a cloud-based data system, you will be expected to manage this system through a hosted system that is not physically located on-site.**

3. **Be prepared to identify baseline numbers for size, storage, growth, and users during the requirements gathering phase, as these factors play into system design.**

4. **Understanding how people will use the data system, and what it is intended to do, will help you understand the goal and other requirements.**

5. **Data systems require CPU and memory, and knowing those minimum thresholds allow teams to make decisions on how much to allocate to a server.**

6. **Gather any existing data that might be stored in various ways all over an organization through the design process to avoid the need to manually add it by hand.**

7. **As a DBA, you must be comfortable reading both technical documentation, like maintenance documentation, and standard operating procedures.**

Lesson 6

Implementing, Testing, and Deploying Databases

LESSON INTRODUCTION

No single implementation of any system is perfectly alike. However, when working with data system implementations, there are common elements that you will likely encounter. These phases of deployment are typically as follows:

- Establish network

- Configure the environment (testing and production)

- Install and configure the database

- Assign permissions and set security

- Conduct testing

- Deploy to production

You may sometimes be responsible for installing and configuring a database, but even if you're not the person in charge of these processes, it's still important to know how it's done. As a DBA, you may also find you are responsible for performing quality checks, both on systems that have been designed and/or implemented by others and systems you design. This can include verifying and validating that properties are set and tables are created as intended by the design. You will also spend time testing systems when new features are added.

Lesson Objectives

In this lesson, you will do the following:

- Prepare for deployment.

- Conduct testing and other quality measures.

- Understand validation techniques and methods.

Topic 6A

Prepare for Deployment

EXAM OBJECTIVES COVERED
2.2 Explain database implementation, testing, and deployment phases.
3.1 Explain the purpose of monitoring and reporting for database management and performance.

Organizations will have databases in various stages of deployment. You will find that there are databases that are legacy (older) but still in use, newly created databases, and also database systems and/or data that has been acquired through mergers and acquisitions. As a DBA, you might be involved in every step of the process, but in some cases, other people are responsible for setting up the environment, and maybe even configuring the database. Even in those cases, the DBA would likely still be responsible for maintenance and settings after implementation. Having a baseline understanding of how systems are installed on servers, and what you may need to check afterward, can be helpful. Even if settings might differ, you will find they are all adjusted in the same way within the software used for your data system.

Acquiring Assets for Deployment

When a company purchases another company, they are not only buying the company name and products, but they are also likely acquiring their technical assets—like databases. For example, imagine that our toy company recently acquired a company that specializes in wooden toys. This acquisition allows the toy company to expand their client list, and their toy inventory, to include those wooden toys. The toy company will work to migrate all the data from the specialty toy shop into their current systems, assessing the software and systems of the specialty toy company to determine if they want to keep or retire those systems.

When you are the database administrator and part of a broader technical team, you will likely have some role to play in figuring out how data from the specialty toy company will be migrated into the current toy company systems. In some cases, you might work on a project to deploy a tool that the specialty company has, migrating the toy company data into that system. Adding data from another system that lives outside your network to your current system is a very different type of project from adding a new system to your network and then adding data. But even so, these two types of projects can share some of the same requirements.

Even if you're not part of the team making decisions on what to keep and what to retire, you will likely still be assigned the task of addressing the data. After all, when one company purchases another, a lot of historical data comes with it. For example, one of the first goals is to obtain the data from the specialty toy company's CRM system. They want to include all their active clients and their historical client data. Suppose the toy company has decided that all of the specialty company's data needs to be moved into the existing CRM system at the toy company, including active and historical clients. Your role might be to query that data from the existing CRM and then append it to the CRM database sitting on the toy company's network.

DBAs often perform user management. Suppose you might also have a list of users from the specialty toy company that handled their inventory, and thus have access to a system that performs the inventory function. These users will need to be given the appropriate level of permissions in the toy company's inventory system; you might be responsible for adding them via script.

As a DBA, you will want to know the system specifications and requirements for the systems that the organization is using. Some questions you might ask are as follows:

- What type of databases do we have?

- Do we use more than just relational databases?

- Where are all the databases currently hosted?

The answers to these types of questions, whether compiled by the DBA or the broader team, can help define what needs to happen with any data system. For systems that will be implemented, this information helps the DBA know what to prepare in the environment for the new system. For example, if the toy company is using a system with an older version of a particular software, you might first need to install the next version of the software on your organization's system before you can prepare to upgrade that data system. In some cases, you will have assets that need multiple rounds of upgrades to meet your requirements.

Types of Deployment

The process of deploying an application, a database, or even just a change to a database is done in phases. There are several steps that need to be taken before a database is installed and configured. First, the network settings are established (either by the DBA or others). Next, you will need to determine the project's requirements. The process of installation will vary depending on whether a brand-new data system is being implemented or an existing legacy system is being upgraded.

New Data Systems

If a brand-new system is being implemented, and everything is being set up for the first time, you might be responsible for installing the new database server, and the databases within, and configuring it for your organization. You could be doing this by yourself, or with the support of a team, depending on the size of your organization.

If your organization is implementing an on-premise solution or IaaS solution, like Azure or Amazon cloud-based services, you would follow the requirements for the setup for those environments and databases. This might mean provisioning the correct amount of space on the server for the database or administering permissions; the scope of what you could potentially work on as DBA will vary. How you do this depends on whether the solution is on-premises or cloud-based.

- When working in an on-premise environment, you will likely have network and server experts on your team who will ensure you have been given enough space and the right amount of access to the server.

- When working with cloud-based tools, the database will be created in accordance with the answers you give to pre-determined questions, and the settings you choose, upon logging into your account for that system.

The ability to set up an environment for a data system without expert knowledge is one of the key benefits of a cloud-based environment. The provider of the tool often holds that expertise and provides it to you as needed or based on your subscription.

Upgrading Data Systems

You may also be responsible for deployment-related tasks on a legacy application, such as preparing for an upgrade of the database, or even just patching it to keep the data system secure. This type of legacy project could involve changes in infrastructure, like going from a legacy on-premise solution to a cloud-based hosted database. Or maybe the database was developed in an older version of software, like SQL Server 2014, and you need to upgrade the server and tools to the newest version. If this project includes moving from an old database to a new database, then there will also be a process to decommission the old data system as the new data system goes live. This often will include importing data from the legacy system to the new system, so that everyone has all the historical data.

As you maintain your database systems, you will find that you also have to deploy modifications to the database. An example would be an on-premise database requiring a security patch, which we delve into in a later lesson.

It is important to note that when you need to deploy modifications to a database that is already in the production environment, you must first ensure these changes will not have unintended consequences. As you will discover later in this lesson, there are processes we follow to minimize potential failures, through testing and verifying. You will most likely work within a test environment, which is a safe place to explore and test, before deploying changes in the production environment.

Considerations for Installation and Configuration

There are certain factors to consider when installing and upgrading your database technology. One such consideration is the operating system (OS) you are using. It's important to remember that systems have to remain compatible through years of use. If you are using a legacy network of tools, it might be due to the fact that an upgrade is a major project for your company. Thus, you want to make sure the software you choose is compatible with the current version of the operating system. This ensures you have the latest features and security enhancements made to the software you are using.

Database software, such as SQL Server, is not a database itself; it is a relational database management system that helps you manage all the tasks you might do with your databases. The process of installing database software differs from an install of other software. While database software is typically installed on a server that others will access, you can also install it on a single local machine that only you use. When you install SQL Server, it will create an instance. You can have a single instance or multiple depending on the needs of the organization, or to address different types of security and configuration needs. Once installed, that server begins to run. Any other services that are needed should be set to run as well. For example, if you want to run automatic jobs, you would navigate to the configuration manager (another database utility that comes with SQL Server) and set it to run, so that you can use it.

As the case is with most software, you will often find installation wizards are available to walk you through the setup and configuration of your database. If you want to use tools like configuration files and command prompt to install and configure your database, you will need to refer to the vendor-specific instructions for the type of OS and database technology you are actually installing. Most vendors will provide guides, templates, and tools for configuring and validating the deployment of network appliances, operating systems, web servers, and application/database servers.

The configurations including security for each of these devices will vary not only by vendor but by device and version as well. The vendor's support portal will host the configuration guides (along with setup/install guides and software downloads and updates), or they can be easily located using a web search engine.

There is also detailed guidance available from several organizations to cover both vendor-neutral deployments and to provide third-party assessment and advice on deploying vendor products.

Typically, these configuration settings are going to be different based on the network, the OS, and the data system itself. For example, a sample database with no real practical purpose other than practice will require a different setup than a production database that is full of sensitive data. After you've prepared your environment for deployment, you're ready to install and configure your database.

Authentication Modes

Every user who connects to the database server needs to do so securely. We will dive into security practices later in the coursework, but for now we will discuss the types of authentication modes used to access the database (or databases) within the database server. It is important to note that users can be not only people, but also other applications that need access to the database server.

When installing SQL Server, you will be presented with two options for authenticating users who try to access the database: Windows Authentication or SQL Server Authentication. The method you choose will likely be dictated by your internal network and the policies in place. Depending on the method of authentication that is chosen, users will either be given dedicated SQL accounts or have roles that are defined by their Windows AD user account.

Tools for account management, like Active Directory, are typically utilized by larger organizations, as they streamline the management of user permissions and are easier to control from a network standpoint. This also helps users, in that they don't have to maintain yet another username and password. A smaller organization, however, will probably use SQL Server Authentication, supplying users directly to the database with a username and password.

When you log into your database, you will be prompted with the credentials and you can select the authentication type.

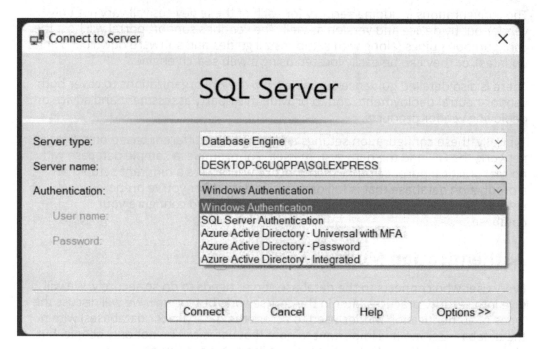

Connect to Server with Authentication Options Displayed in Microsoft SQL Server Management Studio (Used with permission from Microsoft.)

 It is important to note that when you install SQL Server, it will automatically make your Windows user account a system administrator. This is the highest level of permissions you can have. This means that you will be able to do everything on your environment, but at work you might have more limited permissions, and some features may not be available.

The screenshot shows all of the possible selections, whether or not they are available on your network. (For example, Active Directory with MFA shows up even if it's not implemented on your network.) This is the default list that comes with the installation of this database management software. Before you can connect to any server, it must first be installed and configured.

We've discussed so far the choice of using either Windows Authentication or SQL Server Authentication, but there is another option. You can enable both, giving the DBA an alternate method to access the database server. To do this, go to the Security section of the database properties in SQL SSMS. In the screenshot, you can see there is an option you can check to allow the use of both Windows Authentication and SQL Authentication. You will hear this referred to as **mixed authentication mode**, or mixed mode.

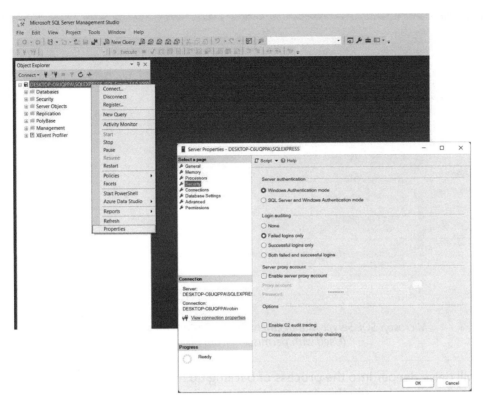

Server Security Options for SQL Server Authentication Mode in Microsoft SQL Server Management Studio (Used with permission from Microsoft.)

Although any of these methods is acceptable, it's best practice to use Windows Authentication for your production databases, as roles make it easier to control user access.

Restoring a Database from Backup

Once our database management software has been installed and configured, we can begin to install our database. We typically use either the GUI interface or a script to create a database and set our properties, but another popular method of installing a database is to restore it from a backup. This allows us to take the backup of a database, like one from a test environment, and restore it to our new production environment. We might even do the reverse, creating a test environment by restoring the backup from a production database, in order to have a safe space to explore and test.

Restoring a database carries over all of the settings that have been set for that database, and any data that it stores will then be available for use in your database server software.

Once we have connected to the new database server, we right-click on Databases and choose Restore Database, which then allows us to navigate to the backup we have saved and restore it.

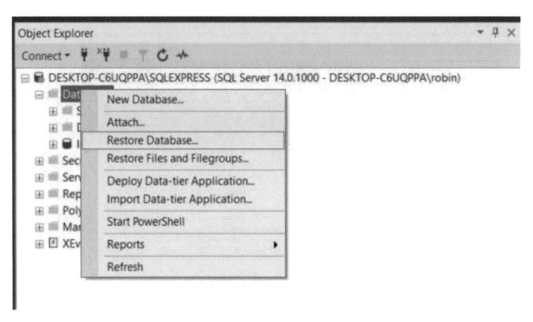

Microsoft SQL Server Management Studio Restore Database Command
(Used with permission from Microsoft.)

We will delve deeper into the process of backing up databases, including the different options, later in this course.

Most DBAs will save the backup of the database in the default backup location. This makes it easier to find it when you are ready to restore.

Configuring a Database

Whether your database has been created from a script or a GUI interface, or restored from a backup, once the database is installed you can explore its different properties and change them as needed.

Properties from the backup database will be set when you restore the database.

If you are using SQL Server, you will configure your database properties by right-clicking the database and selecting Database Properties. The default page includes the general options. It will show items like the last database backup and size (although in our screenshot, there is no last backup date since we have just restored this database).

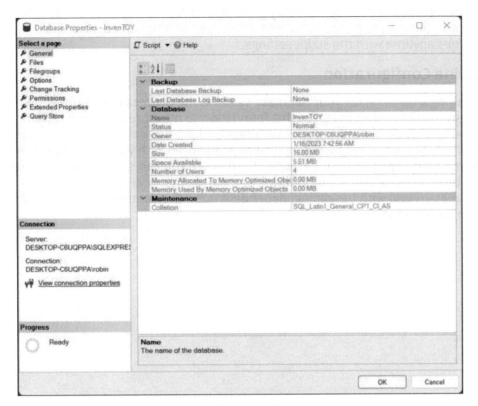

Database General Options in Microsoft SQL Server Management Studio
(Used with permission from Microsoft.)

Using SSMS, you can explore these options and adjust the various settings within the dialog box. Alternatively, you can easily script to discover the various properties of the database. For example, you can make adjustments, like changing OFF to ON, and then execute the script to change the properties. This performs the exact same function as you changing it from a dropdown menu on the GUI.

```
CREATE DATABASE [Sample]
 CONTAINMENT = NONE
 ON  PRIMARY
( NAME = N'Sample', FILENAME = N'C:\Program Files\Microsoft SQL Server\
 LOG ON
( NAME = N'Sample_log', FILENAME = N'C:\Program Files\Microsoft SQL Ser
GO
ALTER DATABASE [Sample] SET COMPATIBILITY_LEVEL = 140
GO
ALTER DATABASE [Sample] SET ANSI_NULL_DEFAULT OFF
GO
ALTER DATABASE [Sample] SET ANSI_NULLS OFF
GO
ALTER DATABASE [Sample] SET ANSI_PADDING OFF
GO
ALTER DATABASE [Sample] SET ANSI_WARNINGS OFF
GO
ALTER DATABASE [Sample] SET ARITHABORT OFF
GO
ALTER DATABASE [Sample] SET AUTO_CLOSE OFF
GO
```

Partial Script of CREATE DATABASE *and Options in Microsoft SQL Server Management Studio (Used with permission from Microsoft.)*

In this screenshot of the automatically generated script from SSMS, the `ALTER` statements allow us to alter the options as we specify. You can adjust these properties anytime with the script settings.

Baseline Configuration

Configuring a baseline for your database server is the process of capturing metrics and system information to establish a foundation to measure against, which will result in effectively monitoring your database and provide consistent service to end users. As a DBA, baselining will get you well acquainted with your database server. Once you have captured your baseline information, you can successfully pinpoint issues by comparing current monitoring to the baseline. There are third-party tools that can assist you with baselining, dependent upon the database management system you're using.

Review Activity:

Deployment

Answer the following questions:

1. What is the default server authentication?

2. A recently restored database would not have which property value?

3. When an organization acquires a new company, what will the DBA spend time reviewing to prepare for a merge?

4. What types of deployments might you work with as a DBA?

5. When configuring a database, you will spend time reviewing what options?

Topic 6B

Conduct Testing and Other Quality Measures

 EXAM OBJECTIVES COVERED
2.2 Explain database implementation, testing, and deployment phases.

Even with the best processes, the most thorough design, and loads of planning, there is still a need to test and confirm that a design is working and providing information as intended. This means testing for quality, addressing code related issues, and confirming the tables and fields meet the schema requirements. Past the initial checks, there are other types of tests you will perform to ensure the database can handle anything thrown at it. All of these various tests and quality checks combined can help create a successful implementation and thus a successful adoption of the application for an organization.

Database Quality Checks

Before a newly designed system is deployed for use in production, it will go through several different checks and balances. As a DBA, you may or may not be responsible for performing any one of these tests. But even if you're not the one conducting a test, you will certainly hear about it. The whole point of implementing a data system is to meet the data requirements for an organization, or for a process in the organization. These types of quality checks can confirm that any system is doing just that.

One of the most basic quality checks involves confirming that the database has been designed to meet the original requirements. One of the ways to test this practically is to confirm that the database has all the defined tables and that the key and referential integrity settings meet the original schema. You can manually perform this test rather easily by using tools like SSMS to expand the database and look at the tables, confirming that you see the intended fields and column settings.

You can also run scripts to pull tables, fields, and attributes either from tables you select or all the tables (to pull data dictionary-style information). You can also explore building custom diagrams in the database to cross compare against the logical schema design.

When performing a quality check, you might have a checklist that could look similar to the following:

1. Are tables and views in the database?

2. Do the tables have the appropriate settings based on the logical schema?

3. Are the fields in the tables as expected, with the appropriate attributes (correct data type, proper name, allow nulls/do not allow nulls)?

4. Do the views that are stored in the database execute and provide expected results?

5. Are the necessary functions and stored procedures available in the database?

If you have ever worked on a software or database development team, then you know that original requirements might also include changes to those requirements that have occurred throughout the design process. Through proper documentation and diagramming, you should be able to easily confirm that the database does meet the original requirements, as well as identify any changes that have been made in the process.

If your organization is using an off-the-shelf offering, you might merely explore any customized features that have been implemented by the vendor development team, at the request of your organization.

Addressing Code and Syntax

Once you have confirmed that the database is intact, with all objects included as expected and designed to specification, then you can begin to test other aspects of the database. One feature to test is whether the code executes as intended based on the triggers that are in place.

If you are working with coding and/or scripting, you will likely troubleshoot syntax errors at some point. We've all dealt with a dreaded missing (or extra) comma, or invalid naming. Something as simple as a misplaced or missing letter can wreak havoc on your code. From the beginning to end of development, anyone who works with a code or script will be troubleshooting code execution errors and syntax errors as they arise.

Most technical error messages will contain error numbers and some information that you can use to research errors. Reading the technical documentation that is provided around the error code you're facing can help you resolve the issue.

Negative Testing

Negative testing is a process where we intentionally add bad data to the inputs (such as on a form or screen, and sometimes in the backend testing fields) to make sure the system does not accept bad inputs and that it works as intended and does what it was designed to do. Negative testing is meant to ensure an application doesn't crash due to unexpected data or usage.

Suppose we want to test whether data constraints are working as intended. In our inventory system, there is a field that allows us to input any number between 1 and 50. If we are conducting a regular test or positive testing, we might type in 25 and verify that the data is accepted. If we are conducting negative testing, we might enter the number 0 or the letter A and see how the system performs when an "unexpected" value is entered. If it accepts the value, we know the constraint is not properly set for the field. If the system crashes or freezes, this indicates the system didn't know how to respond to the data we inputted. All forms of testing will occur throughout the development process.

As a DBA, you might script these scenarios, to then use them for testing on the database. Having an understanding of the users and business rules for the application you're testing can help you formulate appropriate tests.

Software developers also complete positive testing to ensure the software works under normal conditions, meaning all the ways we would expect users to interact with it. If we are conducting positive testing, we might type 25 into our field that accepts numerical inputs between 1 and 50, and verify that the data is accepted.

Stress Testing Applications

The software development team is also responsible for stress testing. A **stress test** is a form of testing that uses a simulation to push an application to its limit to replicate peak times. Applications rely on the network, appropriate hardware, and properly set configurations to run with a good user experience. Having control of these specifications helps control costs, as we can make sure that we have enough memory or processing speed to run while also having the ability to expand as needed. When we stress test an application, the results allow us to know approximately how much our data system can handle before performance is impacted.

Any application that needs to scale up in order to hold more data and handle more people needs to be stress tested. This type of testing will help inform at what point you need to scale the environment, and also allows you to test whether your application will break under stress in a safe environment.

Imagine that our toy company sells an action figure from a TV show that has suddenly become very popular in pop culture. If the company has not conducted proper planning and testing, the increased traffic from customers trying to buy this toy could crash the inventory data system. This can have a devastating impact on sales or even the user experience. Prevention is worth a pound of cure, which is why testing should be performed often, despite the associated costs. It is a critical part of the development and deployment of any new application.

Using Tools for Stress Testing

One of the benefits of working with service offerings is that they provide tools that allow us to stress test our applications and databases within the environment, making testing more available and easier to perform. There are of course costs associated with these tools, but it is money well spent, as it saves you a lot of time from having to create the test yourself.

For example, let's say the toy store's application currently receives approximately 300 visitors a day, on an average day. However, on days when there's a big sale, or a new item launching, it's typical to see 500 visitors. When estimating stress, you will want to use those higher numbers. With the launch of a new, popular action figure upcoming, we might expect to see not only more traffic in general, but more traffic per second—and everyone ordering the new toy. To prepare for this, our stress test might include 15,000 visits per day and 500 visits per minute.

No single scenario is the same, so it's important to check out the various types of tools available and choose the one that fits best with your objective and available funds. Although the exact process of performing a stress test varies depending on the tool used, we typically take the following steps.

1. **Plan the stress testing scenarios.** This planning will involve determining what functionality needs to be tested and the user load required to achieve the desired results. The user load should range from a typical number of simultaneous users to a number representing peak usage.

2. **Configure the scenario in your preferred (or required) tool.** This configuration usually involves pointing the tool to the functions that need to be tested, setting it to start at a certain number of users, and specifying a time frame during which the user load will steadily ramp up to peak levels. If desired, your test can also be configured to spike to a peak number of users at certain intervals and hold there for some period of time.

3.   **Run the test.** Once the test is complete, the number of users will taper off to see how the system recovers from load.

4.   **Using the tool, aggregate the results from the system and present them along with the corresponding load.** This report can be analyzed to determine if changes should be made in the system to handle varying loads.

Once you have performed the test, you will use the tool to aggregate the results from the system and present them along with the corresponding load. You will then want to analyze this report to determine if changes should be made. Ask yourself, what impact did the test have on processing and transactions? At what point did the system start to fail, and were there any deadlocks that you should address? The test initiates the stress and provides you insight on how the application performed, but you are the one who will need to interpret that information and make adjustments to the deployment.

Stress Testing Stored Procedures

Stored procedures, or scripts that run many steps, will likely also need to have their own stress tests. It's one thing to watch a stored procedure execute successfully and quickly on a single run, but what happens if it runs 1,000 times in rapid succession? Further, running a stress test on your stored procedure can be valuable in helping inform further network or system requirements.

Regression Testing

Regression testing is a form of software development testing in which we verify that a change that has been implemented does not break previous working features. This type of testing should occur on any part of the data system where a change might have impacted other objects. For example, removing a field or adding a field can affect views or scripts that might need that field, or may not know how to deal with a new field.

In the toy company's existing inventory process, an advanced set of procedures looks to determine if a product that has been ordered has an associated rebate. This workflow is shown in the diagram below. Suppose the business analysts in the organization have recently discovered that it might be more efficient if rebates are only applied when a customer submits a coupon code. This means the database needs to have a coupon record so that it can identify the rebate and apply it.

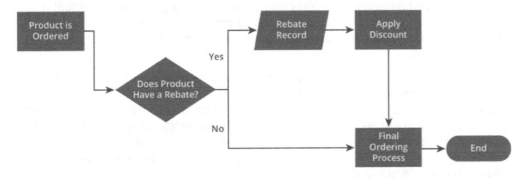

Existing Workflow Diagram Showing the Process for Rebates

In the toy company's inventory system, we will need to add a change to the rebate process that includes a coupon feature. The goal of the feature is to ensure a coupon record exists before it can be associated to a rebate record. The business rule would be that we cannot have a rebate that doesn't have a coupon, which will ensure any coupon record that is generated works within the rebate system. The new workflow is shown in the diagram below.

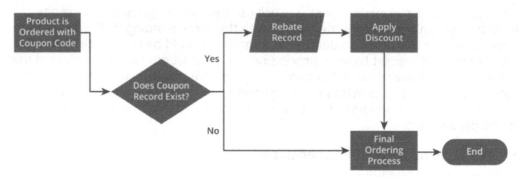

New Workflow Diagram Showing the Process for Rebates to Include Coupons

In this new feature, the order of the process is important. In order to have a rebate record, you must first have the coupon. Thus, you will need to perform regression testing to confirm that in adding the new coupon feature, you didn't break any other processes where the coupon *isn't* required, so that the workflow can move on to the final ordering process. You will also conduct regression testing to ensure existing rebate and coupon processes still work as intended.

Many large and/or growing companies are building systems and using them at the same time. Because of this, you will likely have a test environment where you can build out and test any new features before they move to production.

Version Control

When you're working within a broader team, including the people who are managing the network servers and the application developers whose application works alongside the database or databases that you support, it is important for the team to establish version control.

Version control is a process of keeping up with literally every change in a software application and/or database. Version control tools allow a group or individual developer to "commit" their changes to the repository. Having the source data in source control software provides a lot of value to the entire technology team, including the DBA.

Try to imagine a team consisting of developers and database professionals, of all types. Each of these individuals has an individual or smaller team working on features for the system. This produces a lot of change, and as we have learned, we must always test to ensure that changes do not break existing features of a system. Version control tools that have version control testing will not only keep up with the changes being committed, but will also help ensure you are not implementing features that would break the data system.

For example, suppose when the toy company was building a new app for vendors to submit paperwork, documentation, and purchase orders, they implemented source control by creating a GitHub account and including all the necessary team members. This implementation at the start of the new app development allowed the toy company to have a full history of every change and ensured everyone was working with the most current version of the software.

At the most basic level, whenever you are preparing to work with a database, you will want to ensure that you are working with the current production version. Even if you are not personally involved in the source control process, it is helpful to know it exists, and how to access it, as it is a valuable resource for determining an application's history.

Version Control for Database Objects

Version control is not just for databases, but also for a software application in general. There are some common items that you can find and should likely include in your repository. Remember, tools like GitHub serve as a repository, which is the single source of truth for an application and all its changes. Since it is possible to make changes to the database without storing those change scripts to the repository, a best practice would be to periodically audit what is in the repository against what is in the database, to make sure no changes were made without a corresponding entry in the repository. When conducting version control testing for database objects, we check the following:

- DDL commands used to create the database, users, and permissions

- Database configuration properties

- Custom procedures and functions

- Requirements documentation

Review Activity:

Testing and Other Quality Measures

Answer the following questions:

1. What quality checks are performed to ensure a database meets the original requirements?

2. Using a WHERE clause in a GROUP BY is an example of what type of error?

3. The CustomerID field should only contain numbers. A test is performed on the Product table to see if a value of 'Betty' will be accepted into the CustomerID field. Which type of testing is this considered?

4. A product is being deployed that is expected to result in an increase in sales. What type of testing should be performed before deployment?

5. A company that has introduced an internship program uses a stored procedure to update the Employees table. Which type of testing should be performed to ensure the Employees table remains up to date?

6. What is the primary benefit of version control?

Topic 6C

Understand Validation Techniques and Methods

EXAM OBJECTIVES COVERED
2.2 Explain database implementation, testing, and deployment phases.

Have you ever heard the phrase "garbage in, garbage out"? Our processes and reporting would be problematic if the data behind them was inaccurate, incomplete, or inconsistent. Quality data leads to quality reporting. However, the use of proper data validation methods can turn some of that "garbage" into "one person's trash is another's person's treasure." In essence, we can use data validation to improve the quality of our data, thus ensuring we don't have "garbage out."

In this lesson, we will define quality data, describe quality assurance processes, and explain the reasons we check for data quality through validation. We will describe data quality metrics and walk through different methods to verify and validate the data as we implement new data systems.

Validating Data Integrity

The act of capturing data without integrity is typically phrased as "garbage in, garbage out" in the workplace. As a DBA working directly with data systems, you should seize any opportunity to increase the integrity of your data, as you then also increase its quality.

Characteristics of Quality Data

Quality data can be defined as data that has integrity and is accurate, complete, and consistent.

- **Data completeness means that the data is complete and that all expected and required fields are entered.** For example, if the data set contains first name, last name, and email addresses, does every record have each one of these fields completed? If not, this issue should be further investigated to determine if a quality source of this missing information exists and can be used to correct the missing data.

- **Data accuracy means that the data in the field is correct and accurate.** Imagine that we combined two data sets of products for a company. Although the products are the same, the product names may not exactly match because they were entered in differently. If there are no quality checks, we can get bad groupings on our data (i.e., two distinct products with sales for each, even though they are the same product just renamed) or just invalid data altogether.

- **Data consistency means that the data is consistently entered the same way and as intended based on business rules.** As an example, the staffing data of a healthcare facility contains the credentials of nurses and doctors. These credentials could be entered inconsistently (e.g., MD vs. M.D.; PhD vs. PHD; Lpn vs. LPN). If they have not been entered consistently, then a database administrator (or data analyst) might use transformation techniques to correct them and make them consistent with the required standard for that organization.

Methods to Ensure Data Integrity

There are technical ways to ensure integrity in data.

- **Create required fields.** This guarantees that critical information is not skipped.

- **Create relationships between tables.** By using referential integrity, we can prevent records from being entered without other necessary data. For example, an organization that utilizes referential integrity between the "Employees" and "Payroll" tables could not accidentally send a paycheck to a person who isn't listed as an employee.

- **Verify proper field sizes.** This prevents us from getting inconsistent data. For example, if a field contains an individual's middle initial, then it should only have one character length. Giving this field 20 characters would allow a user to write out their full middle name, when all we wanted was the initial.

- **Confirm proper data types are assigned.** This ensures data is accurate. For example, if a field that should contain a date is not set to a date data type, a user could enter some other value, and the system would not recognize it as being incorrect.

Data integrity controls, like the ones above, provide many benefits. When your data—and corresponding reports—can be trusted to have the correct information, it allows for the organization to make better decisions based off the data.

Validating Data Values

There are times where data is just bad—possibly due to human error, a bad database design, or something that went awry in the process of getting the data from the system to the point of analysis. All data that you work with on a project needs validation and verification throughout the entire project.

- **Data validation** is the process of confirming the type, structure, and accurate representation of the data. An email address is a great example to use for validation. An email address always has an "@" symbol and usually ends with a ".com," ".net," or another variation, all of which can be easily validated with a few logical tests to confirm that the data is valid. If the email address is in the wrong format, then that data is not valid.

- **Data verification** is the process of confirming that the data is accurate or true.

As a DBA, you should always check for data completeness, accuracy, and consistency to ensure the quality of the acquired data. Data quality checks are critical when data is acquired from other sources.

In the business setting, several situations necessitate the need for data verification and validation checks:

- **Mergers and acquisitions:** When companies merge, or one company acquires another, data from multiple organizations is combined. The involved organizations may have some of the same systems, but their data will eventually all need to be migrated to the same organizational data system. It's important to note that when two large organizations merge, they might have different standards developed for their data prior to the merge of the data sets. You will want to ensure that the data meets the correct structure and type (validation) and is correct (verification).

- **Data manipulation:** When data is manually keyed into a system, or manually changed by hand, there is the opportunity for human error. This data needs verification and possibly also validation, depending on the fields used. For example, you may need to confirm that records for email addresses and postal codes meet the requirements for this data (validation).

- **Human error on queries:** Any situation in which human error may have occurred necessitates quality checks for a multitude of reasons. For example, someone may have joined data improperly—a mistake that is difficult to detect in a large data set without diligence. These errors would be difficult to catch without checking for data quality.

- **Data transfers:** The transfer of data between systems is another common reason for quality checks. You will want to ensure that data transfers correctly from one system into the other system. When data flows from one system to the next, it's important to verify that the data actually made it to the intended destination.

Automated Validation

Automated validation is when we utilize the power of software to ensure we achieve a validated result. Email addresses are a perfect example to start the discussion on how automated validation works. When a person attempts to input a bad email address into a field, automated validation can prevent that email address from ever being saved if it doesn't meet the standards of the email field. Automated validation can also ensure that phone numbers or dates are entered in the right format. By ensuring that the data in these fields was entered correctly from the very beginning, this will reduce the amount of verification you must conduct on these fields at a later time. In essence, if you know that there's no possibility a date of birth might use an invalid date format, thanks to automated validation, you will have more confidence that you are working with validated field data.

 It is important to note that automated validation doesn't entirely prevent verification issues. For example, someone could key in a birth date in the correct format, but with a bad date, like 1/1/1900 instead of 1/1/1990.

There are software tools dedicated to helping organizations validate their data. These tools use processes that look at groups of records and confirm the completeness by creating a master record. Data validation software tools can be set up to provide automated reporting about data processes. For example, reports can be generated to confirm what data was transferred from the source system to the data warehouse. Data validation tools will let you know how many records passed through successfully and also how many failed to go through. These reports will also often provide reasons why records may have failed to transfer that can give meaningful insight into how to solve the failure. Can you imagine the process of loading millions of records without automated validation? It would be very time consuming and prone to errors.

Let's walk through an example of how data validation tools help ensure data quality. To support an older company that has recently adopted a new customer relationship management (CRM) software, you are tasked with ensuring that all the historical invoices are loaded into the CRM. The system requires data on all accounts, contacts, products, and invoices. You will not manually enter these records, but will use an API that is built to work with the CRM. You create various exports of all the necessary data sets and load them into the system. Because the older CRM system did not have any controls on the account names, you anticipate some duplicated accounts. The automated validation in the new CRM system provides a list of potential duplicates and allows you to merge these fields with no issues, giving a higher quality data set. Automated validation also would allow you to check for data loss. When you load information into the new CRM system, if you expected to see an account and failed to find it, the system could provide a list of the invoices that could not load because of missing values.

Data Verification Methods

As you now know, verification is the process of confirming that data is accurate. The lines between verification and validation can be blurred, and in some cases both are in order for the data you might be working with. There are some verification steps you should perform on all data sets.

Verifying Field Level Data

Field level data can be incorrect for many reasons. It sounds simple, but verifying field data can become complicated very quickly when you have a large amount of data. Looking for data that seems to be outside the norm, or having a discussion with the team that is responsible for that data, can add clarity and help you verify the data. When field data is incorrect, we can attempt to provide a verified value if needed. This process is strongly dependent on whether you have information that can be used to verify the data and thus provide the correct information.

Verifying Record Counts

Data loss is the intentional or accidental loss of information through human error or an ineffective process. Data loss occurs when records are lost, are incomplete, are poorly named, or may have accidentally dropped out.

A discrepancy between data types in the source system and the system where data is transferred can also result in missing data. If the date field in the source system is a text data type, but the system where the data is headed contains an actual date field, data loss will occur if you do not convert the date field to a recognizable format—or all the records might fail when you attempt to load them.

When you know your data, the people in your organization, and the quality standards for data, you can build quality check queries that check for null values or information that is missing.

Verifying Calculations

The mathematical equations within the programs that will be used by the DBA and other data professionals, like data analysts, are nothing short of amazing. They perform complicated computations that require little more from us than correctly inputting the right values into a formula. In your role, you might be tasked with providing data to someone else in your organization, and will likely script some of the functions into your queries. Numbers can show up sometimes, but that doesn't mean they are always correct. We can introduce errors by making mathematical mistakes, using the wrong equations, or applying the wrong logic. It is always important to verify calculations, such as spot-checking for the intended outcome and that the correct information was supplied to formulas and equations.

Data Mapping

Data mapping is the process of mapping data to data at the field level. In other words, you are mapping the field that represents some specific information (like SalesOrderID) from one data set to the field that contains this same information in the data set you are importing or appending to the database.

Something as simple as importing data into an existing table will likely require mapping, or at least a review to ensure that it does in fact map correctly. Suppose that we are loading prior invoices into the inventory database for the toy company. These invoices have been exported out of the accounting system and are in .csv format. The accounting system has slightly different field names, so we must match the fields in the accounting data to the appropriate fields in the SalesOrderDetail table.

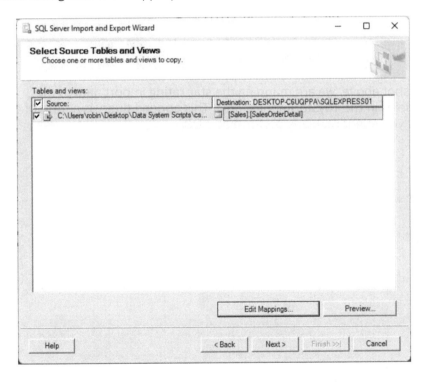

Edit Mapping Importing Invoices into Inventory in SQL Server Management Studio
(Used with permission from Microsoft.)

When we write append queries, we are using the query to pass information between tables at the field level; effectively, we are telling SQL to set the field to the value of the other field.

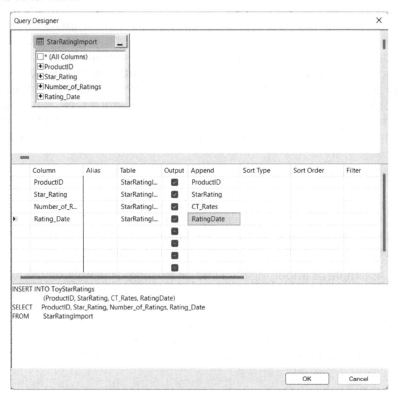

Append Query Set Value in SQL Server Management Studio
(Used with permission from Microsoft.)

In our screenshot above, we are mapping the star rating import data to the appropriate fields in the ToyStarRatings table. This append query is a form of data mapping that you might regularly perform as a DBA.

Review Activity:

Validation Techniques and Methods

Answer the following questions:

1. Which data quality constraint follows business rules on naming conventions for a field?

2. A subtotal field set as a text type would likely lead to which data quality issue?

3. Data validation is the process of confirming _____.

4. Which process entails confirming the type, structure, and accurate representation of the data?

5. Confirming the record count for data before and after a data transfer is a step in which process?

6. A confirmation email is sent when a new user signs up for a newsletter. This is an example of which process?

Lesson 6

Summary

After this lesson, you should have a better understanding of how to prepare for the deployment of a database. You should be familiar with the types of deployments and their related nuances, whether assets are being acquired, a system is upgrading, or the organization is switching to an improved tool. You should also be familiar with the types of quality checks and testing you will be expected to perform to ensure the database design is working as intended. Although you will not be the only person responsible for ensuring data integrity, you should still be comfortable with ways to verify and validate not only data properties, but the data itself as well.

Guidelines for Implementing, Testing, and Deploying Databases

Consider these best practices and guidelines when preparing databases for deployment, testing database design, and validating data.

1. **Spend time reviewing the specifications and requirements of any new software before installing it on your network.**

2. **Gather and review historical data to determine how it will be migrated into your environment.**

3. **Make sure you understand the minimum specifications for software, and identify whether acquired software needs to be upgraded to meet your organization's requirements.**

4. **Perform various types of testing to ensure that the data system works as intended.**

5. **Work with a team to implement version control to ensure that changes, from changes in data to application changes, are being captured.**

6. **Determine what data integrity measures are already in place within your data system, and consider what else could be added.**

7. **Use validation and verification methods to ensure data is accurate and meets requirements.**

Lesson 7

Monitoring and Reporting on Database Performance

LESSON INTRODUCTION

Monitoring and reporting on the performance of a database can keep it happy and healthy—and its users too. After all, databases exist for a purpose, and they are often very important to an organization. Understanding where a database is hosted, and how to access it, will help support you in monitoring the database. It is also important to learn how to leverage log files and alerts to identify failed processes and drive critical next steps. Over time, you will become familiar with the normal usage of your database, and thus be able to detect abnormal usage. We monitor the performance and health of our database because it allows us to identify any issues quickly and get users back to business.

Lesson Objectives

In this lesson, you will do the following:

- Consider database connectivity needs.

- Explore log files and alerts.

- Understand and address deadlocks.

Topic 7A

Consider Database Connectivity Needs

 EXAM OBJECTIVES COVERED
1.3 Compare and contrast scripting methods and scripting environments.
2.2 Explain database implementation, testing, and deployment phases.

When you are connecting to a server or a database, it is always a good idea to know what you are connecting to and where it is coming from. For example, are you logging into a database that's hosted on a cloud server or an internal network? It also is important to have a thorough understanding of the infrastructure to which you are establishing this connection. This applies to databases as well. You should know where your database lives and what its architecture looks like. Knowing these things will help you identify the appropriate team member or service provider to work with when an issue arises.

Client-Server Architecture

Client-server architecture is the roadmap for how the server communicates with the client. Most database servers use this type of architecture. The client is the device an end user uses to run their applications, and the server is the device that contains the information or service the client is requesting. The client-server computing environment provides business-critical information as requested by the client systems. Users access the database server either through a front-end application that displays the requested data on the client machine, or through a back-end application that runs on the server and manages the database. When part of the application is a client software program, installed and run on separate hardware to the server application code, the client interacts with the server over a network.

A web application is a particular type of client-server architecture that leverages existing technologies to simplify development. The application uses a generic client (a web browser) and standard network protocols and servers (HTTP/HTTPS). The specific features of the application are developed using code running on the clients and servers.

Client-Side and Server-Side Scripting

As you have discovered tools for scripting, it is important to keep in mind that because we have client-server architecture, we also have client-side scripting and server-side scripting.

Client-side scripting is actions that are run on the client machine. This could be an application that is run from a browser, or a client application that is used within the organization via its network. For example, the toy company has an application that people open up from the network (not the browser), which interacts with the SQL database that we maintain. When we run scripts that occur in this application, it would be considered client-side scripting.

Suppose the toy company also hosts a website that lets potential vendors explore various rate calculations. The vendor keys in the values on the page, and then a basic client-side script runs, performing a calculation from the information entered into those boxes on the web page. This script runs on the client's machine and doesn't require any information from the server. The benefit of this is that it doesn't have to call the server to produce the calculation, which means that it doesn't have to use any server resources to produce the necessary information for the user.

However, suppose our vendors don't want to merely explore rate calculations, but have access to their actual rates. In order for vendors to log in and have access to their information, we use server-side processes to pass information. **Server-side** processes happen directly on the server side. Server-side scripts can interact with the server, the database, or back-end web applications. When you log into the site, you are sending a message from the web page (client side) that passes to the server and confirms through server-side processes that you have access.

Server-side scripting is used to send additional information back to the client. It's what gives the toy company vendors the ability to log into the system through their browser and see their historical data (such as orders and invoices), with options to add and change profile information.

Database Server Location

In a client-server architecture, the database will live on the server-side of the architecture, on the database server. Server location is where a database or multiple databases are hosted. For example, in a client-server architecture, the database will live on the server-side of the architecture. Once connected to the server that hosts the database, you will then connect to the appropriate database server software, and from there select your database server.

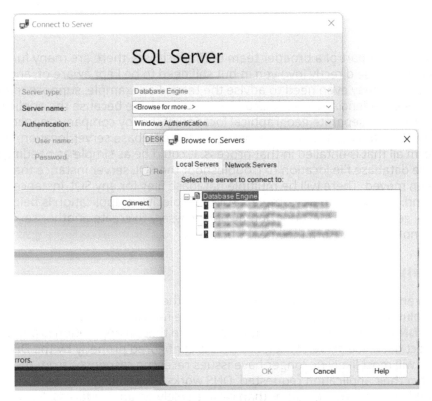

Browse for Database Servers in Microsoft SQL Server Management Studio
(Used with permission from Microsoft.)

Selecting your database server allows you to then work with the databases that are on that server. Each database has a database file location. It's important to remember that these locations are where each database lives on the machine.

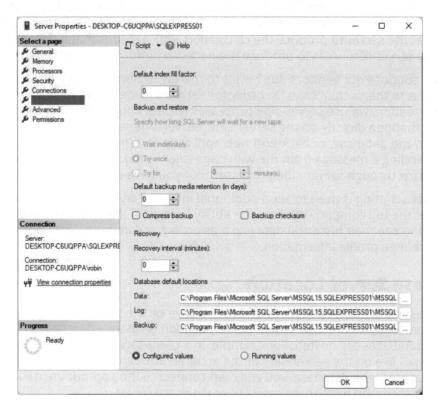

Server Properties Displaying the Database File Locations in Microsoft SQL Server Management Studio (Used with permission from Microsoft.)

When working as part of a broader team of IT specialists, there are many functions that you will not be directly involved in but still need to be kept aware of, and sometimes you may even need to advise the team. For example, suppose the toy company is experiencing **latency** issues with its database because the application is being used in a separate geographical location. If the toy company's application development team has requested a change in the database server location, the DBA can inform all that is entailed in that process. It could be as simple as needing to locate the database file location to troubleshoot the SQL server instance that may have been moved. There will be multiple database files for any SQL instance. On the other hand, it could be more complex. For example, if the application is being used in several geographical locations, it may be necessary to create another server in the area not suffering from the latency problem.

Domain Name Service (DNS)

When an end user runs into connectivity issues, they are going to call on the DBA for a resolution. Because of this, a DBA should be familiar with the **domain name service (DNS)**, which allows you to quickly ensure that an application is pointing to the correct database server. When the DNS is configured properly by the DBA, the end user will most likely no longer have issues receiving responses from the correct server that their application requested. DNS works by enabling the creation of a memorable domain name, rather than relying solely on an IP address. For example, instead of your users typing `116.45.66.23` to access a database, they could alternatively type `sql.AwesomeCompany.com` for access. The latter is easier to remember.

Familiarity with DNS is helpful when setting an instance of SQL Server or changing server settings. You will need to be aware of TCP/IP properties, and you will also need to determine whether your instance should be set up with static ports or dynamic ports. SQL Server can allocate one of the many ports on a computer to communicate with other servers or systems. This process of selecting any available port is known as dynamic ports, because the port used to communicate is dynamically allocated when a connection is created. SQL Server by default is set to dynamic ports, but it can also be assigned a single port number that will be used any time it communicates to another server or system. Assigning a static port to SQL Server can be beneficial when an organization's firewall settings are more restrictive. Using a static port means that the firewall will be configured to only allow communication from SQL Server over that single, assigned port. When using dynamic ports, the firewall would need to allow communication over a range of ports, leaving a network more exposed. (We discuss how firewalls work in more detail in a later lesson.)

As a DBA, when a database is moved to a new server location, you will work with another member of your team to update the IP address.

Review Activity:

Database Connectivity Needs

Answer the following questions:

1. What type of architecture is the roadmap for how the server communicates with the client?

2. Suppose visitors to the toy company's website can sign up for an account and save their wish-listed items. Which side of the architecture would this website represent?

3. A database is stored in what type of server?

4. The toy company has created a new website. What service will convert it to an IP address?

Topic 7B

Monitor the Database

EXAM OBJECTIVES COVERED
3.1 Explain the purpose of monitoring and reporting for database management and performance.

There are a lot of actions that can be taken both proactively and reactively when it comes to database management. As a DBA, it is critical that you know what to monitor, and where to look for notifications and alerts. In this section, we will explore the type of information you need to monitor, such as how many connections are currently using the database and whether your routine procedures ran or failed. We will also discuss how to review log files and stay on top of alerts, notifications, and other resources that help us maintain a healthy data system. When it comes to database issues, time is of the essence, so it is imperative to be prepared.

Monitoring Connections and Sessions

In order to do anything with a database, you must first connect to the server and then connect to the database. When a database connection has been formed (meaning you have connected to the database server), you have established a connection and a session.

A **connection** is the physical connection/communication to the database server. A **session** is the authenticated interaction with the database server for the exchange of information.

Connections and sessions can also be created by applications that communicate with the database. For example, your organization most likely will have some application that sends data to a database you manage. In that scenario, the application is opening a connection to the database server and then starting a session to the database to write data.

Typically, if you have one connection you will have at least one session, although a connection can have multiple sessions. Every time anyone or anything connects to the database server, it will cause a session to open. Using Microsoft SQL Server Management Studio, once you are connected to the database server, you can execute the script named `sys.dm_exec_sessions` in the master database. When executed, this script shows each open session. You can connect to SSMS and run this query at any time to see open sessions; when they close, and you execute the query again, that session will roll off the list.

Other Users Connecting with Tools

End users and other employees will connect and create sessions as well, although they will likely use different tools than the DBA. Popular visualization tools, statistical tools, and even spreadsheet programs like Excel will allow users to connect to any database that they have permission to access.

Results from Running `sys_dm_exec_sessions` in Microsoft SQL Server Management Studio (Used with permission from Microsoft.)

In the screenshot, we've executed `sys_dm_exec_sessions` in Microsoft SQL Server, and the query results show us that a user is connected to the database server in multiple different ways—using ODBC, Microsoft Office, Mashup Engine (which is Power BI), and several other Microsoft SQL Server Management Studio sessions. This scenario is known as concurrent connections, because the same user has connected to the database server multiple times. If this user were to close any of these sessions, they would roll off the query list.

Different Types of Connections

Suppose the toy company you work for has 100 users, all with unlimited access to the database. As you might imagine, that's a lot of connections and sessions to monitor, and this is just one part of the daily usage of the database that must be monitored. But it's important to monitor concurrent connections, as well as failed connections, to ensure the database runs properly and is protected.

Concurrent Connections

A database server has connection limits, and by default it is unlimited. If a concurrent connections limit has been specifically set, then once this limit is reached, the database can no longer operate for the next user or application that attempts to connect. For this reason, it's important to monitor concurrent sessions, and even set the number of connections that can be established to the database server, when possible. While it might not always be your responsibility to define the number of acceptable concurrent connections, these properties can be set in SQL Server Management Studio under **Properties**, in the **Connections** section. For example, if you want the toy company's 100 users to be able to have up to three concurrent connections, then you would set that limit to 300. When you do not set this number, it will default to zero, meaning that it will have unlimited connections.

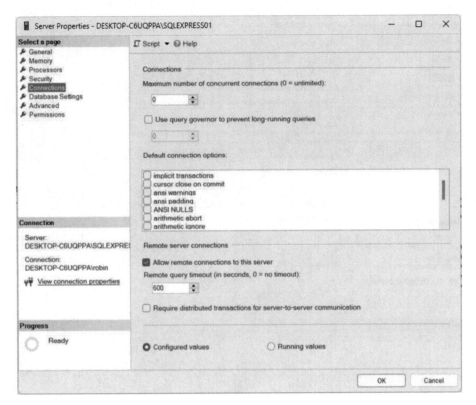

Concurrent Sessions Setting in Microsoft SQL Server Management Studio
(Used with permission from Microsoft.)

When a server is overwhelmed by connections, no one else can get in. This can happen accidentally, if the concurrent connections per user is set to unlimited, but this is also how a denial of service (DOS) attack functions—a server is hit with numerous connections to intentionally disable it. We'll learn more about this type of attack in a later lesson.

Failed/Attempted Connections

When a user attempts to log into a database server but cannot connect because they forgot their password or their Windows credentials, a failed connection is created. While we expect to see this happen occasionally, it's important to monitor for failed connections because a lot of them can indicate a nefarious attempt to gain access to the database server.

In the screenshot below, our database is tracking failed logins only. We often choose this setting because hundreds of users will successfully connect to the database, and including both failed and successful attempts on our log would certainly increase its size.

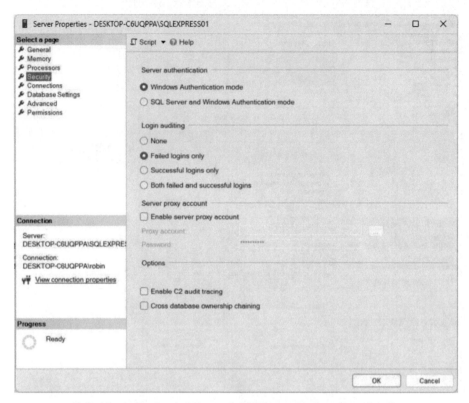

Failed Login Setting in Microsoft SQL Server Management Studio
(Used with permission from Microsoft.)

The SQL Server log file below shows the results of this filter to show only failed attempts. We can see in the log file that one user tried to use SQL Server Authentication but did not succeed.

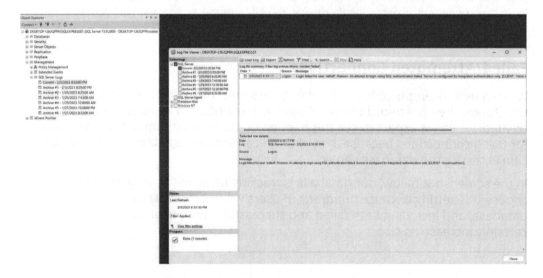

Log File Viewer Filtered to Show Failed Login Attempts in SQL Server Management Studio
(Used with permission from Microsoft.)

As mentioned earlier, it's not abnormal for people to forget their login information, but it is important to monitor these failed connections for security reasons.

Growth and Storage Limits

Daily interactions with a database by many users can impact the size and growth of the database, which the DBA should monitor and report on. Further, storage limits for a database, and settings for growth, should be defined during configuration, and before installation. Not monitoring database growth and failing to set accurate storage limits can cause performance issues, and if left unchecked it often leads to application disruption for your end users. For example, when a database has met its storage limit, no further data can be saved to the database. Also, allowing a database to just grow and increase storage continually can increase costs.

There are a few settings to be aware of when monitoring and reporting on the growth of your database. Some database management systems allow for an automatic increase in the size of your database file when it exceeds the initial size allocation. In SQL Server, this setting is Autogrowth; in Oracle, it is called Auto Extend. Even with these options, adjustments to the default settings should be considered carefully, because every database grows at a different pace and size.

There are different queries/scripts that can be run in different database management systems that will essentially let you gauge how big your database has grown and how fast it is growing.

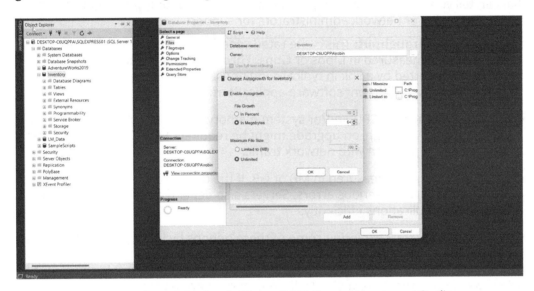

Inventory Growth Settings in Microsoft SQL Server Management Studio
(Used with permission from Microsoft.)

This screenshot shows the growth settings for the inventory database in SSMS. As the DBA, you might not be responsible for deciding the final values of these settings, but you will certainly be the one setting the values.

 By default, SQL server databases grow by percentage. However, the growth setting should be set to a fixed value to avoid performance issues.

Resource Utilization

The operating system and hardware will work together to provide the best experience for users. When you are experiencing poor performance, you should investigate and monitor the resources that are being used on the hardware with metrics that are provided by the OS (operating system). These two core components work together to give space, memory, and processing to any system, including any data systems that are on that shared resource. Memory and CPU are part of the hardware, but without the OS sending commands, we not only can't monitor them, but we can hardly use them. Hardware, operating systems, and data systems will have the best performance when we start with the correct resources, then continue to monitor them as the system and its usage grow.

If you have hit a threshold, the resource will no longer be available to others. For example, if a user runs a query that has been poorly drafted, and it takes a lot of CPU or memory to run, then other processes will have to wait.

It is typically the server administrators or network administrators who will monitor and perform the maintenance of the hardware and network. However, as a DBA, you will likely be monitoring a database, and there are several performance metrics that can tell you whether everything is operating normally, or if you might need to turn to the server or network administrators for support.

- **Bandwidth/throughput:** This is the rated speed of all the interfaces available to the device, measured in Mbps or Gbps. **Throughput** is the amount of data transfer supported by a link in typical conditions. This can be measured in various ways with different software applications.

- **CPU and memory:** If CPU and/or system memory utilization (measured as a percentage) is very high, an upgrade might be required. High CPU utilization can also indicate a problem with network traffic.

- **Storage:** Storage is measured in MB or GB. If the device runs out of storage space, it could cause serious errors. Servers also depend on fast input/output (I/O) to run applications efficiently.

You will be able to start exploring some of these options by looking at various tools or reports that have been adopted at your organization. For example, SSMS has built-in performance reporting that you can navigate to and explore. In the report below, we can see the System CPU Utilization and other metrics, like current activity and historical information.

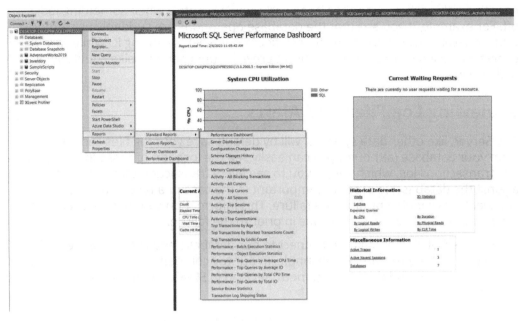

Built-In Performance Report in Microsoft SQL Server Management Studio
(Used with permission from Microsoft.)

The performance report below shows information about the CPU, including all the databases on the server and waiting requests.

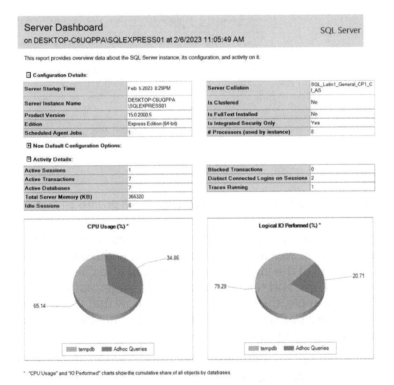

Built-In Server Report in Microsoft SQL Server Management Studio
(Used with permission from Microsoft.)

As with anything, if you monitor it regularly, you will notice when something looks off. For example, if you see that the database operations are suddenly using more CPU, you would then explore further to figure out what is causing it. While we expect increased processing when users grow, an unexpected spike could signal a bad process.

Reviewing Log Files and Alerts

SQL Server, like other data systems, will by default save your log files separately from your database (although you can easily see the location of those log files). The transactions log, which allows you to see every transaction that has been run against the database, is especially important in the case of a failure, as it can show you what was running prior to the failure. This information can then be used to get the database back to the state it was in prior to the failure.

To view the SQL Server logs, we connect to our database and then navigate to the log viewer of that program. For example, in our toy company, we would connect to our database, expand the **Management Section** in SSMS, and then expand the **SQL Server Logs**.

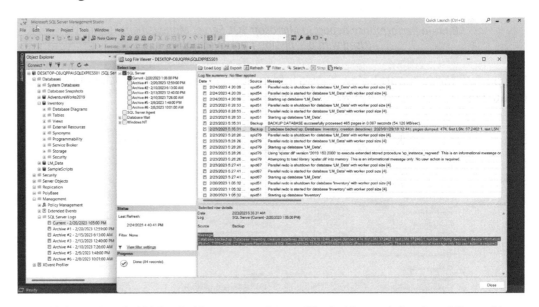

SQL Server Logs in SQL Studio Management System (Used with permission from Microsoft.)

In the above screenshot, we are connected to the database engine and are able to select the current log, as well as the past few days of archived logs. This allows us to filter and review all of the log information. We can also check different scenarios, like our backups, and read various user messages associated with the log information. For example, the one below lets us know that this backup has occurred, tells us where it's at, and provides the name of the file. It also alerts us that no further information is required.

"Message Database backed up. Database: Inventory, creation date(time): 2023/01/29(18:12:44), pages dumped: 474, first LSN: 37:2462:1, last LSN: 37:2465:1, number of dump devices: 1, device information: (FILE=1, TYPE=DISK: {'C:\Program Files\Microsoft SQL Server\MSSQL15.SQLEXPRESS01\MSSQL\Backup\Inventory. bak'}). This is an informational message only. No user action is required."

Filter Log Files

If you are looking for something specific in the log, you can leverage the filter settings to narrow it down. In this scenario, we are filtering for a few days of information, and specifically looking for **Backup**, which is the source of the logs we are looking to explore. We can designate our settings, apply our filter, and select **OK**.

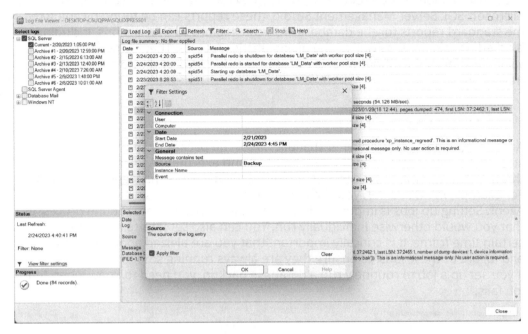

Filter Settings for SQL Server Logs in SQL Studio Management System
(Used with permission from Microsoft.)

For our time frame, we see two messages, showing us that the inventory database has successfully been backed up in two occasions.

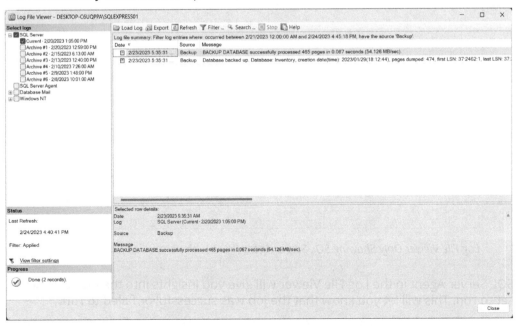

Backups Only in Filter Settings for SQL Server Logs in SQL Server Management Studio
(Used with permission from Microsoft.)

Your organization will have various rules and requirements around different types of jobs, procedures, and automatic backups. The logs will provide you with valuable insight into the success or failure of many different processes in the database.

Transaction Reports

In addition to exploring the log files from transactions, you will find value in looking at the transaction-related reporting provided by the data systems you use. In Microsoft SQL Server Management Studio, these reports can be found by going to the standard reports for the database. You can explore all transactions, including blocked transactions, as well as the user statistics reports. These reports contain valuable information about what is open, what is blocked, and who are running transactions.

Job Completion and Failures

A job in SQL Server is a container that allows for the packaging of one or more steps in a process that needs to be scheduled and executed. A job can be created through scripts, or in some cases set up using the database management system. For example in SQL Server, you can create and monitor jobs using the SQL Server Agent. Setting up jobs is important because it can help automate routine processes that you would otherwise individually run. You can also set jobs to run during a certain time frame. It is critically important that you are alerted about the success and failure of these jobs, to ensure they are always running smoothly. For example, if you set up a job to routinely run a database backup, you need to know when that job fails.

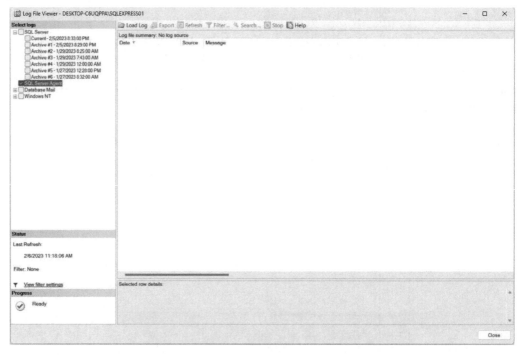

Log File Viewer Only Showing SQL Server Agent (Used with permission from Microsoft.)

SQL Server Agent in the Log File Viewer will give you insights into the jobs that are set to run. This will let you know that the job was successful or failed to run.

If a scheduled job fails to run, and the DBA discovers this, one of the first steps is to notify impacted users. For example, if ratings updates fail to run, we might notify the marketing department that the ratings data did not update and that we are working to identify the issue. The next step would be to start investigating why this process did not run. It could be that another process failed to complete, which prevented other jobs from running as intended. It could also be that bad data, or data that didn't meet the requirements for the record, existed. Once the issue has been identified, the DBA will address the issue and run the job again to determine if the fix indeed corrected the issue. The DBA then monitors that job to determine that it is back to running as intended.

The problems that can occur can be simple or complex, requiring unique fixes based on the problem that cause the job to fail. Further, they always require notification to impacted users/departments based on the organizational policy.

Review Activity:

Monitor the Database

Answer the following questions:

1. **What information is available through the Log File Viewer?**

2. **True or False. A connection cannot have multiple sessions.**

3. **A sales team of 50 people connects to a report with data sourced from SQL Server that is accessible on their company desktops, tablets, and mobile devices. In order to accommodate the possibility of each user connecting on each of their devices, what should the minimum for concurrent connections be set at?**

4. **What is a drawback of automatic size increase settings?**

5. **SQL Server Management Studio's Performance Dashboard report focuses primarily on which performance metrics?**

6. **A database has a sales table that is updated each night through a scheduled job. You check this process and determine that it has failed. Which SQL application is responsible for managing this job?**

Topic 7C

Understand and Address Deadlocks

EXAM OBJECTIVES COVERED
3.1 Explain the purpose of monitoring and reporting for database management and performance.

In an earlier lesson, you learned how transactions can lock tables—a positive measure to ensure data quality, and one that follows ACID principles. However, this is only one type of lock. Another, less positive type, is deadlocks. Deadlocks are exactly what they sound like: a dead-end and locked-down work. When these occur in your production databases, it means that the processes and/or tables are locked. Locked tables can cause data loss, since data cannot be added to locked tables. If a critical process that ferries data from one location to the next is unable to perform, this means that the process has failed. Being able to identify and address deadlocks is an important measure in maintaining and running data systems.

How Deadlocks Occur

Deadlocking typically occurs when the locking of two or more co-dependent tasks causes them to block each other, creating a stalemate in a cyclic fashion. When this happens, all activity is stopped until the conflicting locks are prioritized or rolled back. This kind of disruption will result in poor application performance, such as slow response times and repeating/retrying application actions. Knowing how to identify and address deadlocks when they occur is critical to the health of any database.

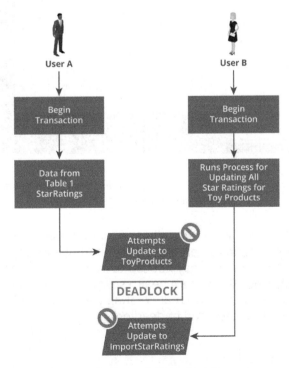

Diagram of a Potential Deadlock Scenario

In our example diagram of a deadlock scenario, User A begins a transaction to update the rating data for a few products from the StarRatings table. At the same time, User B has begun a process that runs an update to adjust all the ratings. Because both of the processes are trying to use the Toy Products table, a deadlock is produced.

When you experience a deadlock, one of your first steps will be to try to determine what is causing the deadlock.

Identifying the Cause of a Deadlock

Identifying a deadlock is not only the first step in resolving the issue, but also the first step in prevention. When a deadlock has already occurred, a DBA will most definitely be notified by application users, who will experience an error due to locked resources.

In the toy company, a massive report runs each month that reports on year-over-year performance, and it is on an automatic schedule. This report leverages many tables in the database, including order tables, and when it runs these tables are locked. Suppose that in advance of the holiday season, the toy company opens up a presale for the hottest new toy of the year. However, because the schedule for the performance report was not turned off, it runs, and produces a conflict with the application where orders are placed. This will immediately stop orders from being processed while the report continues to run.

In SQL Server, there is a default event session called `system_health` that collects information about deadlocks that can be used to query the deadlock issue prompted by the end user or development team.

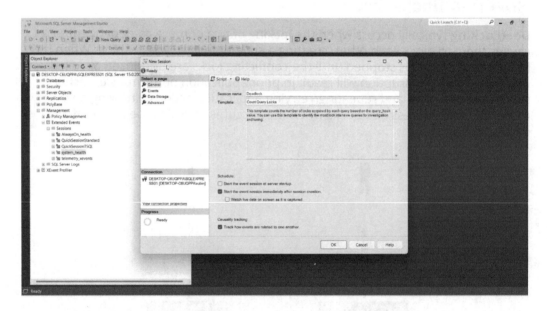

Creating a New `system_health` *Session in SQL Server Management Studio*
(Used with permission from Microsoft.)

If your team doesn't already have a deadlock extended event created, then creating one would be another step in the process of monitoring and identifying deadlocks. The `system_health` session may not capture all deadlocks because of file limitations, especially since the system health session is collecting more than deadlock information. You may find that creating your own deadlock event session will isolate the information captured to deadlocks.

Obviously, as DBAs we would ideally want to identify deadlocks before the end user experiences application errors. SQL Server Profiler allows us to identify deadlocks and also to add graphs for deadlock analysis. Also, setting alerts for deadlocks based on previously resolved deadlock errors is a best practice to prevent reoccurrence.

Addressing a Deadlock

Every deadlock is not created equal, and addressing them is dependent on what's causing the deadlock. You must first determine what is causing the issue, and based on the cause then make the necessary correction.

In our previous example, the hot new toy presale occurs at the same time as the scheduled report runs, which locks the table and causes no orders to be fulfilled through the website. In this case, adding a (NOLOCK) statement to the queries might just do the trick; that way, when they run, they do not lock the tables.

However, a deadlock could also be caused by someone opening a transaction and failing to commit or roll it back, thereby just leaving it open. You might have hundreds of users, so in order to identify the transaction that is causing the deadlock, we begin our investigation by viewing open transactions.

```
SELECT * FROM sys.sysprocesses WHERE open_tran = 1
```

This code will allow you to look for any open transactions, so that you can determine your next steps.

The sysprocesses table is the powerhouse of most of this work. This particular query only returns records where `open_tran` is 1. But if that does not return any results, then we dig a bit deeper into this system table.

This next query returns the blocking_session_id (among other things). This is the session ID of whatever connection is blocking. The `wait_type` column tells you what kind of block it is that has caused the deadlock. For normal scenarios, the most usual suspects will be the wait types that begin with LCK.

The following is a sample script that allows you to start to investigate what potentially might be causing the deadlock, with some additional details.

```
SELECT
    session_id, start_time, [status], command,
    blocking_session_id, wait_type, wait_time,
    open_transaction_count, transaction_id,
    total_elapsed_time,  Definition = cast(text as
    varchar(max))
FROM SYS.DM_EXEC_REQUESTS
cross apply sys.dm_exec_sql_text(sql_handle)
WHERE blocking_session_id != 0
```

Once we've run this query, we make note of the `blocking_session_id`, as we need this information to look up this session to see what application is connected and who is logged in. Keep in mind that there may be multiple blocking sessions, so trying to figure out which one was first can be a challenge. But sometimes it will be obvious.

```
SELECT * FROM SYS.DM_EXEC_SESSIONS
```

To find the session ID that matches the blocking session IDs found previously, we use the above query, which will actually show you the application that is causing the blocking.

There is no catch-all solution for deadlocks, but there are ways to identify them and work to address them using the various tools and scripts available to you in the data system. The goal is to make sure your data systems are running and available, so getting on top of whatever blocks the usage is important.

Review Activity:

Deadlocks

Answer the following questions:

1. A _____ causes processes to be blocked, slows performance of the data system, and creates rollbacks in the data.

2. When experiencing a deadlock, or any lock for that matter, where might you begin to identify the cause of the issue?

3. What is the most typical cause of deadlocking?

4. Why is it important to address deadlocks?

Lesson 7

Summary

After this lesson, you should have a better understanding of how to keep a database healthy through monitoring and leveraging reports. You should be familiar with how web applications use client-server architecture to work with our data systems and how websites are converted to meaningful names using DNS. You should be able to determine where a database is hosted, and know how to access it so you can monitor its performance and review the various log files that support you in the investigation of issues. You should have a thorough understanding of connections and sessions. You should also understand how to investigate and address deadlocks.

Guidelines for Monitoring and Reporting on Database Performance

Consider these best practices and guidelines when monitoring the performance and health of a database.

1. **Be familiar with the front-end application that allows your organization's users to interact with the back-end systems—whether it's a website, custom software, or something else.**

2. **Know whether programming processes occur on the client side or the server side.**

3. **Determine whether your instance of SQL Server uses static or dynamic ports.**

4. **Review the normal number of connections and sessions from the user population regularly, recognizing that an increase in normal usage can signal an issue.**

5. **Monitor the resources that your data system uses, setting limits or increasing them to maximize space for your data system.**

6. **Be familiar with the types of jobs that run on your data systems and what they perform, so you can plan your next steps should they fail.**

7. **In the event of a deadlock, be prepared to leverage reports, insights, and queries to determine where the issue originated and what needs to be done to resolve it.**

Lesson 8

Understanding Common Data Maintenance Processes

LESSON INTRODUCTION

Maintaining a system, or set of systems, at an organization can include several types of maintenance, ranging from basic patch management for updates to software to patches for critical vulnerabilities. Simply installing updates is not the only maintenance a DBA will perform. You will also likely find yourself engaged in performance tuning, which will increase the performance of your queries by deploying strategies for query optimization, and performing index analysis and optimization.

Lesson Objectives

In this lesson, you will do the following:

- Explain patch management.

- Ensure database performance.

- Understand database integrity and corruption checks.

Topic 8A

Explain Patch Management

EXAM OBJECTIVES COVERED
3.2 Explain common database maintenance processes.

Each type of OS and applications software has vulnerabilities that present opportunities for would-be attackers. As soon as a vulnerability is identified in a supported product, the vendor will (or should) try to correct it with a **patch**. Databases are no different; they require patch management processes as well. The challenges we face in patching live database systems and closing vulnerabilities are a fact of life for any DBA.

Patch Management

Patch management refers to the procedures put in place to manage the installation of updates for hardware and software. It is important to make a backup of the system before performing an update or upgrade.

Updates will typically be marked as critical or optional. Patch management is done throughout the entire technical department regardless of domain. If you are responsible for software and/or hardware, then you will likely be involved in patch management.

Although this might vary from one organization to the next, patches, not unlike any change to a database, will typically be installed and tested in a test environment before being implemented into production. Just like any other upgrade, patches will go through the organization's defined change management process (described in more detail in Lesson 10). Patching can be complicated at times, so it is important for all involved to communicate effectively during implementation.

It's also important to consider when patches should be implemented. You may find that only critical security patches get installed quickly, due to the nature of securing the data system. Other patches will not be implemented the minute they are released. Many organizations will wait for a certain amount of time before applying a new, noncritical patch, making sure it is stable before implementing it into their environment. This helps to reduce the downtime and overhead of fixing things when teams are small and lean.

While patch distribution can be done manually, scheduling it is a best practice when it comes to security patches. Because security patches must be installed quickly, a schedule helps make sure they are prioritized and never overlooked. A patch management process that is structured and includes rollouts on a consistent schedule is often more effective. For example, Windows rolls out monthly security updates to maintain and patch security vulnerabilities. Following your organization's patch management process will help avoid, prevent, and decrease the chance of performance slowdowns or database vulnerabilities. When planning the rollout of a patch, you must check with your development team for a suggested downtime window, as well as be aware of your database's workloads, to avoid overloading the system. Patches should first be implemented in a test environment and monitored before applying to the production environment. It's important to note that when working with cloud vendors, patch distribution will be performed automatically.

Types of Patches

As a DBA, you may not be responsible for implementing every type of patch for all of the hardware or software on the network, but it is still important to understand the most common types of patches that you will likely encounter within your organization's technology solutions.

- **Operating system updates:** Operating system (OS) updates are critical to the operating system and may include either performance upgrades to the OS or security patches. When software vendors identify an improvement, or security issue, they will typically respond with a patch to improve or secure the issue. Security patches in particular should be implemented right away to protect systems from vulnerabilities.

- **Vendor-specific patches:** When using software or hardware from a vendor, you will need to be aware of how that vendor provides updates. How you implement these patches will be specific to the vendor and the software used, as they will provide the patch and the instructions. For an OS like Windows, we use Windows Updates to install necessary updates or "patches" to our OS.

- **Database-specific patches:** Database patches are typically comprised of bug fixes, additional features, and discovered vulnerabilities that have been identified for a specific database software, which are then released to patch that version of the software. SQL Server uses Cumulative Updates (CUs) for patching, regularly issuing critical updates every 30–60 days. Oracle uses Bundle Patch (BP) and releases once a quarter. Three of these quarterly patches are RUR (Release Update Revision) that include smaller sets of changes. The fourth, released once a year, is a major patch called an RU (Release Update). While each software company will handle releases differently, you should be aware of how the software you're using releases patches so that you can plan accordingly.

Review Activity:

Patch Management

Answer the following questions:

1. What process involves installing an update to fix an issue that has been discovered?

2. What critical type of patch should be implemented immediately?

3. True or False: Only operating systems receive patches.

Topic 8B

Ensure Database Performance

EXAM OBJECTIVES COVERED
2.2 Explain database implementation, testing, and deployment phases.
3.2 Explain common database maintenance processes.

All technology professionals, regardless of their domain or specialty, would likely agree that technology should operate as fast as we can afford. The process of increasing the performance of our data system will include reviewing our queries to make sure they execute efficiently, as well as reviewing our indexes to confirm that we are leveraging them for better performance.

But measures to improve performance aren't restricted to queries. As a DBA, you may work with technical professionals who support the hardware, network, and tools that support data systems, so it's a good idea to have a high-level understanding of what they are meant to do and how they do it. When talking about the performance of our data systems, we shouldn't neglect to discuss scalability; a data system that properly performs for 50 users may perform terribly at 5,000 users.

Performance Tuning

Performance tuning is the process of increasing the performance of queries in a relational database. Before we go into how to conduct performance tuning, we must first ensure an understanding of the types of things that can slow the database down. It's important to note there are several different types of issues that can cause slow performance. For instance, poorly designed databases that do not follow proper normalization can have a lot of data redundancy. More data, and especially duplicated and redundant data, will cause performance issues. Poorly designed queries are another cause of slow performance, such as a bad query running inside a stored procedure slowing the system down. You may find that you have a design that requires a lot of processing but does not have a lot of processing power.

Consistently monitoring database transactions and I/O (Input/Output) is crucial to performance tuning as well. When monitoring transactions, you should not only be paying attention to successful and failed transactions, but also the number of transactions being processed (or the transaction workload). Identifying the workloads will allow you to appropriately remove poor-performing indexes that result in high I/O and create indexes for the right queries, resulting in increased performance. High I/O typically is an indicator that your disk subsystems are overworked, which is commonly a sign that you have poorly written queries and/or insufficient indexes.

As a DBA, if you're experiencing a performance issue, you should investigate the issue, try to determine where the problem might be stemming from, and then attempt to correct it. There are some simple techniques that you can use as DBA to help increase the performance of your data system, which we will cover next.

Index Analysis and Optimization

When a database is designed properly, fields that are commonly sorted, queried, or filtered will likely be indexed. Indexing is a field property setting that tells the database that a field needs to be indexed. It's an internal process that controls how much data must be looked at when processing the data for queries. When fields are indexed, it makes data processing faster and ultimately speeds up the performance of the query.

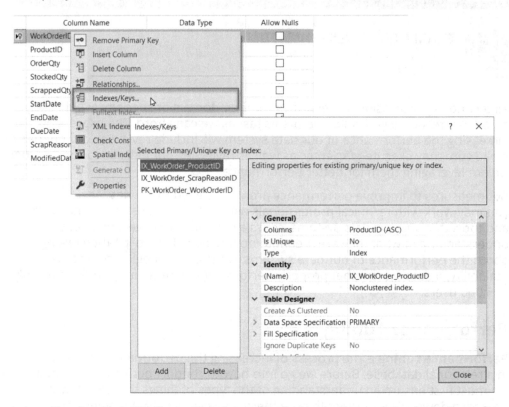

Indexes/Keys Screen via SQL Server Management Studio (Used with permission from Microsoft.)

Index analysis is the process in which indexes are analyzed for performance. This process will initiate during the implementation and testing phases of design, but it will be an ongoing process over the life of the database. When databases are designed to include primary keys, these keys are already indexed by default. However, any field can be set to be an index. When a field is set as an index in SQL, we can see some performance gains when we query.

However, more indexes are not always better. When we conduct index analysis, we must determine if the indexes are effective for the goals of the project, and make decisions that provide the best performance for the need. As a result of index optimization efforts, you may discover that tables with many indexes can actually negatively impact the performance of your database. For example, a table can only have one clustered index, which is defined when you establish the primary key for that table. If you were to create many non-clustered indexes, believing it to enhance the speed, and that data grows over time, those non-clustered indexes would have to constantly rebuild themselves with the new data coming in. You might discover that these types of indexes need to be removed to increase performance.

There is an appropriate balance, or trade-off, in indexing, depending on what you need to accomplish.

Query Optimization

In some organizations, there are database professionals whose entire role is to ensure that queries are running as fast as possible. Imagine that traffic on the network is like rush hour on the highway. If one car on the highway is going half the speed of the other cars, all the cars stuck in the lane behind the slow car are also impeded, even if other cars are flying by in other lanes. In this same way, sluggish queries block up network traffic and make everything else run more slowly, so we want to avoid them as much as we can.

In Microsoft SQL Server Management Studio, every time we run a query, we are given the amount of time it took to execute that query. In the screenshot below, we are running the view Sales.vIndividualCustomer from AdventureWorks2019 in SSMS. In the bottom-right side of the query window, we can see that this query executes in one second and is returning 18,508 rows of individual customer records. This is one of the first places you should look when trying to determine whether a query is slow.

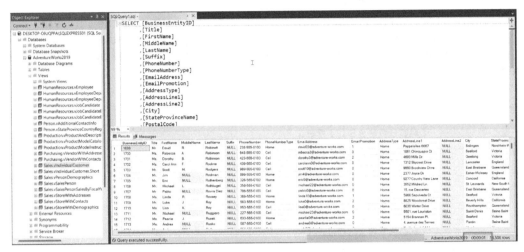

Sales.vIndividualCustomer in Microsoft SQL Server Management Studio (Used with permission from Microsoft.)

Sorts, unfiltered data, and querying on a large number of records are a few of the most common reasons for slow queries. Addressing these issues can help improve performance.

Removing Sorts

Including the `ORDER BY` clause in a query that pulls hundreds of thousands of records is going to slow the query down. If the sort can be performed somewhere else, it should be. For example, suppose the toy company's business analyst is doing historical orders research. They will likely use various sorting scenarios with the tools they work with. Removing that sort is a simple form of performance tuning that would optimize the query to run more efficiently.

Filtering

You can improve performance by filtering data using the WHERE clause, as long as you understand the objective for the data. For example, suppose the toy company's director of finance has asked the DBA to provide them with historical order data so they can perform some year-over-year analysis. One of the first questions the DBA should ask is whether the director needs all of the history or if the last three years would be sufficient for their analysis. Being able to filter down to the last three years of information, rather than pulling everything, would have immediate benefits to the speed of execution.

Using Temporary Tables

A **temporary table** is a table that is stored on the database server until a user disconnects from the server. Similar to a permanent table, temporary tables provide records, but they are for temporary use only. These temporary tables can improve processing speeds for queries simply because they likely contain a smaller number of records than the permanent table.

Temporary tables can be created through SQL statements. We use the CREATE TABLE syntax, and then add records to the temporarily created table using INSERT. You would create the temporary table when querying the permanent table.

```
SELECT [AddressID]
      ,[AddressLine1]
      ,[AddressLine2]
      ,[City]
      ,[StateProvinceID]
      ,[PostalCode]
  INTO #LosAngelesAddresses
  FROM [AdventureWorks2019].[Person].[Address]
  Where City = 'Los Angeles'
```

Create Table Syntax for a Temporary Table in Microsoft SQL Server Management Studio (Used with permission from Microsoft.)

In the screenshot above, we are creating a temporary table that we can then use to automatically filter the addresses to only include those who are in Los Angeles. Then we can use this table within other queries, without having to always use the entire address table. Remember the size of a database will increase over time as the number of records increases, so slow performance early on becomes even slower performance later.

Query Execution Plan

A **query execution plan** is the order of steps in which a query is processed, and it can give you more insight into how to improve the performance of any given query. It is a visual representation that provides details about how the query executes. The query execution plan includes an **estimated execution plan** of possible requirements for executing the query and the **actual execution plan** that is known once the query has been executed.

The estimated execution plan can reveal areas of high server usage to process the information. It will be the DBA's responsibility to review the estimated execution plan and fine-tune queries that run inefficiently.

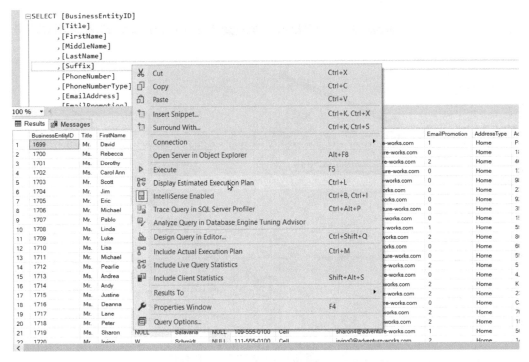

Display Estimated Plan in Microsoft SQL Server Management Studio
(Used with permission from Microsoft.)

In the case of queries that take a long time to execute, you can choose to view the estimated execution plan beforehand (as shown in the screenshot above). When running the query, choosing to include the actual execution plan (as shown in the screenshot below) gives you a tab that lets you review said execution plan.

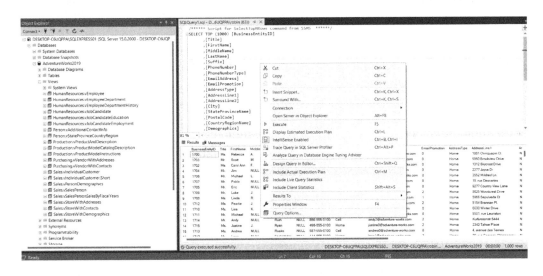

Include Actual Execution Plan in Microsoft SQL Server Management Studio
(Used with permission from Microsoft.)

When viewing the query execution plan, each part of the graphical representation can be hovered over for a more detailed view of the associated step and its impacts. When you build queries for large data sets, you will want to deploy strategies like this to execute your queries faster.

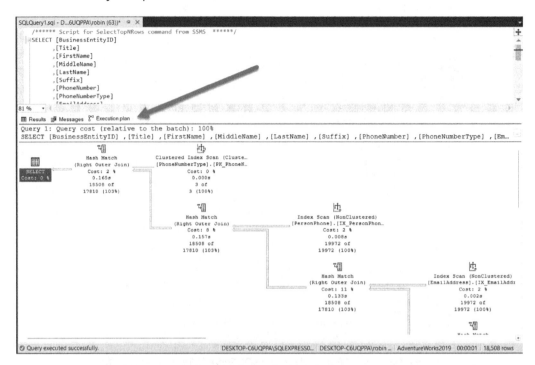

Visual View of the Query Execution Plan in Microsoft SQL Server Management Studio (Used with permission from Microsoft.)

When you include the actual execution plan, it will add a tab to the results. In the image below, we can see our clustered and non-clustered indexes. We can look at the different percentages of cost to determine if each index might be one that we consider removing.

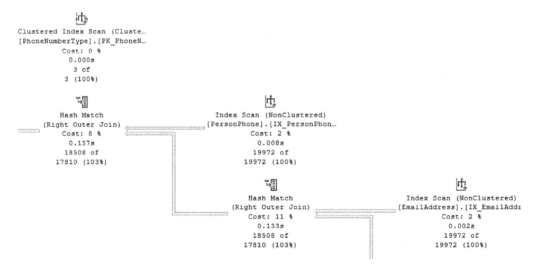

Visual View of the Query Execution Plan in Microsoft SQL Server Management Studio (Used with permission from Microsoft.)

This gives you a starting point to look at, but each part of how this query executes will give you the next step. When trying to optimize, each scenario you face will be different. It's as much investigation as it is correction, if not more.

Load Balancing

Just as it sounds, database **load balancing** is the distribution of incoming traffic or workload across multiple databases to prevent downtime and to enable **scalability**. Load balancing is an important part of a fault tolerant system, as is **failover**, which we'll discuss in a later lesson.

A **load balancer** can be deployed as a hardware appliance or software instance to distribute client requests across servers. Load balancers can be used in any situation where there are multiple servers providing the same function. Examples include web servers, databases, front-end email servers, web conferencing, A/V conferencing, or streaming media servers. The load balancer is placed in front of the server network and distributes requests from the client network or Internet to the application or database servers. The service address is advertised to clients as a virtual server. This is used to provision services that can scale from light to heavy loads, provision fault tolerant services, and to provide mitigation against distributed denial of service (DDoS) attacks.

Load Balancing Techniques

The algorithm that is used to distribute incoming client requests to the various load-balanced servers determines the type of load balancing, or load balancing technique, that will be used. There are many load balancing techniques, with some of them being variations of others. These techniques can be divided into two categories: dynamic and static techniques. Dynamic techniques use algorithms that take into account the state of each server when determining how to distribute traffic. Static techniques distribute traffic without any consideration for the server state. Below are a few examples of some of these techniques:

- **Round robin** is one of the most common load balancing techniques. This simple, static technique distributes client requests to servers in a rotation. The first request is sent to the first server, the second request is sent to the second server, and so on. When the last server has been sent a request, the next request is sent to the first server again, and the sequence continues.

- **Sticky round robin** is a variation of round robin and is also static. In the sticky round robin technique, the initial client request is distributed exactly as it is in round robin. The variation is that once a particular client has been distributed to a server, each subsequent request from that same client will be distributed to the same server.

- The **least connection technique** is a dynamic technique in which the servers are checked to see which one has the fewest connections at the time of the request. Then the client connection is distributed to that server.

Validating Scalability

Scalability validation involves confirming that an application, which includes the database, can scale up or down as needed. Scale applies at every level: the network, hardware, server, application, and database. When performed accurately and consistently, scalability will ultimately improve the availability of your database to users. Technical teams will typically deploy third-party tools to test for scalability.

Validating for scalability might seem to serve the same purpose as stress testing, which tests how many users can connect to a database before it breaks. However, while stress testing intends to seek out the limits of the system, scale validation seeks to ensure the network has the right amount of resources both for typical use and also for growth. A system designed to work for 100 users might not scale effectively to 1,000 users. At the same time, designing a system for 1,000 users when it will only have 100 users results in increased cost for no real purpose. Thus, we validate for scalability to ensure that our system can handle increased needs while also not overdeveloping. If a system made for 100 users suddenly has 1,000 users, and we have not planned for this scaling, we can anticipate that it will stress the system. This means we could face processes that do not run and transactions that do not get processed. We might just experience terrible performance overall.

Review Activity:

Database Performance

Answer the following questions:

1. What are issues that can lead to poor database performance?

2. Which process is used to determine how an application or data system performs with a large number of users?

3. True or False: You can have many clustered indexes in a table.

4. What can you include when you execute a query to determine if and where it is slow?

5. What is the process of optimizing performance also known as?

Topic 8C

Ensure Database Integrity

 EXAM OBJECTIVES COVERED
3.2 Explain common database maintenance processes.

A database that is lacking integrity will provide very little benefit to an organization. There are several ways to ensure consistent data is being entered into a database. We can leverage primary keys and assign proper relationships, thus ensuring that the database is not capturing bad data by design. All DBAs should be familiar with how built-in table locking measures maintain integrity. Databases can also have corruption issues due to network crashes or server failures. Finally, learning how to monitor and explore corruption issues due to a network crash or server failure can be a useful skill.

Designing for Data Integrity

When a database is designed, primary keys and relationships are typically put in place to prevent bad data from being accidentally added and quality data from being inadvertently deleted. We introduced the concepts of keys and relationships back in Lesson 1, but it's worth revisiting here to talk more specifically about how these areas of database design affect data integrity.

Primary Keys

Primary keys have properties and constraints that limit what data can be entered into the database. When we make a field a primary key, it ensures that any new record entered must hold a unique value in that field; essentially, another record cannot be entered with the same value in that field. For example, suppose your organization assigns each employee a unique identifier that is used in all the systems, and that identifier is set as the primary key of the "Employees" table. If you tried to enter any employee's information into the table for a second time, the system would produce an error message warning you that primary keys should not be duplicated.

Relationships

When working with relational databases, we can also use primary keys to establish relationships between tables to achieve another level of integrity. Let's refer back to the example of unique employee identifiers. When you relate the "Employees" table to another table (let's say "Payrolls") through a relationship, you can only add an employee to the payroll table if they already exist in the employee table. This prevents us from adding an employee to the payroll table that shouldn't be there, thus providing table integrity.

Even if you do not design your own databases, you still may want to check for these settings on any database you are charged to work with. These are not the only integrity steps that can be performed, but they are the most basic to enact and confirm for when reviewing a design. Here are a few others:

- A field can be set in the properties to not allow a value to be null or blank.

- Default values can be set so that a field that is commonly the same value doesn't have to be manually typed by a human.

- A field can be established to hold a unique value even though it may not be the primary key field.

- Fields can be required to be populated before a record is saved.

Locking Order

If you try to open a file on a server drive that someone else already had open, you will likely receive a message stating that the file is locked for editing. This same idea holds true for databases.

When users of a database are performing transactions, like updates and inserts, table locking occurs by default. Two people cannot edit the same record at the exact same time, because it's locked for editing. This type of isolation ensures data integrity, as all other objects have to wait for the lock to be released before any other edits can be applied. The locks are released when the transaction is committed.

In the diagram below, we show the locking order of a database. The database is locked from being dropped when even just a row is open for editing.

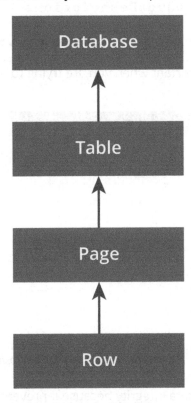

Locking Order of a Database

Imagine it this way: A row locks a page, a page locks a table, and a table locks the database. This locking order prevents a lot of "accidents" in our data. For example, if someone has a table locked by default, the database is also locked so that no one can drop the database. You can't delete the database because someone is using it, not unlike our file example. The same goes for editing a table and a record. You can't drop a table when that table is being used, and you can't remove a record if it's locked because someone is editing it through a process or application.

Consider the transaction below. Once it is executed, but before it is committed, it will lock the ToyProducts and ProductDescriptions tables, because they are both in use.

```
BEGIN TRANSACTION

INSERT INTO ProductDescriptions
                (ProducID, ProductDescription)
SELECT     ProductID, 'Lorem ipsum dolor sit amet, consectetur adipiscing elit,
sed do eiusmod tempor incididunt ut labore et dolore magna aliqua. Volutpat cons
FROM        ToyProducts

COMMIT

ROLLBACK
```

Transaction Script Updating the ProductDescriptions Table in SQL Server Management Studio (Used with permission from Microsoft.)

If another user tries to drop the ProductDescriptions table with the following code, it will run forever but never actually drop the table.

```
DROP TABLE ProductDescriptions
```

We can use the All Blocking Transactions report in SQL Server to see details about active transactions, including what SQL statement is being blocked. Knowing the locking order can be important when you are trying to determine the source of a lock.

All Blocking Transactions Report in SQL Server Management Studio (Used with permission from Microsoft.)

Locking helps establish data integrity because it prevents objects that are currently in use from being harmed when commands are running and working on the data system. This is why using TCL commands is an important best practice.

Data Corruption Checks

There are many reasons why a database might become corrupt, from server-related failures to malicious acts. But no matter the cause, you will want to know how to check for **data corruption**. As with many other activities you will conduct, this process typically begins with investigation. A knowledge of how to perform corruption checks is crucial because data corruption can result in unexpected results, such as damaged data or data loss. If left unchecked, in some cases it will even result in a system crash. Thus, taking actions to be notified about and being prepared to take action on corruption in a timely manner is essential to database maintenance.

There are several different ways to monitor and detect corruption. In SQL, the DBA can run queries or commands to check the database for damage. The following stored procedure can be queried to check for any corruption in the SQL database.

```
SELECT * FROM msdbo.suspect_pages
```

This is a quick way to check for corruption that has previously occurred. When using Microsoft SQL Server, another method to determine corruption is the DBCC CHECKDB command. This command is part of the Database Console Commands for SQL Server, which will return details on why a corruption may have occurred.

Even with the ability to check a database for corruption, it is still important to set up alerts to notify you of these corruptions using SQL Server Agent. For example, if you have a stored procedure that fails and corrupts the database, you can establish an alert to notify you if that happens again. The quicker we know a system is corrupted, the faster we can fix it for people to begin using it again.

Once you have identified the presence of corruption, through any method, there are several third-party database repair tools that help make the repair effortless.

 Data corruption is one reason to have a proper backup strategy. When you find that your database is corrupted, the presence of a backup allows you to minimize downtime and data loss by putting the backup into production.

Review Activity:

Database Integrity

Answer the following questions:

1. We would establish a _____ to ensure that a record has a unique identifier.

2. True or False: Creating a relationship between two tables allows us to add records to one of the tables without needing a primary key in the other table.

3. What prevents a table from being dropped or altered while in use by another person?

4. Which Database Console Command for SQL Server can be used to check for corruption?

Lesson 8

Summary

After this lesson, you should be familiar with the processes involved in maintaining a system, or set of systems, at an organization. You should have a better understanding of patch management, which can include maintenance activities ranging from basic software updates to patches for critical vulnerabilities. You should have a better understanding of how queries can impact performance, and different methods of performance tuning. You should know how to increase the performance of your queries by deploying strategies for query optimization and performing index analysis and optimization. You should also have a better understanding of what database integrity is and how to achieve it.

Guidelines for Performing Data Maintenance Processes

Consider these best practices and guidelines when performing various maintenance activities.

1. **Know the most current version of your data system and be aware of any updates that are issued, even if it's not your responsibility to update or upgrade the system.**

2. **Gather and explore patch management for vendor-related software and identify how it could impact your data system.**

3. **Be aware of the performance tuning options that are set within your organization.**

4. **Explore and work with indexes in your database design that might impact performance.**

5. **Be on the lookout for slow-performing queries and review the code for efficiency.**

6. **Discover what load balancing options have been used with your data system.**

7. **Determine typical usage of your data system so you can consider scalability.**

8. **Be familiar with the data integrity properties that have been set in your data system's design.**

9. **Check your database routinely for corruption and use alerts to bring your attention more quickly to damage.**

Lesson 9

Understanding Governance and Regulatory Compliance

LESSON INTRODUCTION

Data governance is the process of managing the availability of data, defining how data can be used, identifying who can access the data, and determining how the data is secured. The purpose of data governance is to ensure the integrity and proper use of data.

A successful data governance plan should prevent inconsistent data among departments or business units. It should allow an entire organization to create and share a common set of data definitions and prevent data from being misused. Data errors and inaccuracies can be more easily fixed or prevented with a successful data governance plan.

This lesson provides an overview of governance and compliance. Governance and compliance are typically misunderstood as being the responsibility of only one division (information technology, security, leadership, or development). This is a great place to discuss how governance and compliance is the responsibility of the entire organization. Ask the students how different areas/divisions of an organization can affect governance and compliance.

Lesson Objectives

In this lesson, you will do the following:

- Understand the importance of protecting data and preventing data loss.

- Use data retention policies.

- Classify data.

- Consider global and regional regulations.

Topic 9A

Understand the Importance of Protecting Data and Preventing Data Loss

 EXAM OBJECTIVES COVERED
4.2 Explain the purpose of governance and regulatory compliance.

The responsibility for protecting the integrity of data, ensuring the privacy of data, and preventing the loss of data does not just belong to a single team. It lies with multiple teams within an organization and ultimately with everyone in an organization in one way or another. But before we take the steps needed to perform these actions, we must first identify what data needs to be protected and determine the level of protection that data needs. In order to do this, we must identify the type of data we're working with and recognize what state the data is in.

Why We Protect Data

Historically, many organizations viewed data as simply a by-product of doing business. However, modern organizations are realizing it is time to view data as a critical and strategic resource. When valuable information and actionable insights can be extracted from data, it becomes an economic asset that will help the business evolve and achieve its objectives. Protection of that data is therefore a top priority for companies. In some cases, the protection of data is not just a priority for the business, but a requirement of the regulations that affect the business or the industry.

Protection of the data, or protection from the loss of the data, can take multiple forms. This is referred to generically as **data loss prevention (DLP)**. Policies, procedures, and technology must be put in place to ensure data is only accessible to the appropriate people and systems. Loss of data can occur because of corruption, exfiltration, data breaches, or just the misuse of data, whether accidental or intentional.

The increased use of digital and disconnected devices, as well as the rising popularity of a remote workforce, have made the job of protecting against DLP even more difficult. Data is transferred between, and stored in, multiple places, including mobile phones, tablets and laptops, and other smart devices. DLP policies must now expand beyond the confines of the business environment into homes and social venues.

Identifying Private Data

When considering the amount of data owned by an organization, it might seem impossible to protect it all. However, not all data needs to be protected in the same way. What data needs to be protected, to what extent, and where it is located, will be dependent on the business.

There is an exception to this rule; in some cases, government regulations dictate how certain data must be protected, regardless of the organization's policies.

This process is rarely the sole responsibility of the DBA. In fact, developing data governance policies is usually a company project involving IT, leadership, legal, and other departments. The DBA is just one of many members of a larger team working on the project.

Where to Start

The first step in determining what data needs to be protected is to identify all the data assets owned by an organization and where those data assets are stored. Not all data that should be protected resides in a database, which is why there is a need for a larger team beyond just the DBA. Data can reside in files on storage media and even as printed documents that are archived. Once all the data assets have been identified, the data must be categorized to determine what individual data elements should be, or are required to be, protected. Often this means identifying and categorizing data as sensitive or confidential, collectively referred to as **private data**. **Confidential data** refers to data that is material to the operations of a business or government organization, which cannot be learned outside of that business or governmental organization. The definition for *sensitive data* is not as clear-cut and can differ across regions. There are common data elements that are considered sensitive, such as a person's social security number or bank account number. But a particular business might identify additional data as sensitive in the context of that business. A potential extension of this may be any data that would allow the inference of private data through indirect data relationships. Further, there are regulations and industry standards that may require certain data to be considered private.

By identifying a subset of the entire collection of data assets as private data, the amount of data that must be protected can be reduced to a more manageable set.

Documenting and Sharing Data Classification

Once the types of data that are to be categorized as private are identified, this information should be documented as part of the organization's data governance framework, and that documentation shared with the entire organization. A shared understanding of what data is considered to be private is imperative to ensuring it is managed, tracked, and protected in the same way across the organization, regardless of where that data is transferred or stored. A lack of communication regarding the identification of private data could potentially expose it to potential loss or misuse. For example, a lack of agreement regarding what data should be considered private might allow the misuse or loss of that data by a department that does not understand it to be private.

Data at Rest

Once data has been identified as private data, that data must be protected. But data can be in more than one state, and the considerations for how the data should be protected may be different in different states. **Data at rest** is data that is neither being actively used nor being transferred, and it is one of the states data can be in. The most common recognition of data at rest is data that is stored either on physical storage media, on a device, or in a cloud service, such as Microsoft Azure or Amazon Web Services (AWS).

However, there are less obvious examples of data at rest that must be taken into consideration when implementing DLP strategies. Consider data that is backed up or archived, data that has been printed, or even data that was emailed and is still in the recipient's mailbox. These are all examples of data at rest that must be included in the overall governance policies regarding protecting private data.

Data at rest is the easiest state of data to secure. However, it is also the most common target for hackers, because data spends most of its time at rest (and thus, the volume of data at rest is greater). It is also the most likely target for threats that are internal to a business, like disgruntled employees.

As more organizations allow employees to use their own devices for work-related activities, commonly referred to as **bring your own device (BYOD)**, the difficulty in securing data at rest increases. Sensitive data that exists on mobile devices is particularly difficult to secure due to the naturally distributed nature of these devices and their possible connection to insecure networks. Another threat to the protection of data at rest is the use of third-party services, like collaboration services, messaging services, and file sharing services. Data is often shared with and through these third-party services, but the storage of that data is outside of the user's control. This means the storage of the data is outside the scope of the owning company's policies. In order to account for third-party services, an organization should include policies regarding the use of third-party services. In order to ensure data protection in a nuanced environment, a comprehensive set of policies and practices must be put in place.

Data in Transit

Data in transit, also known as data in motion, is data that is actively being transferred between one or more computer systems, and it is the second state of data we'll be covering. The data is considered to be in motion as it is being transferred between RAM and the physical storage media or when it is being transferred from a smart device, or any network-enabled device, to a web-based service. A more relatable example is when you log into your email account. Your password is sent to a third party for validation, and then your email messages are transferred back to you to read. Data is also considered in motion while being transferred between applications or application instances. The transfer of the data may occur within a trusted, private network or an untrusted, public network (like the Internet).

Data in transit is vulnerable to a type of attack called an **on-path attack**, alternatively known as a man-in-the-middle attack. An on-path attack happens when a hacker inserts themself in between the source of a data transmission and the target of a data transmission. In doing so, the hacker can intercept the data as it is being transferred. The data can then be stolen, modified, or rerouted to an unintended target. Sometimes just being able to access and observe the data as it is being transferred is enough to cause damage. As an example, consider what could happen if an attacker was able to observe a user's username and password, a bank account number, or sensitive medical information.

Data that is in transit becomes data at rest once the transfer is complete and the data has reached its destination.

Data Endpoints

An endpoint is a remote computing device that communicates data back and forth across a network to which it is connected. In other words, any device that is connected to a network can be an endpoint. These data endpoints should be included in security plans that encompass data at rest and data in motion.

Traditionally, the perimeter of a network could be protected by perimeter security devices, like firewalls. However, as computing devices have become more mobile and more powerful, the increased number of devices accessing data remotely has created a constantly changing security perimeter for modern organizations. It is difficult, if not impossible, to completely define boundaries of the network now, meaning perimeter security devices are less effective as a security solution by themselves. Laptops, tablets, mobile phones, and even remote storage devices need to be included in data security and data governance plans. If an organization fails to consider data endpoint devices in its data security plan, it loses control of any sensitive data that is copied to the external device. In addition, an endpoint that is not properly secured provides an easy point of access for someone looking to compromise, access, or exfiltrate sensitive data.

 Think beyond the obvious when it comes to endpoint devices. Newer devices like smart appliances, voice-controlled digital assistants, and more can be endpoints.

Data Leakage

Data leakage refers to the unauthorized transfer of data from inside an organization to a destination outside its secured boundary. Data leakage can refer to electronic data, which may be transmitted across a network, or physical data, which may be stored on a portable storage device or a smart device (like a mobile phone) with internal storage. In fact, the data that is transferred may not even be digital. Printed data that is not properly destroyed can be retrieved from an organization's waste disposal.

The effects of data leakage on an organization can be devastating.

- **If proprietary data is lost, a competitive advantage can be forfeited.** Imagine a medical records company looking to partner with an organization with which they will share private customer data. Do you think a company like this is going to choose an organization that has had prior data loss incidents? Most likely not.

- **If customers' private data is lost, the reputation of the organization will be damaged.** Customers trust that any organization they do business with is properly caring for their personal and private data. Customers will not do business with an organization that has a reputation for being careless with their data.

- **Depending on the regulations affecting an organization, the fines that must be paid when data leakage occurs may be financially crippling.** In addition to fines levied by the regulatory bodies, an organization that fails to maintain compliance with regulations becomes a target for direct and class-action lawsuits, which can also be financially crippling by themselves.

Employees are the biggest threat to an organization's data. The threat becomes even greater as more and more employees work remotely. The tools and techniques being used by hackers to get access to data continue to evolve and improve. But often, it is an employee who will inadvertently deliver or give them access to data.

There are many different types of data leakage. Data protection policies and procedures need to address multiple areas to ensure that the most common data leakage threats are prevented.

Accidental Data Leakage

Most data leakage incidents are accidental. An employee may incorrectly choose the wrong recipient when sending an email containing sensitive or private data. Data containing sensitive information might be copied to a USB storage device that is accidentally dropped on the way home. Most instances of data leakage do not occur over an electronic medium, however, but rather via printers, photocopiers, video or still cameras, or even dumpster diving. A printed report with sensitive data left on a desk could be viewed by unauthorized individuals like a third-party vendor or a company visitor. Even if there's no malicious intent, unintentional data leakage is still data leakage and can still result in the same penalties, reputational damage, and loss of competitive advantage.

Data Exfiltration

It's important to note that while most data leakage is accidental, this isn't always the case. Any type of unauthorized data theft is considered **data exfiltration**. One common example involves disgruntled employees. While an employee may have signed an employment contract that effectively signifies trust between employer and employee, there is nothing to stop them from later leaking sensitive or confidential data if they are disgruntled or offered large sums of money by criminals or competitors.

Another less common and highly technical example of data exfiltration uses what is called air-gapped communication channels. Air-gapped communication channels are special types of covert communication channels that enable an attacker to exfiltrate data from isolated, network-less computers using technology such as electromagnetics, acoustics, optical properties, and thermal properties. As an example, even if a computer has no network connection, an attacker can use malware on the computer to manipulate the fan in the computer to vibrate the surface the computer is placed on. These vibrations can be picked up by an infected phone that is placed on the same surface. The variations in the vibrations can be used to transmit data from the computer to the phone, which then sends the data to the attacker.

A more obvious scenario might be simply a computer that is infected with malware of some sort. This malware can exfiltrate data disguised as legitimate network traffic. For example, some malware can embed data in an image and then transmit that image to a remote network location where the attacker can retrieve the data embedded in the image. Often, security software might not interpret the image being transferred as a problem, because it is just an image.

These are just a few examples of the ways data can be exfiltrated from an organization. This is why it is important for an organization to have a robust data loss prevention plan in place.

A real-world example of data leakage damaging the reputation of a company and ultimately impacting them financially occurred toward the end of 2022. A well-respected provider of password manager software was the victim of a cyberattack. The attackers were able to exfiltrate the encrypted passwords of their customers. While these password files were encrypted, it was determined that it might be possible for the attackers to decrypt the encrypted passwords. Users who trusted the password manager company were faced with the possibility that all of their passwords were now exposed to hackers. News of the incident was spread through news and social media. The company suffered a major impact to their reputation, and no doubt lost many of its users. At the time of this writing, it is still not known what the ultimate impact will be to the company.

Review Activity:

The Importance of Protecting Data and Preventing Data Loss

Answer the following questions:

1. What is the first step that must be taken in order to determine how to properly protect data?

2. What are two states of data that must be considered when determining how to protect data?

3. Data in which state is vulnerable to an on-path attack?

4. Why are traditional perimeter security measures no longer sufficient for protecting network endpoints?

5. What is often the biggest threat to data security?

Topic 9B

Understand Data Retention Policies

EXAM OBJECTIVES COVERED
4.2 Explain the purpose of governance and regulatory compliance.

It is imperative to have policies and procedures to protect data that is no longer actively being used from unauthorized access, unauthorized modification, and leakage. These policies and procedures should also address how, where, and for how long this data is stored. This part of data management is called **data retention**. And the policies that define these rules are data retention policies. While data retention policies are often considered part of an organization's overall data governance, there are also practical reasons for having a data retention policy. In addition to an organization's internal data retention policies, there may be regulatory requirements for data retention that an organization must comply with. In fact, one of the main reasons organizations create data retention policies is to comply with regulatory requirements.

The Purpose of Data Retention Policies

A data **retention policy** may serve many purposes, but it ultimately serves to define how inactive data is protected. Local, state, or federal laws may require an organization to maintain a data retention policy. There may also be industry standards that require a data retention policy. A data retention policy may be used to better prepare a company for business continuity and disaster recovery. A data retention policy typically defines the following:

- How data is stored for regulatory or compliance purposes

- How long it must be stored

- How it is disposed of when no longer needed

- What format the data records are stored in

The retention policy should specify what happens to the data after the retention period has been exceeded (such as whether it must be destroyed, and how). However, the retention policy may not have specific rules for what happens to the data after the retention period. This is often the case when regulations dictate that data must be kept for a minimum amount of time but do not state what must happen after that minimum. If an organization's retention policy does not require data to be destroyed, data that is past the retention period may simply be moved to a different long-term storage location. Unfortunately, the absence of a policy in place for how data is disposed of can lead to data loss. Private data has been found in the garbage of companies that don't have a policy for how data should be destroyed when no longer in use.

Remember that a data retention policy may also apply to non-digital data. For example, an educational institution that requires paper forms from students may have a data retention policy that specifies how that paper form is stored and later destroyed.

Elements of Data Retention Policies

An effective data retention policy should start by describing the purpose in retaining the data once it is no longer being used. It should also include details about the retention period, such as where the data must be stored during the retention period and who can access it during the retention period. For example, the retention policy should specify whether data needs to be available for access or if it can be archived. Further, the policy should describe any laws and/or regulations with which the organization must comply.

As mentioned earlier in this lesson, the retention policy will also include guidelines for the destruction of data that is past the retention period. While there may not be a requirement for the policy to contain directives on how to destroy data, a good data retention policy should contain this information.

The last part of a retention policy is a set of procedures to be followed in the case of a violation of the policy. The policy should identify a point of contact in the event any of the policies are violated, and may specify ramifications for individuals, business units or departments, and the organization when a violation has occurred. The ramifications of a policy violation can range from heavy fines imposed by a regulatory body to an employee being fired.

Examples of violations would be someone not shredding a document containing private data prior to throwing it out or someone not demagnetizing a storage drive before disposing of it.

Policy Maintenance

Any policy or procedure should be audited or reviewed on a regular basis to verify that the reasons the policy exists are still present and valid. Over time, laws and regulations change, and the type of data collected by an organization may also change. Therefore, it is necessary for an organization to periodically audit a data retention policy and make updates as necessary.

To ensure this process isn't overlooked, an organization should provide a change management policy alongside its data retention policy. The change management policy should include a schedule of when the data retention policy will be reviewed under normal circumstances. It should also describe when it will be reviewed if a regulation or law changes that it was made to enforce.

If a change needs to be made to a data retention policy, that change needs to be communicated to all affected parties in an organization. It might also be beneficial to communicate that no change was required after review. Communicating any changes, or lack thereof, will make sure that everyone that is responsible for following the policy is aware of any updates.

Review Activity:

Data Retention Policies

Answer the following questions:

1. What does the data destruction part of the data retention policy specify?

2. Why should a data retention policy be reviewed periodically?

3. What does the retention period dictate?

4. True or False: A data retention policy only applies to digital data.

5. What are the ramifications of violating a data retention policy?

Topic 9C

Classify Data

EXAM OBJECTIVES COVERED
4.2 Explain the purpose of governance and regulatory compliance.

In order to effectively identify and protect sensitive data, organizations classify their data by categorizing it according to its sensitivity level. Data categories can come from industry regulations, industry standards, or internal processes. While classification is required to abide by regulations, there are additional benefits for organizations. In the event of an audit, a breach response, or even an investor request for information, having data that has been properly identified and categorized can reduce risk, reduce response time, and provide a perception of preparedness. Further, properly classifying data prevents an organization from wasting time protecting data that is not important or sensitive in nature. The category in which we classify data affects whether that data needs to be protected and how that data must be protected.

Confidential Data

Confidential data can be a confusing category because it is often used interchangeably with private data or sensitive data. In fact, the same piece of data may be categorized as confidential by one company and private by another company. Both categorizations can be correct given the context in which the particular company uses the data. Think of it this way:

- **Sensitive data** is any data that needs to be given additional consideration with regard to how it is treated. All the data that is addressed by a governance policy is sensitive because there are special rules, or policies, for how it is to be treated.

- **Private data** is data that belongs to an individual or company but is collected, stored, and used by someone else. The owner of the data would want it protected from being used or accessed in any way they did not consent to. Examples would be a bank account number or a phone number.

- **Confidential data** is data that is restricted from general knowledge or access and is considered secret data. Examples would be a restaurant's award-winning proprietary recipe or the algorithm behind Google's search engine.

Personally Identifiable Information

Personally identifiable information (PII) is one of the most common categories of private data, and as such, it is the subject of many regulations. Organizations in a wide range of industries collect and store PII. A person's social security number, name, address, telephone number, and email address are all examples of PII.

PII can sometimes be difficult to classify when considering data that can indirectly identify an individual. For example, a person's gender, race, date of birth, or place of birth could not, on their own, be used to identify an individual. But when combined with other information, they could. For example, consider a vehicle's registration number. By itself this number cannot be used to identify an individual, but it can be linked to other information about the registered vehicle—like its owner's address, which of course can then be used to identify that person. This means that an organization must consider not only the data itself, but also the relationships among the data, when classifying data as PII.

Many of the regulations dealing with PII are designed to protect the information of consumers in a particular region, country, or state. However, a company located outside of that particular region may still be affected by those regulations if they collect the data of people in that region. For example, the California Consumer Privacy Act (CCPA) protects the use of PII of California state residents, regardless of where the business using the data resides. Another regulation concerned with PII, which will be discussed in more detail in a later lesson, is the General Data Protection Regulation (GDPR). The GDPR applies to any organization that provides goods or services to citizens in the European Union.

Personally Identifiable Information (PII) vs. Personal Information (PI)

While many organizations refer to PI and PII collectively as PII, there is technically a difference between the two. However, this is muddled by the fact that some regulations use the term PI, while others use PII, to mean the same thing. To make it even more confusing, different regulations may also define these terms differently. There is one thing they do agree on, however—in general, PII is considered PI, but not all PI is considered PII.

The California Consumer Privacy Act (CCPA) defines PI as "information that identifies, relates to, describes, is capable of being associated with, or could reasonably be linked, directly or indirectly, with a particular consumer or household." This doesn't include information that has been made publicly available by the local, state, or federal government.

We know that PII is any information about a person, including data, that can uniquely distinguish their identity, and any information that can be linked to them—such as medical data, financial data, or data about their employment. PI, on the other hand, does not always consist of all those identifiers.

The biggest difference between PI and PII is that PII is often used to differentiate one person from another, while PI includes any information related to a unique individual, whether it distinguishes them from another individual or not. To use an example, consider a person named John Smith. His name is PI because it is related to him. But his name is not PII, since he is not the only John Smith that exists.

Personal Health Information

Personal health information (PHI) includes demographic information, medical histories, test and laboratory results, mental health conditions, insurance information, and other data that a healthcare professional collects to identify an individual and determine appropriate care. It is data that relates to the past, present, or future health of an individual. It may also relate to an individual's payment for healthcare.

The **Health Insurance Portability and Accountability Act (HIPAA)** of 1996 is the primary law that oversees the use of, access to, and disclosure of PHI in the United States. HIPAA regulates how this data can be created, collected, transmitted, maintained, and stored by any organization that is covered under HIPAA.

Keep in mind that HIPAA does not protect all health information, nor does it apply to every person who may see or use health information. HIPAA only applies to covered entities and their business associates. The definition of covered entities is complex, and sometimes confusing. But in general, covered entities are defined in the HIPAA rules as health plans, healthcare clearinghouses, and healthcare providers who electronically transmit any health information in connection with transactions for which the U.S. Department of Health & Human Services has adopted standards.

Payment Card Industry Data

Payment card industry (PCI) data refers to any data related to a payment card, such as cardholders' names, credit card numbers, and other financial information.

PCI data is protected by state and federal laws. The **Payment Card Industry Data Security Standard (PCI DSS)** is a set of requirements intended to ensure that all companies that process, store, or transmit credit card information maintain a secure environment. The PCI DSS defines how PCI data must be stored, transmitted, and destroyed.

It's important to note that bank account data, such as branch identification numbers, bank account numbers, and routing numbers, is not considered PCI data. However, if a bank account number matches or contains a **primary account number (PAN)**, then regulations around PCI data apply.

There are 12 compliance requirements in the PCI DSS regulations, each of which has multiple sub-requirements. A few examples of the compliance requirements for PCI DSS are as follows.

- Configure firewalls restricting access to systems containing cardholder data.

- Mask the primary account number, showing only the first six and last four digits.

- Destroy cardholder data when it is no longer necessary and perform a scan for cardholder data at least every three months to find data that is no longer necessary.

If you would like to read more about PCI DSS compliance, the PCI DSS resource hub is a great resource at https://blog.pcisecuritystandards.org/pci-dss-v4-0-resource-hub.

PCI DSS only applies to payment cards (like credit cards, debit cards, prepaid money cards, and other similar cards). This is why bank account numbers and routing numbers are not covered. However, in the case where a bank account number is actually the primary account number (PAN), then it is covered under PCI DSS, simply because it happens to match the number on the credit card.

Review Activity:

Data Classification

Answer the following questions:

1. What is one of the major variables that affects whether data needs to be protected and how it must be protected?

2. Data that is not generally known and should be considered secret is generally categorized as what?

3. What is the primary law that oversees the use of, access to, and disclosure of PHI in the United States?

4. What regulation defines how credit and debit card data must be stored, transmitted, and destroyed?

5. What is data that can be used to identify a unique individual?

Topic 9D

Consider Global Jurisdiction and Regional Regulations

EXAM OBJECTIVES COVERED
4.2 Explain the purpose of governance and regulatory compliance.

More social and economic activities take place online these days than ever before. The importance of privacy and data protection is increasingly being recognized by local, regional, and global organizations and governments, with over 70% of the world's countries putting legislation in place to address it.

This is good news for anyone whose private data is collected and stored by organizations doing business online. The organizations that collect and store this data need to be keenly aware of whether they are affected by any of these regulations, and if so, in what way. In a global economy, it is no longer sufficient for organizations to assume they are only affected by local and regional laws.

Global Jurisdiction

There are no worldwide laws that directly address the privacy of individuals, but there are territorial privacy laws that are applicable within certain countries or regions. These laws mandate how organizations can collect, use, and store the personal data of natural persons.

These laws, as a rule, are applicable within the boundaries where they are adopted. However, some data privacy laws also include special provisions that make it possible to apply the laws internationally. This means an organization that collects or stores data could still be affected by a law even if said organization does not reside in the territory where the law was created. If the organization offers goods or services to, or monitors the online behavior of, individuals in that territory, then the organization must comply with its laws, despite being established outside the territory.

International Jurisdiction

Due to the online nature of many organizations, and the international nature of the Internet, organizations may be affected by international laws that they are not even aware of. In some cases, they may not become aware of these laws until problems arise and they are determined to be in noncompliance. Identifying laws that might affect them is a major challenge for organizations that collect, store, and use data online.

When considering how regulations apply globally, it is less about truly global regulations and more about the jurisdiction of a state with regard to how data flows across national borders. So while there are currently no globally recognized regulations, understanding jurisdiction and data sovereignty is necessary for organizations doing business at a global level.

Data sovereignty is the idea that the country in which data is stored has control over that data. It describes the legal dynamics of the collection and usage of data in a global economy. Laws vary widely from country to country. Some impose restrictions on how data can be used, how it can be moved from one country to another, and what type of encryption can be used to protect it.

Jurisdiction is the official power to make legal decisions and judgments. Organizations must monitor any applicable laws in the regions in which they conduct business and be aware of how these laws affect them and their operations.

Examples of Jurisdictional Regulation

Consider an online store based in Canada that sells goods or services to consumers in the European Union (EU) and Brazil. This store will have to comply with the **General Data Protection Regulation (GDPR)** and the Brazilian General Data Protection Law (LGPD), since it sells to people in these territories (and these laws set out provisions that are applicable outside of the territories). Further, because the organization is based in Canada, it will also be bound by the Personal Information Protection and Electronic Documents Act (PIPEDA). If the same company offers services to and handles the personal data of more than 50,000 California residents, it will have to comply with the California Consumer Privacy Act (CCPA) as well. You can see now why maintaining data privacy compliance is a tall order for many organizations.

It's worth mentioning that the GDPR is the toughest privacy and security law in the world. Though it was drafted and passed by the EU, it imposes obligations onto organizations anywhere in the world, as long as they target or collect data related to people in the EU. The regulation was put into effect on May 25, 2018, and levies harsh fines against those who violate its privacy and security standards, with penalties reaching into the tens of millions of euros. While GDPR is one of the most well-known global regulations due to the large number of companies affected by its policies, many countries have regulations that might affect your organization. Below are some examples:

- *__HMG Infosec Standard 5:__ This is the British government standard that specifies how digital media must be destroyed.*

- *__BSI-GS:__ This standard is used by the German Federal Office for Information Security. It also specifies how data should be destroyed.*

- *__New Federal Act on Data Protection (nFADP):__ Switzerland's regulation on data privacy was updated in 2020.*

- *__Personal Data Protection Act 2019 (PDPA):__ This is Thailand's first law dedicated specifically to data protection.*

Regional Regulations

While relevant global regulations may be difficult for organizations to identify due to their extraterritorial nature, regional regulations are usually more familiar. However, even regional regulations pose challenges for many organizations.

Regional regulations may not apply to all the regions or territories where an organization has a presence. In most cases, adhering to the most restrictive regional regulations becomes a common strategy, unless doing so is financially burdensome or resource intensive. Thankfully, regional privacy and data security regulations typically do not vary greatly.

Health Insurance Portability and Accountability Act of 1996 (HIPAA)

There are too many regional regulations to mention, but one of particular importance is the Health Insurance Portability and Accountability Act (HIPAA) of 1996. It is a U.S. federal law that requires the creation of national standards to protect sensitive patient health information from being disclosed without the patient's consent or knowledge. The U.S. Department of Health and Human Services (HHS) issued the HIPAA Privacy Rule to implement the requirements of HIPAA.

The Privacy Rule standards address the use and disclosure of individuals' health information, or PHI, by entities subject to the Privacy Rule.

The Privacy Rule also contains standards for individuals' rights to understand and control how their health information is used. A major goal of the Privacy Rule is to make sure that individuals' health information is properly protected while still allowing the flow of health information needed to provide proper healthcare, and to protect the public's health and well-being.

Review Activity:

Global Jurisdiction and Regional Regulations

Answer the following questions:

1. **True or False: Regulations only affect companies located in the regions in which the regulations are defined.**

2. **Why do many organizations find identifying the privacy laws that affect their business challenging?**

3. **How do we know that the importance of privacy and data protection is increasingly being recognized by local, regional, and global organizations and governments?**

Topic 9E

Understand Third-Party Agreements and Release Approvals

EXAM OBJECTIVES COVERED
3.4 Given a scenario, implement data management tasks.

When adhering to regulations, you will find that there are types of third-party agreements that support the use and sharing of information. These important agreements will need to be in place to outline what data can be shared, who it can be shared with, and how it can be used. As a part of being compliant, you will also find there are approval processes that grant the use of data and provide the permission to move forward. From use agreements to approvals, a DBA should be aware of these critical details at the start of any data project.

Data Sharing and Usage

A **data use agreement** is an agreement between two parties about the exchange of data that specifies what data will be shared and how that data can be used. Typically, a data use agreement is a legal agreement. Some variations include contracts, nondisclosure agreements, memorandums of understanding, and other legal instruments. Any document that addresses the use and exchange or sharing of information is a form of a data use agreement.

Nondisclosure Agreements

A **nondisclosure agreement (NDA)** defines the conditions under which an entity (such as a person or supplier) cannot disclose information to outside parties. An NDA includes specific descriptions of the legal ramifications for breaking the agreement, which provides a legal basis for protecting information assets and serves as a deterrent to the sharing of information.

Acceptable Use Agreements

An **acceptable use agreement** describes not only how data can be used, but also for what purpose. For example, suppose a company is giving a vendor access to its customer data for the purpose of researching the customers. However, the company would not want the vendor to use that data to create its own target customer list. In this case, an acceptable use agreement can be created to define the acceptable ways the vendor can use that data.

Acceptable use agreements also establish requirements for de-identification, or the removal of personal data, especially when privacy regulations like GDPR or HIPAA apply to the data. The goal is to reduce the risk that data can be re-identified.

Memorandums of Understanding

A **memorandum of understanding (MOU)** is an acceptable use agreement that establishes the rules of engagement between two parties and defines roles and expectations. They are used for describing and enforcing the data usage agreements between two parties. An MOU is a nonbinding agreement, meaning it is difficult to enforce in a court setting because it is not a formal contract. It is mostly used when the involved parties do not intend to enter into a legal agreement with each other, but still want to engage in a formal agreement of certain practices and policies surrounding the data that is to be used.

An organization that is in the early stages of engaging with another party will typically create an MOU as a first step toward a more formal agreement or a legal contract. An MOU establishes the guidelines for how the parties will work together and lays out each party's expectations and responsibilities, in addition to the purposes for which the data will and will not be used. The goal is to achieve a mutual understanding of the partnership, so both parties can confidently move forward thereafter into an enforceable contract.

Release Approvals

As a DBA, you will have access to information that can be considered private or confidential. When working with private information and data that has sensitive and confidential classifications, you will likely be involved in the process of release approval, which intends to protect the organization and everyone involved in the process. Before an organization can release data to others for analysis, or before you can release it to others for any reason, these actions must be approved.

For example, suppose someone in your organization's accounting department asks you to send them the data for all employees, including payroll data and social security numbers. If proper release approvals are in place, that request would come through proper channels, and there would be no question whether you could deliver that information to that person in accounting.

 When personal and sensitive or confidential data is released without proper approval, there are serious consequences (even if the release was accidental). Always err on the side of caution when preparing to work with personal data. When in doubt, reach out to your manager to inquire about the appropriate process at your organization.

Review Activity:

Third-Party Agreements and Release Approvals

Answer the following questions:

1. What type of agreement exists between an organization and another party that requires both parties to avoid disclosing information to any other party?

2. What type of agreement exists between two parties that specifies what data will be exchanged and how that data can be used?

3. What type of nonbinding agreement establishes the rules of engagement between two parties, defining roles and expectations?

4. True or False: It's a best practice to share your insights with everyone as you discover them.

Lesson 9

Summary

After this lesson, you should understand that data is an important resource that must be protected from loss or misuse. Thus, a strong data governance plan can create guidelines for how it is protected and used. You should understand some of the challenges associated with protecting data in an environment in which so many nontraditional storage devices interact. You should also understand that the data needs to be protected in all the states it can exist in, like during transit and when it is being stored. The obligation to protect data does not end when it is no longer being used, and thus you should be able to describe what makes up a data retention policy. And finally, you should know that how you protect and use data is not always completely within your control. Local, regional, and global regulations may dictate how certain data is to be protected.

Guidelines for Understanding Governance and Regulations Regarding Data Protection

Consider these best practices and guidelines when building a plan to protect data.

1. **Identify the particular data that needs to be protected by properly classifying it as one or more types of private data.**

2. **Be sure to consider data both in transit and at rest when creating a data protection plan.**

3. **Determine what regulations affect your organization and be sure to follow the policies outlined in those regulations.**

4. **Confirm that a data retention plan exists to define how data is protected once it becomes inactive.**

5. **Make certain your data governance plan is communicated to everyone affected in your organization.**

Lesson 10

Securing Data

LESSON INTRODUCTION

Whether an organization is required to adhere to global, regional, or industry laws and regulations, securing data is an important part of collecting and storing data. Securing data can take many forms. One of the most common activities involved in securing data is encryption. But there are other ways to secure, or protect, data.

The act of securing data results in the data being restricted. It is made unavailable to persons or systems that should not have access to it. Some data may be secured by simply hiding it or making it unreadable or unrecognizable. In addition, data that no longer needs to be stored must be properly destroyed.

It is also important to be able to observe who has access to the data that has been secured, and how it is being accessed. In addition to techniques used to secure data, there must also be a way to audit access to the data. In this way, an organization can ensure that the measures used to secure the data are actually effective.

Lesson Objectives

In this lesson, you will do the following:

- Understand data encryption.

- Understand data masking.

- Describe data destruction techniques.

- Audit data access.

- Audit code.

Topic 10A

Understand Data Encryption

EXAM OBJECTIVES COVERED
4.1 Explain data security concepts.

The process of encryption uses sophisticated algorithms to convert data to unreadable text. The original data is typically referred to as plaintext, while the transformed, or encrypted, data is referred to as ciphertext. This transformation prevents unauthorized users or systems from accessing the data unless they have the appropriate information to decrypt it. Typically, data encryption is used to secure data that is being stored. Those who spend time browsing on the public Internet may also consider securing data as it is being transmitted over the network.

Encrypting Data in Transit

Recall that **data in transit** is data that is actively moving from one location to another. This would include data being transmitted across the Internet, data being transmitted within a private network, and data being transferred to and from the cloud. To ensure the data is secure, the endpoints of the communication must be authenticated. The data must be encrypted before transmission and decrypted upon arrival at the destination, as well as verified that it was not modified.

Data that is being transmitted to and from a database over a secure connection is typically secured using **Internet Protocol Security (IPSec)** or **Transport Layer Security (TLS)**. Let's walk through the process using TLS first.

Encryption at the Client

Before data is transmitted to the server, it must be encrypted at the client. When using TLS, the initial communication between a client and a server is called the TLS handshake. The client sends an initial transmission to the server containing the cipher suites it supports, along with some additional information. The server responds with the cipher suite it wants to use and a certificate containing the public key of the database server (or database instance, in the case where each database has its own certificate). The client verifies the certificate, either by indicating trust in the certificate or having the certificate in its certificate store. Once verified, the client creates a master key, encrypts it using the public key from the certificate, and sends this back to the server. This master key will be used to encrypt the data. The server then responds with its acknowledgment. Now the client can encrypt the data it wants to transmit using the master key that was sent to the server.

Step 5 in the figure below shows the point at which the data is encrypted at the client prior to being transmitted to the database server.

Encryption in Transit

After the data is encrypted at the client, the client will transmit the encrypted data to the server. During the TLS handshake, the server received the encrypted master key from the client and decrypted it using the private key that corresponds to the public key sent to the client in the certificate. The data is protected during transmission due to the encryption using the shared master key. Once the data arrives at the server, the shared master key will be used to decrypt the data.

The line between steps 5 and 6 in the image below shows the encrypted data transmitted from the client to the server. The encrypted data will utilize a secure network protocol like TLS.

 SSL used to be the protocol most commonly used for secure communication. However, due to a security vulnerability in SSL3, TLS 1.2 or 1.3 is now recommended.

Encryption at the Server

When transferring data from the server back to the client, the master key shared by the client during the TLS handshake is used to encrypt the data prior to transmission. This shared session key will also be used to decrypt the data once it has arrived at the target, or client side, of the transmission.

Step 6 in the image below shows the point at which the server would use the shared master key to decrypt the data once it has been transmitted.

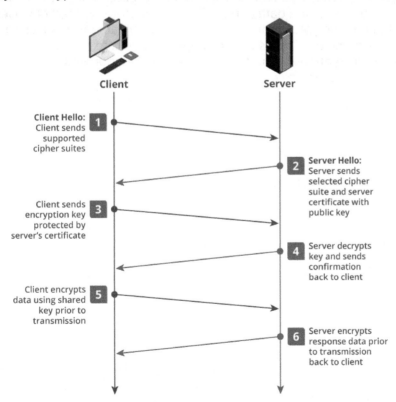

TLS 1.2 Handshake to Establish Shared Encryption Key and Encrypt Data Transmitted Between Client and Server

Encryption in Transit Using IPsec

While not as common as TLS, IPsec is another protocol that can be used to secure the data sent between two computers (such as an application server and a database server). While TLS is typically used to secure data transmission on a per user and per application basis, IPsec can be used to provide continuous message encryption between computers for any user or application transmitting data between them. For example, a user connecting to an application over the Internet would most likely use TLS, but IPsec might be used to secure the communication between an application server and a database server within a private network.

Encrypting Data at Rest

Data at rest is data that is being stored on a storage device, cloud storage, or archived in some other way, and not actively moving from device to device or network to network. When data is encrypted while at rest, it is protected from people who might attempt to wrongfully access it. If the data at rest is properly encrypted, it cannot be decrypted even if the storage device containing the encrypted data is stolen. Most data breaches occur when a storage device, laptop, or smart device is lost or stolen and the data contained within is not properly encrypted. While data is generally less vulnerable at rest than in transit, a hacker might find the data at rest more valuable, because there is a larger volume of data at rest.

There are multiple techniques that can be used to encrypt data at rest. But in most cases, data at rest relies on **symmetric cryptography** for encryption. Symmetric cryptography is typically chosen when speed and responsiveness are the priority, which is often the case with data at rest. Since symmetric cryptography uses a single key to both encrypt and decrypt the data, many databases will use a layered approach to securing data at rest. For example, a certificate may be used to protect the symmetric encryption key, and then a password or another key may be used to secure the certificate, and so on.

Review Activity:

Data Encryption

Answer the following questions:

1. **What is data in transit?**

2. **If a storage drive containing data is being transferred to an off-site archive facility, is that data considered data at rest or data in motion?**

3. **What protocols are used to establish secure communication to protect data in transit?**

4. **What type of cryptography is used to protect data at rest, usually chosen for speed and responsiveness?**

Topic 10B

Understand Data Masking

EXAM OBJECTIVES COVERED
4.1 Explain data security concepts.

While encryption is ideal for sensitive data that is being stored or transferred, another solution is required to protect data that is currently in use. **Data masking** enables us to use data without exposing the original data values. It is a data security technique used to hide data by modifying it so that there is no correlation to its original value. The main reason for applying masking to a data field is to protect data that is classified as PII, sensitive personal data, or commercially sensitive data. Data masking meets the requirements of most privacy laws.

Pseudonymization

There are two main techniques used for data masking, the first of which is data pseudonymization. **Data pseudonymization** is a technique that replaces or removes information in a data set that identifies an individual. The personal data is replaced with a pseudonym, or a value made up of numbers, letters, special characters, or a combination of them. In another table, that pseudonym would be associated back with the original value. It's important to ensure that the table containing both the pseudonym and the individual's private information is stored separately from the pseudonymized data, and is only accessible by appropriate personnel. This process effectively makes the data more generalized and prevents it from identifying the original individual.

Before

Customer	CustomerName	City	PostalCode	OrderDate
21768	Cole Watson	Metchosin	V9	2011-05-31 00:00:00.000
28389	Rachael Martinez	Pantin	93500	2011-05-31 00:00:00.000
25863	Sydney Wright	Lebanon	97355	2011-05-31 00:00:00.000
14501	Ruben Prasad	Beverly Hills	90210	2011-05-31 00:00:00.000

After

Customer	CustomerName	City	PostalCode	OrderDate
0x895344AC2B57574FB76010D6A2F3D1F5479F3F2...	6BDCB234-D3D2-47BE-8815-8EA069BF6D05	Metchosin	V9	2011-05-31 00:00:00.000
0x510A3768AA427A5B70EB7A6B0C1C0C959792560...	5857CFF3-B4DF-4E28-A3EA-CAA7D03C2D65	Pantin	93500	2011-05-31 00:00:00.000
0xFC2D61B95AE0D33A12520F2E59264ADDC90F14...	41F16D41-86E9-4CFB-9DAD-A9E60A1AEC2F	Lebanon	97355	2011-05-31 00:00:00.000
0x601CF76101FA17F5CB558D5713A552C40AE75D2...	F3F3D01E-D67F-40F3-8086-9B0E1B99924C	Beverly Hills	90210	2011-05-31 00:00:00.000

*Data Before and After Pseudonymization in Microsoft SQL Server Management Studio
(Used with permission from Microsoft.)*

The screenshot shows both original data and data after pseudonymization. The data in the customer column was converted to a hash, and the customer name was replaced with a random value (which is mapped to the original value in a separate table).

Pseudonymizing sensitive or personal data can reduce the risks to the data subjects and help you meet your data protection obligations. When the data is pseudonymized, the possible risk of exposing personal data is minimized, since the data record is no longer identifiable. The record remains available for data processing and data analysis without the personal data being exposed, and the process is reversible. Pseudonymization does not change the fact that the data is personal data—it simply hides any personal identifiers. Keep in mind that since pseudonymizing the data is reversible, if the entire database is stolen, the original value will still be obtainable. So using this data masking technique will not completely eliminate the risk of exposing the private information.

Anonymization

The second technique typically used for data masking is **data anonymization**, which is the process of protecting sensitive or personal information by erasing or encrypting the identifiers that connect an individual to the data that is being stored. As an example, consider personally identifiable information (PII) such as names, social security numbers, and addresses.

Before

Customer	CustomerName	City	PostalCode	OrderDate
12631	Clarence Gao	Paris	75012	2012-03-26 00:00:00.000
12631	Clarence Gao	Paris	75012	2013-10-15 00:00:00.000
12631	Clarence Gao	Paris	75012	2013-10-23 00:00:00.000
12631	Clarence Gao	Paris	75012	2013-11-07 00:00:00.000

After

Customer	CustomerName	City	PostalCode	DateRange
B1C26E00	Omar Goel	Paris	75017	Feb 22 2014 12:00AM - Mar 15 2014 12:00AM
2BCF507E	Carolyn Malhotra	Paris	75009	Feb 18 2014 12:00AM - Mar 11 2014 12:00AM
3C79DD8F	Ross Patel	Lille	59000	Feb 3 2014 12:00AM - Feb 24 2014 12:00AM
C626A03A	Dawn Deng	Paris	75003	Jan 22 2014 12:00AM - Feb 12 2014 12:00AM

Data Before and After Anonymization in Microsoft SQL Server Management Studio
(Used with permission from Microsoft.)

The screenshot shows data before and after anonymization. The customer column was replaced with a random value, and the order date was replaced with a data range based on the original order date.

Anonymization prevents the data from being linked back to the original individual, since that personal data no longer exists or is fully encrypted. Unlike pseudonymization, there is no additional data available in another location that would allow for the reassociation of the anonymized data back to the individual it originally identified.

Anonymization is usually defined as being "irreversible." But depending on how the data is anonymized, experienced hackers may still be able to reverse the process. For example, suppose data is anonymized by replacing each character of the alphabet with another one. While the data is obscured at first glance, if the replacement character is not randomized, it might be possible to figure out the pattern and reverse the anonymization.

The Challenges of Data Discovery

Not all data needs to undergo anonymization or pseudonymization. Before the process of de-identifying data begins, organizations must first determine which data could be considered identifiable and which data can safely remain in its original form. While this may appear to be straightforward, sensitive data is subjective and can vary depending on a range of factors, from the individual evaluator's opinions to any standards applied to that industry. For example, the IP address of a user visiting a website might not mean much to the manager of a marketing firm, but it may be viewed as highly sensitive information by security personnel.

Data discovery becomes even more challenging when multiple sets of seemingly anonymous data can together be personally identifiable. For example, consider marketing and sales data for a toy company. When a toy is sold, the order data contains date and time information identifying when the order took place, the shipping address where the purchaser has shipped the toy, and the name of the particular product purchased.

By itself, each piece of data might seem insignificant in the context of identifying an individual. But suppose a bad actor uses social media to identify people who follow the toy company's social media accounts and is also able to locate mentions of purchased products in their feeds. That bad actor could potentially identify individuals in the marketing and sales data by comparing it to the social media data (such as by comparing the date that a product purchase was posted on social media and comparing it to the purchase dates in the marketing and sales data). Once this connection has been made, it might be possible to then discover more personal information by using additional relationships in the original sales and marketing data. This example demonstrates the challenges facing organizations that store and share data.

Before blindly masking data that exposes private information, many companies will perform a risk analysis on the likelihood of that data being exposed inappropriately. Private data that is not used in reporting or data analysis might not need to be masked. Challenges and risks, like those described in this section's example, must be identified to determine how to appropriately mitigate the risk of data exposure in the context of how the data will be used. This mitigation may result in a decision to pseudonymize or anonymize the data (or do neither).

Review Activity:

Data Masking

Answer the following questions:

1. **As an alternative to encryption, what de-identification method can be used to protect data that is currently in use?**

2. **Between pseudonymization and anonymization, which data masking technique is reversible?**

3. **Which data masking technique has been used if the original user data is not recoverable from the masked value?**

Topic 10C

Describe Data Destruction Techniques

 EXAM OBJECTIVES COVERED
4.1 Explain data security concepts.

At some point in your life, you've likely shredded or incinerated documents that were no longer needed. While that action used to be enough to ensure that information did not fall into the wrong hands, it no longer holds true with the rise of digital data. Data destruction involves the complete annihilation of information, specifically when it is contained within a digital storage device. There are two main types of data destruction, categorized by how the destruction occurs: logical destruction and physical destruction.

Logical Destruction

Although data that lives on a digital storage device (such as hard drives, flash drives, computers, tablets, smart devices, and magnetic backup media) can be deleted from the device, this alone is not sufficient when data needs to be destroyed due to its sensitivity or according to regulations. When you delete a file, the only thing removed is the master file table reference, which tells the operating system where the file was located. Removing this reference allows new data to be written to the location of the previous file, replacing the data that was there previously. But until new data is written to the location, the old data is still present, just not visible to the user. It is possible, and in some instances simple, to recover deleted data from digital media. **Logical destruction** directly targets the data in the memory storage locations of the device to completely destroy it. There are three standard techniques used for logical data destruction.

Overwriting

Overwriting destroys existing data by overwriting it with characters, like 0s, 1s, or even random characters. This most common logical destruction technique is implemented using specialized data overwriting algorithms. Typically, an overwrite standard will specify how many times, or passes, the data must be overwritten to be considered destroyed.

Block Erase

If the data is stored in a solid-state-drive (SSD), the **block erase** technique (designed specifically for SSDs) can be used to fully erase the memory blocks in the drive. Block erase involves increasing the voltage levels on each memory block to a considerably higher value than the standard operating value and then suddenly dropping it to zero.

Cryptographic Erase

If the data is stored on a self-encrypting drive (SED), the **cryptographic erase** technique will erase or replace the media encryption key of the drive, thereby rendering the ciphertext, or encrypted data, illegible. The technique actually does not destroy the data; it only destroys the encryption key. The effectiveness of the technique depends on the robustness of the SED's encryption algorithm. While this technique is efficient because it only needs to erase the encryption key, it may carry some risk. If a backup of the media encryption key was made and is found, the data can still be decrypted using this backup key.

Physical Destruction

Physical destruction of data involves damaging the digital storage device itself, in such a way that it is no longer usable. Unlike logical destruction, which maintains the physical integrity of the media or drive while still ensuring the information it contains is not recoverable, physical destruction destroys both the device and the data contained within. Physical destruction may be preferred over logical destruction if an organization does not have the expertise to properly pull off logical destruction (as someone with the correct technical skills could reverse the process and get access to the data). Physical destruction is also the best method for destroying data on a damaged device, as a technique like overwriting can only be performed on a device that is writable and undamaged. There are two physical destruction techniques that are frequently used.

Degaussing

Degaussing involves exposing the storage device to a strong electromagnetic field that essentially scrambles all information present on the device, thus rendering the data completely unreadable. Degaussing is one of the most common and cost-effective ways to destroy data on a storage device.

Physical Media Destruction

Physical media destruction involves the decimation of the storage device, which can be performed using chemicals, through incineration, or by shredding the device. These are not the only methods of physical destruction, but they are some of the most common.

A storage device that is destroyed chemically is submerged into hydrochloric acid (HCl) or nitric acid (HNO_3), which effectively melts all components of the device. A storage device that is fed into a specially licensed incinerator and burned at high temperatures is reduced to ashes, again rendering the data unrecoverable. In the same way that paper shredders destroy pieces of paper or similar hard copy, specialized shredders for storage media break down the electronic and mechanical components of the device into very small pieces, as small as two to four millimeters (mm). In all of these cases, the data stored on the media is destroyed because of the device's physical disintegration.

It should be noted that many regulations require certain methods of destruction and certain parameters within which that destruction must occur. For example, when destroying magnetic media, the National Security Agency (NSA) allows degaussing, incineration, or shredding. But incineration must be performed at or above 650 degrees Fahrenheit, and shredding must result in pieces no larger than two millimeters on edge.

Keep in mind that most organizations do not have the specialized equipment to perform these physical destruction techniques. And some techniques, like incineration and chemical destruction, may produce environment, health, and safety (EH&S) hazards. So most physical destruction techniques are performed by third parties that are licensed to carry out the correct procedures safely.

Physical Data Destruction

While we've been discussing physical data destruction in the context of destroying the device to also destroy the digital data within, it's important to remember that not all data is digital. Sensitive data can be found in a physical copy, such as in a printed report or log. The standards for destruction of data found in hard copy are more homogenous because the results are more easily verifiable. Most standards regarding destruction of hard copy information specify the size of the shards that result from shredding or that the data must be incinerated to ash.

 Physical data can also take other forms besides printed documents. As an example, PVC printers, which are often used to print employee badges, can leave mirror images of the printed data on the printer ribbon. That printer ribbon is typically thrown in the garbage intact, but it really should be properly disposed of.

Regulatory Impact on Data Destruction

There are multiple regulatory standards for data destruction, and they can vary by geographical region and industry. Thus, when a company is creating its data destruction policy, it must ensure that it follows all industry, state, and federal regulations that apply to it.

Data Destruction Standards

The **National Institute of Standards and Technology (NIST)** 800-88 is widely recognized as the current industry standard in the United States and is among the most well-known and followed data destruction guidelines in the world today. If you are interested in reading more about the standards defined by NIST, you can find the (NIST) 800-88 document here: https://csrc.nist.gov/publications/detail/sp/800-88/rev-1/final.

PCI DSS and GDPR (which were discussed in a previous lesson) both have sections that define data destruction requirements for compliance. Some additional standards from multiple industries and regions are as follows:

- **HMG Infosec Standard 5:** This is the British government standard that specifies an option of a one-pass or three-pass overwrite.

- **BSI-GS:** This standard is used by the German Federal Office for Information Security. It calls for one overwriting pass with random data.

- **Air Force System Security Instruction 8580:** The latest U.S. Air Force standard requires two pseudo-random overwrites, followed by an overwrite with a set pattern of ones and zeros. At least 1% of the final overwritten data must be visually inspected to guarantee overwriting success.

- **Navy Staff Office Publication (NAVSO P-5239-26):** This is a three-pass standard in which the U.S. Navy uses two predetermined characters, then a random character, and verifies them at the end of the process.

Review Activity:

Data Destruction Techniques

Answer the following questions:

1. What data destruction technique sanitizes the data but leaves the storage media usable for future storage?

2. True or False: Deleting a file completely removes the data from the storage media.

3. In what scenario is logical data destruction absolutely not an option?

4. Why shouldn't most companies attempt physical device destruction themselves?

5. What organization is responsible for creating the most widely known and globally recognized standards for data destruction?

Topic 10D

Audit Data Access

EXAM OBJECTIVES COVERED
3.2 Explain common database maintenance processes.
4.1 Explain data security concepts.

So far in this lesson we have discussed securing data by encrypting it or obscuring it while it is active, and properly destroying it when it is no longer needed. All these activities prevent sensitive data from being accessed by unauthorized individuals. But how can we be sure that the policies and practices we put in place are working? To do this, we need to also monitor, or audit, the access to sensitive data. Auditing your databases enables you to track how your records are being used and gives you visibility into any risks of misuse or breaches.

Account Authorization

A big part of protecting sensitive data is restricting and controlling access to that data. When managing databases, you should make sure to limit a user's permissions to just what the user needs to do their jobs. Doing this ensures that if the user's account is compromised, the attacker would have access to the smallest amount of data and functionality. It is important to regularly audit users' access rights to determine whether each user that has access to the data still needs access, and if the level of access they have been given is what they truly need. Many regulations and security policies will require authorization audits to be performed on a regular recurring basis, in addition to when significant changes occur in a user's job responsibilities or employment status. The audit may result in a user's access being removed, or the user's rights being decreased or increased based on their current need.

A typical audit of account authorization would involve querying a list of all user accounts with any access to the database, along with the roles and permissions given to that user account. Each of these user accounts will need to be confirmed to be valid. This means making sure that the user still needs access to the database and that the user still has the correct level of permissions.

A DBA will often not be able to make determinations regarding a user's ongoing need for access. You will need to work with supervisors and managers to get confirmation on the level of access the users need to the database.

During the audit, you will also need to look for user accounts that seem out of place. If there are any user accounts that are not recognized or should not exist, logs should be investigated to determine how they were created and by whom, in order to ensure they were not created by an attacker or a malicious service.

The results of auditing the account authorization will be a list of action items—accounts that need to be removed and permissions that need to be adjusted. In many cases, though, there will be no changes necessary and thus no action items.

Connection Requests

Even if you've verified that all users have proper access rights, it is still important to track what users are coming in and going out of a database. Of equal importance is tracking where these connections to the database are originating from, so that we may identify suspicious activity on the database and hopefully prevent unauthorized access to sensitive data. It's important to recognize that connection attempts originating from an unrecognized location are not always malicious, but they should be scrutinized to determine if the connection is valid or not. Even if a connection is not identified immediately as an invalid attempt to access the data, it might be valuable information when investigating missing data or another security event. Having information about where connections to the database are coming from can provide a good starting point for investigating issues.

In most cases, it might not be possible to review every connection request to the database. You will likely rely on your organization's IT staff to retrieve either a sampling of connection requests or a list of anomalous connections. This will create a more realistic list of connection requests to review.

 An example of an anomalous connection would be a connection from a location that is not recognized or that occurred very late at night (as most connections occur during the day).

In reviewing the requests, you will usually work with the IT staff to make sure that each connection request is coming from a known source and has been made by a known user. Another thing you may look for when auditing connection requests is any that seem outside the parameters of normal business operations. For example, are there connection requests unexpectedly happening outside of normal business hours? Are the connection requests being made by the same user account from multiple locations at the same time?

A connection request audit will result in a list of connection requests that need to be investigated further. The investigation of these requests is beyond the scope of the role of the DBA. But you will usually work closely with IT and security staff during a more thorough investigation.

While you will usually work with the IT staff to take advantage of the network monitoring tools that they should have in place, there are some things that you can do with existing tools in the database. As an example, in a Windows-based database, you may start by looking at data provided to the SQL performance counters. Executing the below query will display the number of user connections to the database.

```
SELECT *
FROM sys.dm_os_performance_counters
WHERE counter_name = 'User Connections';
```

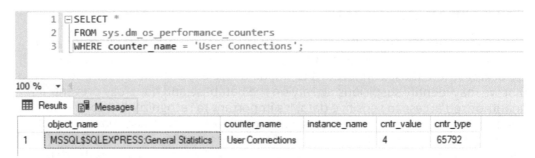

```
1  □SELECT *
2   FROM sys.dm_os_performance_counters
3   WHERE counter_name = 'User Connections';
```

100 % ▼

⊞ Results 📄 Messages

	object_name	counter_name	instance_name	cntr_value	cntr_type
1	MSSQL$SQLEXPRESS:General Statistics	User Connections		4	65792

Total Number of User Connections to the Database from Performance Counters View in Microsoft SQL Server Management Studio (Used with permission from Microsoft.)

Once you know how many active user connections you have, you can look at the current users, sessions, state of those connections, and processes involved. You can get this information by executing the following sp_who command, which returns the following data.

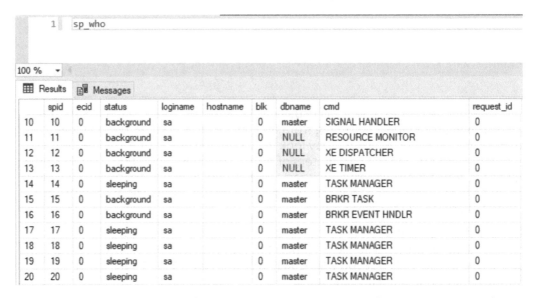

```
1   sp_who
```

100 % ▼

⊞ Results 📄 Messages

	spid	ecid	status	loginame	hostname	blk	dbname	cmd	request_id
10	10	0	background	sa		0	master	SIGNAL HANDLER	0
11	11	0	background	sa		0	NULL	RESOURCE MONITOR	0
12	12	0	background	sa		0	NULL	XE DISPATCHER	0
13	13	0	background	sa		0	NULL	XE TIMER	0
14	14	0	sleeping	sa		0	master	TASK MANAGER	0
15	15	0	background	sa		0	master	BRKR TASK	0
16	16	0	background	sa		0	master	BRKR EVENT HNDLR	0
17	17	0	sleeping	sa		0	master	TASK MANAGER	0
18	18	0	sleeping	sa		0	master	TASK MANAGER	0
19	19	0	sleeping	sa		0	master	TASK MANAGER	0
20	20	0	sleeping	sa		0	master	TASK MANAGER	0

Results of Executing sp_who Showing Current Users, Sessions, and Processes in Microsoft SQL Server Management Studio (Used with permission from Microsoft.)

If you need a higher level of detail regarding sessions and the processes being executed in those sessions, as well as more information about the network connections and users, you can use the following statement.

```
SELECT [host_name],
      [client_net_address],
      [client_tcp_port],
   [program_name],
   login_name,
   COUNT(c.session_id ) num_sessions,
   GETDATE()
FROM sys.dm_exec_connections c JOIN
   sys.dm_exec_sessions s on c.session_id =
   s.session_id
GROUP BY host_name, client_net_address,
client_tcp_port, program_name, login_name ORDER
BY 6 DESC
```

The query can be modified to pull all of the columns, instead of these specific columns, but this will provide more detailed information about the connections and sessions, as can be seen below.

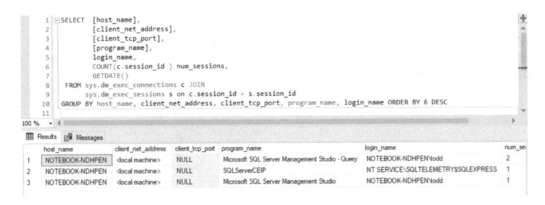

Detailed Information from the Connections and Sessions Views in Microsoft SQL Server Management Studio (Used with permission from Microsoft.)

Expired Accounts

When conducting an audit of authorized accounts to a database, you may come across expired user accounts whose access rights need to be removed. You might wonder, why should we bother with expired accounts? After all, if an account is expired, the owner of the account no longer has access to the database. While that's true, expired accounts still need to be audited so they can be purged, and soon-to-expire accounts should be tracked and managed, to prevent unnecessary access.

Another reason to audit expired accounts and remove any that are no longer needed is to reduce the risk of unauthorized access to data. For example, if an attacker is able to activate an expired account, and that expired account has a higher level of access to private data, that data would then become available to the attacker. While this kind of technique might seem complex, it is commonly used to gain access to data and functionality.

On the other hand, you may also need to confirm that an expired account should indeed be expired. If you're running into expired accounts, it's likely that user's access to the database is automatically disabled after a specified date—a common setup for consultants, summer workers, and other users who require only temporary access. While we want to prevent unnecessary or unauthorized access to data, we also want to make sure those who still require access to the data don't lose it.

We usually begin an audit of expired accounts by using database system queries or database tooling to identify all of the expired accounts. Once the list of accounts has been identified, each account should be reviewed to determine if the account should be removed, reactivated, or set to be reviewed again during the next audit. To make this decision, we may need to contact a manager, supervisor, or someone else who can help verify whether the account is still required.

For example, the account of a user who has left the company will likely need to be removed. A user who only works one week a quarter, like a student intern, might need their account to be reactivated. A user who is taking an extended leave of absence, and whose account likely expired due to inactivity, will go on a list to be reviewed again during the next audit. This is because this user's account shouldn't be removed, but also shouldn't be reactivated until the user returns to work.

As you can see, there are often no absolute rules when auditing. Your goal should simply be to identify potential issues or risks and then determine the best way to mitigate them.

While many database platforms contain features to audit expired and inactive accounts, there are also commercially available packages that are often used to perform these audit activities.

Review Activity:

Data Access Auditing

Answer the following questions:

1. Auditing _____ will identify accounts that have more permissions than is necessary.

2. In what scenario might you leave an expired account found during an audit as-is?

3. An attacker attempting to gain access to your database performs attacks very early in the morning, hoping to go unnoticed. What type of audit activity could help catch this?

4. True or False: When an audit identifies an anomaly, it means that illicit activity was occurring.

Topic 10E

Audit Code and Changes

EXAM OBJECTIVES COVERED
3.2 Explain common database maintenance processes.
4.1 Explain data security concepts.

While auditing the access to and use of data is important, it is equally important to review and audit the code that is executed in the database in order to access the data. Artifacts stored in the database that can affect data, like executable queries and logic, should be audited to verify any changes made to them are expected and acceptable. There are also automated processes and integrations with other systems and servers that need to be audited to verify they don't expose or access data that they should not. Depending on the processes and procedures in place for the deployment or modification of these types of artifacts, there may be multiple users, and change management processes that can create or update objects of the database.

Structured Query Language (SQL) Code

Depending on your role in an organization's technology groups, you may have a different concept of "code" when it comes to accessing and modifying data. A software developer, writing an application, probably considers "code" to be the program logic that is being written in whatever programming language they are using. In a database server, we typically refer to the content of stored procedures, functions, automated processes, and any other stored logic as "code." This code most often takes the form of structured query language (SQL).

In some cases, a DBA will be the only person who can implement changes to code in a database. But in many cases, other users will have the authority to implement changes. For example, developers are sometimes authorized to deploy code changes to a database. Support staff or configuration teams may also have the authority to make changes to stored procedures or other code in the database. These code changes are often not reviewed by a DBA before being implemented, and the modifications might inadvertently put private data at risk of improper exposure or loss.

This is not to say that those authorized to make changes to database code would intentionally do harm. In fact, many problems with database code are accidental or are due to a lack of expertise in the proper implementation of SQL.

Best practice suggests that the number of people who can make changes to database code be limited as much as possible. User roles and permissions, which will be discussed more in depth in a later lesson, are used to restrict who can make changes to database code. If the number of people who can make changes cannot be limited, a process can be put in place to require that code changes be reviewed prior to implementation. These types of restrictions or processes are usually put in place and enforced by the DBA, working with those making the code changes. These measures can help prevent inadvertent or inappropriate changes to code that might expose or allow unauthorized modifications to sensitive data.

However, even with good processes in place, it is important to verify that no unexpected changes have been made to the code in a database via auditing. Reviewing change logs is one way to determine if unexpected changes were made to code. But a more common technique to audit changes is to compare a known version of the code with the actual code in the database. To do this, the DBA creates and retains a copy of all the code in the database. As approved changes to code are made, this copy of the code is updated. During an audit, we compare the code in the database to the copy of the code to confirm they still match. Any differences would highlight an unapproved change. We would then investigate these changes to determine who made the change and why the change was made.

Credential Storage Checks

When a database integrates with other databases or systems, it must first identify itself to those databases or systems. This identification process usually involves authenticating, using stored credentials assigned to each integration, to verify that the database is authorized to perform the integrations. These credentials are typically stored in a special secure storage area—not in the same database tables where other data is stored.

Since these credentials are used to access and authenticate to other systems from the database, it is possible that the credentials provide elevated access to those systems. A hacker that gets access to the database could potentially use these stored credentials to gain access to the integrated systems.

Thus, it is very important to audit any credentials stored within a database, treating them just like any other authorized user. Credentials should periodically be reviewed to make sure the associated integrations are still needed, and that the minimum acceptable level of authorization required for the integration is provided. The auditing of these credentials may involve working with other IT staff in order to verify the level of access credentials may have throughout a network.

Change Management

Change management refers to the controlled identification and implementation of required changes within a database. One of the most important words in this definition is "controlled." Change is inevitable; the functionality provided by a system and the use of the data within will change over time as requirements and regulations are updated and revised. Thus, it is important to properly manage these changes to databases. At a minimum, updates to software are ongoing, and since databases use software, the changes must be maintained. You will always need a change management plan and process.

Typically, the DBA will be responsible for developing change management documentation relating to changes in the database or database server. A good change management plan should be documented and shared with anyone in the organization that might be affected.

Direct changes to data are typically not what change management is concerned with. However, it is possible that configuration changes to a database might indirectly affect data that is dependent on the configuration. And in this case, those anticipated changes to data should be included in the change management documentation. In the context of a database or database server, change management is used to manage configuration changes and data access changes. And with regard to data access, change management targets any changes to users who can access a database and to the permissions granted to users who access the database.

The implementation of database change management processes is usually accomplished by the DBA, or at least in conjunction with the DBA. As an example, a software development team may work with the DBA to include database change management processes in their **software development lifecycle**.

Keep in mind that change management is used to manage any change to a database. A change management process can manage changes to database configuration, data, and/or code. Any change that could affect the operation of a database can be managed by a change management process. For the most significant or major changes, organizations should attempt to test the change first. Every change should be accompanied by a rollback plan, so that the change can be reversed if it has harmful or unforeseen consequences.

Change Management Process

Proper change management involves creating processes for managing how changes are requested, approved, implemented, reviewed, and tested. When ready, the change will be in the **release schedule** for actual deployment. The release schedule also defines the individuals who are responsible for steps in the process, as well as those with approval rights for the change (including those who are authorized to deploy any changes to the database). At a company, any time a change is to be made to the database, it must be approved by the appropriate teams starting from the top. This change approval process protects all the people involved, from the managers who approve the change, to the DBA who is required to implement it. Obtaining approval then allows the company to add this change to the release schedule. The release schedule communicates what is in the release when changes are made. As a DBA, you will find that properly documented features in a release are invaluable to you.

The change management process should also include communication at every step. A good change management process will likely include some of the following main steps:

1. A request is made for a change. Where the request originates is usually not restricted, meaning it may come from any part of the organization.

2. The request is reviewed by a project manager, product manager, or whoever approves changes. The change request will be either approved or denied. This is the change approval step of the process.

3. If the change is approved, someone will actually design and implement the change. The person who makes the change could be a DBA, a database developer, or another appropriate resource.

4. Once the change has been made, it will be reviewed and, if possible, tested. Among other things, this step will help ensure that the change can meet the timeline set in the release schedule by measuring the time involved with the implementation.

5. Finally, the change is deployed to the production database. Ideally, as discussed elsewhere in this section, the number of people that can deploy changes is kept to a minimum.

The resources involved in the change management process will vary and depend on your organization. Typically, change management will involve project management resources, development resources, security resources, quality assurance resources, and, of course, the DBA.

Having a change management process in place should ensure that all changes to the database are verified and confirm that the changes will not expose or allow unauthorized changes to sensitive data. Its presence does not mean that audits are not necessary, but it should make audits easier to perform and review, since all changes to the database would have gone through the change management process. There should be no unidentified changes found in an audit; if unidentified changes are found, they should be minimal.

Change Management Considerations

In addition to the considerations previously discussed, there are additional, tangential considerations that will impact the successf of a change management process.

Capacity Planning

The DBA will work with the networking resources to determine if there are any changes to the network or host server. These kinds of changes may affect the capacity of network, remote storage, or machine resources needed during or after the change. It is important to take any changes in capacity into account during change management. This type of **capacity planning** needs to be done if the change requires more memory, disk space, or processing power, for example. If you fail to account for capacity changes when planning for change management, it is possible that catastrophic failures could occur due to a lack of resources. It's important to note that the effects of ignoring capacity planning during change management are not always so dire; in some cases, there are merely economic ramifications. Without planning ahead for any increased capacity needs, an organization may find itself with higher expenses than budgeted.

Vulnerability Remediation

The DBA will work alongside security resources to consider vulnerabilities and the **vulnerability remediation** plan. The goal of this plan is to determine whether the change will create a new vulnerability in the network or inappropriate access to the data. The vulnerability remediation plan, typically developed by an organization's security team, will document the process of identifying potential vulnerabilities and performing a risk analysis on these vulnerabilities, as well as discuss the determination of mediation plans based on the results of the risk analysis. If an identified vulnerability can be avoided altogether, that is the best case mediation strategy. Therefore, it is common to include the security team in change management so that the introduction of new vulnerabilities may be identified during the planning (and thus avoided.) If a change would introduce a new vulnerability, or increase the exploitation risk of an existing vulnerability, the team must identify what modifications can be made to keep that from occurring. When it's time for the **database refresh**, during which you are replacing the existing system with your new changes, this type of change management process will ensure the outcome is exactly what is expected. The goal is for the system to be updated, and the changes put in place, with virtually no downtime to the client who uses the application.

Scheduling Changes

Changes should also be scheduled sensitively if they are likely to cause system downtime or other negative impact on the workflow of the business units that depend on the database or system that is being modified. Most organizations have a scheduled maintenance window period for authorized downtime. Unless there is a circumstance to do otherwise, such as the need for an emergency patch or upgrade, all changes should occur during this predetermined window of time, including software and hardware changes to the servers. If software or hardware changes need to be made, they too should go through the change management process. The changes should be planned and tested in a test environment prior to being implemented in a production environment. After a change has been implemented, its impact should be assessed, and the process reviewed and documented to identify any outcomes that could help future change management projects.

Review Activity:

Code Auditing and Change Management

Answer the following questions:

1. What is considered best practice when identifying the number of people that can make changes to database code?

2. Besides restricting the number of people who can make changes to database code, what else can be done to help prevent code changes from inadvertently exposing private data?

3. How does a database identify itself to another database or system it integrates with?

4. What is the main goal of change management?

Lesson 10

Summary

After this lesson, you should understand the purpose and importance of encrypting data when it is in transit and at rest. You should also understand that data masking is an alternative method to protect private data when it still needs to be human readable. You should recognize why it is important to be able to properly destroy data. You should also understand that auditing is necessary to confirm that private data is protected and only accessible by properly authorized users.

Guidelines for Securing Data

Consider these best practices and guidelines when planning for changes to a database.

1. **Database code changes should be regularly audited in order to identify unexpected changes and confirm the changes won't cause data loss or unauthorized data exposure.**

2. **If possible, limit the number of people that can make code changes to a database.**

3. **Use data masking to remove private data when access by unauthorized personnel is necessary for business functions, such as data analysis.**

4. **Use a change management process to help control the changes being made to the database.**

5. **If credentials are being stored in the database for integrations, audit them regularly to confirm the level of authorization provided by the credential is appropriate.**

Lesson 11

Securing Data Access

LESSON INTRODUCTION

An important part of data security is ensuring that only those who should be seeing the data have access to it. Data can be encrypted and obscured, but if it can be accessed by someone who should not have access to it, these encryption techniques may not be enough to properly protect the data. Thus, the practice of securing data must also include protecting data from inadvertent modification or deletion. The way to do this is to control who has access to view and modify the data.

Lesson Objectives

In this lesson, you will do the following:

- Understand identity and access management.

- Understand access controls.

- Understand password policies.

- Work with service accounts.

Topic 11A

Understand Identity and Access Management

 EXAM OBJECTIVES COVERED
4.3 Given a scenario, implement policies and best practices related to authentication and authorization.

When discussing security, the term "identity" refers to the set of physical and behavioral characteristics by which an individual is uniquely recognizable. To protect the integrity and the privacy of data, it is important to be able to uniquely identify an individual and then determine what level of access that individual has to data.

Authentication and Authorization

When securing access to data, two questions need to be answered: who is accessing the data, and what can they do to the data? Authentication and authorization, respectively, are the techniques used to answer those questions.

Authentication

Authentication is the process of determining whether someone is who they say they are. Authentication technology provides access control for one or more systems by comparing a user's credentials with the credentials in a database of authorized users or in an authentication server. While there are several types of authentication, for purposes of user identity, users are typically identified with a user ID or username. Authentication occurs when the user provides credentials, such as a password that matches their user ID or username. This type of authentication is called single-factor authentication (SFA). The "factor" in single-factor authentication is a categorization of the different technologies used to define credentials. The three credential factor categories most often used are the following:

- **Something you know:** A factor that is based on something you know is referred to as a *knowledge factor*. The most common knowledge factor is the information you use to log into a system, composed of a username and a password. The username is typically not a secret (although it should not be published openly), but the password must be known only to the account holder. Therefore, this is a knowledge factor. Another example of a knowledge factor is a pin.

- **Something you have:** An *ownership factor* is characterized by something the user possesses that no one else does. For example, a mobile device such as a smartphone can be used to receive a uniquely generated access code as a token. Unlike a password, these tokens are only valid for a single use, typically within a brief time window. The fact that this unique token is only available for limited access on a particular device means this is an ownership factor.

- **Something you are/do:** A *biometric factor* uses either physiological identifiers, such as a fingerprint or facial identification, or behavioral identifiers, such as the way someone moves (gait). These identifiers are scanned and recorded as a template. When the user authenticates, another scan is taken and compared to the template.

Many security policies nowadays require the use of more than one factor during user authentication. For example, a user might be required to enter their username, their password, and a numeric code received on their smartphone. The password would be the first factor (knowledge) and the numeric code, or token, would be the second factor (ownership). This is known as **two-factor authentication (2FA)**. Any authentication technology that uses more than one authentication factor is considered **multifactor authentication (MFA)**.

Multifactor authentication requires a combination of different technologies. It is important to recognize that MFA requires at least two different types of factors—it is not just the requirement of several of the same type of factor. For example, an authentication that requires you to enter a PIN number plus your date of birth is certainly stronger than requiring a PIN alone, but these are both knowledge factors, so this would not be considered multifactor authentication.

Authorization

Authorization is the process of giving a user permission to access a specific resource or function. Authorization will always follow authentication, meaning that a user's identity must be confirmed before they can be granted any permissions. During authentication, a user proves that they are who they say they are. But just because a user's identity has been confirmed does not mean that user has any privileges in the database.

So while authentication allows access to the database, authorization determines what the user can do, or what resources they can use within that database. Authorization is usually accomplished by assigning privileges to a user account associated with an identity.

Identity and Access Management

Identity and access management (IAM) is a framework of business processes, policies, and technologies that facilitates the management of digital identities. With an IAM framework in place, user access to critical information within an organization can be centrally managed.

The part of an IAM that manages access is made up of a set of technical controls that govern how subjects may interact with objects. Subjects in the context of a database are typically users, but may also be devices, applications, or anything else that can request and be granted access to a resource. Objects are the resources. In the context of a database, these objects could be database servers or databases; in other situations, objects could be entire networks or individual files.

An IAM system is usually described in terms of four main processes:

- **Identification** involves creating an account or login that uniquely represents a user.

- **Authentication** is the process of proving that a user is who they claim to be when they attempt to access a resource.

- **Authorization** determines what rights or permissions a user should have on each resource, and enforces those rights.

- **Accounting** includes tracking, and often logging, authorized usage of a resource, and creating an alert when unauthorized use is detected or attempted.

IAM enables the definition of attributes that make up a subject's identity, such as its purpose, function, security clearance, and more. These attributes subsequently enable access management systems to make informed decisions about whether to grant or deny a subject access. If granted, the system decides what the subject has authorization to do.

Each individual employee may have their own identity in the IAM system. The employee's role in the company factors into their identity, such as what department the employee is in and whether the employee is a manager. For example, suppose your organization is setting up an e-commerce site and wants to enroll users. The appropriate controls need to be selected to perform each function.

- **Identification:** All customers must be confirmed to be legitimate. For example, the site might need to verify that billing and delivery addresses match, and that anyone placing an order is not trying to use a fraudulent payment method.

- **Authentication:** It must be confirmed that each customer can manage their own orders and billing information, within their unique account.

- **Authorization:** Rules must be set that allow customers to place orders only when they have valid payment mechanisms in place. The organization might also operate loyalty schemes or promotions that authorize certain customers to view unique offers or content.

- **Accounting:** The system must record the actions a customer takes for accounting (to ensure, for instance, that they cannot deny placing an order).

It is usually not the responsibility of the DBA to install, maintain, or configure an IAM system. However, many IAM systems can integrate with the authentication and authorization mechanisms of databases. So a DBA may collaborate with other IT departments or personnel in configuring the authentication and authorization requirements for one or more databases.

Review Activity:

Identity and Access Management

Answer the following questions:

1. **What type of authentication factor is a user's fingerprint?**

2. **What is the difference between authentication and authorization?**

3. **Which security policy requires more than one factor to be used during user authentication?**

4. **What are the four main processes of an identity and access management (AIM) system?**

Topic 11B

Understand Access Controls

EXAM OBJECTIVES COVERED
4.3 Given a scenario, implement policies and best practices related to authentication and authorization.

A user who has been authenticated and allowed access to a database cannot perform any actions or access any data unless they are authorized to do so. This authorization comes in the form of permissions or privileges. In a database where there are a large number of functions or objects a user can be authorized to access, it could mean giving a user account potentially hundreds of permissions. Thus, it is imperative to find ways to manage permissions efficiently.

Permissions and Roles

Permissions are the smallest unit of authorization in a database. They define the actions that a user can perform in a database and the database objects that the user can interact with. Privileges are assigned permissions. When a permission is assigned to a user, we say that the user has been granted a privilege. Common examples of privileges are those that give a user the ability to select, delete, or alter data in particular database tables; execute stored queries; or alter the columns in a database table.

While permissions are typically used to grant a user the ability to perform an action or access an object, they can also be used to deny a user the ability to perform an action or access an object. In this case, a revoke operation is used to deny the user's privilege. If a permission has been both granted to and denied from a user, the deny will take precedence over the grant, and the user will not have that permission.

A role provides a way to group multiple permissions together and minimally consists of a name and a list of permissions. A role can also be assigned to users. A user that is assigned a role receives all the permissions of that role. It is more efficient to assign roles, rather than having to assign individual permissions to multiple users. Users can have more than one role, and they can even have different roles in different databases.

Roles are typically aligned with business functions or job roles. For example, in the database that supports the toy company's inventory, an administrator or developer is going to have more privileges than a sales engineer. Likewise, a sales engineer will have different privileges than a marketing manager. To manage these varying privileges, roles would be created and named according to the business function (such as Administrator, Developer, Sales Engineer, and Marketing). Then users belonging to any of these business functions would simply be assigned to their corresponding role. This allows you to manage the privileges of multiple users in a business function without needing to remember which user is assigned which individual permissions.

It is best practice to use roles when assigning permissions, as then individual permissions can be granted or denied based on exceptions. Most users performing the same or a similar job role will need to perform the same set of functions. If a role is created based on a job role, then most users performing that job role will need the same set of permissions. Without the use of a role, an administrator will need to remember which specific permissions should be assigned to any user performing a certain job function. This will inevitably lead to users with too few, or too many, permissions. In addition, maintenance of these users and their assigned permissions would become difficult. Anytime the users performing a particular job role needed a different set of permissions, the permissions assigned would need to be changed for each user. But, if the permissions were grouped into a role, and the role was assigned to the users, then any changes could be made just to the role—and those changes would thus automatically apply to all users assigned that role.

There are, of course, always exceptions to the rule. Perhaps a single user in a role may need one or two additional permissions, or maybe one or two of the permissions assigned through the role are not actually needed. For example, suppose any new sales engineers hired at the toy company need to be restricted from updating product pricing until they have at least six months of on-the-job experience. The new sales engineer could be assigned to the Sales Engineer role, but the permission that enables updating the pricing table could be denied for that user. This is considered best practice for handling the assignment of permissions and the management of small exceptions. Allowing for an exception in the permissions associated with a role for an individual user is more efficient than creating separate roles. If a new role were created every time an exception was identified in the grouped permissions, then you would wind up with an infinite number of roles representing all the permutations of permissions.

Most databases provide a set of default roles, but you can add additional roles to suit your business needs. Some databases allow for permissions (and roles) to be applied at an individual database level, while others extend to the database server level. Roles and privileges applied at the database server level affect all databases that are located on that server.

Schemas

A **schema** is a distinct namespace to facilitate the separation, management, and ownership of database objects. Think of a schema as a virtual container where you can group database objects like tables, views, stored queries, functions, and indexes.

Privileges and roles can be applied to schemas, making them an effective way to apply permissions to multiple objects at the same time. In the same way that a user can have multiple roles, a user can also be given access to multiple schemas (and thus their associated privileges).

Although both schemas and roles are often used as a data access administration mechanism, they are not the same thing. Schemas are simply a useful mechanism to segregate database objects for different applications, access rights, and the management of security administration. Since roles can be applied to a schema, grouping database objects in the schema and then assigning a user to that role can give the user access to all the objects in the schema. But the schema itself does not allow or deny any privilege. This is a common area of confusion. Thinking about the schema as an organizational tool can help prevent this misunderstanding.

 Microsoft SQL Server provides default schemas in each database that are named the same as the default roles. Don't let this naming convention cause confusion; schemas and privileges are not the same.

The Principle of Least Privilege

Least privilege means that a user is granted sufficient rights to perform their job, and no more. This mitigates risk if the account should be compromised and fall under the control of a threat actor. If an account that is attacked has only minimal rights or permissions, then there is less information and data the attacker will have access to using that account.

Over time, as a user's role or job function changes, they may be given additional permissions or added to additional roles. As this occurs, it may be possible to remove permissions no longer necessary, either directly or by removing the user from certain roles.

As an example, suppose one of the support staff at the toy company has been promoted to the software development team. As a member of the support staff, they were given the permissions to access customer contact data, so that they could verify and contact customers who were reporting support issues. As a member of the software development team, they will be given new permissions to access the source code of the inventory software. But they no longer have a need to access customer information, and those permissions should be removed. If the permission to access customer information is not removed, they will now have more permissions than necessary to perform their duties as a software developer, thus violating the principle of least privilege. This is an example of **authorization creep**, which refers to a situation where a user acquires more and more rights, either directly or by being added to security groups and roles. Least privilege should be ensured by closely analyzing business workflows to assess what privileges are required and by performing regular account audits.

Change management can help prevent authorization creep by properly planning for the addition of a user account to a database, a change in a user's permissions, or the removal of a user account from a database. During the planning for the change, the principle of least privilege should be applied to verify that the change in question will not allow more access to the data than the user requires to do their job.

Review Activity:

Access Controls

Answer the following questions:

1. **True or False: Permissions can contain one or more roles that allow a user to perform certain actions in a database.**

2. **What is occurring when a user acquires more and more rights over time, either directly or by being added to security groups and roles?**

3. **What activity involves planning what privileges should be assigned to a user prior to adding them to a database?**

4. **When following the principle of _____, a user is granted sufficient rights to perform their job and no more.**

Topic 11C

Understand Password Policies

EXAM OBJECTIVES COVERED
4.3 Given a scenario, implement policies and best practices related to authentication and authorization.

A secure digital environment requires all users to use strong credentials. As of the writing of this book, the most common credential is the password, even in types of authentication using multiple factors. A **password policy** is a set of rules designed to enhance security by encouraging users to properly use strong passwords and is often part of an organization's official regulations. While working as a DBA, you would not be responsible for creating your organization's password policies, but you should be familiar with them, as those policies will be applicable to any database user accounts.

Recently, there has been a shift in the security industry toward the technique of "passwordless authentication" as the most effective way to reduce risky password management practices and prevent credential theft attacks. Instead of entering passwords, users provide some other proof of their identities, like fingerprints, face scanning, or a hardware token code. While there is no single standard for passwordless authentication yet, there is plenty of information on current implementation techniques that can be found by searching for "passwordless authentication."

Common Password Policies

While most organizations have their own requirements for the complexity of passwords, there are also standards bodies that publish recommendations for password policies. Some global regulations, like PCI DSS, specify minimum password policies. Examples of standards bodies that publish minimum password policies include the **National Institute of Standards and Technology** at the U.S. Department of Commerce (NIST) and the **International Organization for Standardization (ISO)**. The latest NIST password policy recommendations are published in NIST special publication 800-63b (nvlpubs.nist.gov/nistpubs/SpecialPublications/NIST.SP.800-63b.pdf). ISO password policy recommendations can be found in the ISO 27001/27002 frameworks.

A password policy will document requirements for user-selected passwords. Some of the most common password characteristics that are featured in requirements are as follows:

- **Password length:** Password policies almost always enforce a minimum length for passwords. There may also be a maximum length.

- **Password complexity:** Password complexity rules ensure the password is varied. For example, they might require that the username does not appear within the password, or that the password contains a combination of at least eight uppercase/lowercase alpha-numeric and non-alpha-numeric characters.

- **Password aging:** The majority of password policies force users to select a new password after a set number of days.

- **Password reuse and history:** This prevents the selection of a password that has been used already. The history attribute sets how many previous passwords are blocked.

- **Common passwords:** To prevent password guessing, commonly used passwords (e.g., p@ssw0rd) and dictionary words are often restricted from use. Lists of commonly used passwords are maintained by multiple security organizations, and some can be obtained for free online.

While the above attributes are all still in wide use, the most recent guidance issued by NIST deprecates some of the "traditional" elements of password policy:

- **Complexity rules should not be enforced.** The user should be allowed to choose a password (or other memorized secret) of between 8 and 64 ASCII or UNICODE characters, including spaces. The only restriction should be to block common passwords, such as dictionary words, repetitive strings (like 12345678), strings found in breach databases, and strings that repeat contextual information, such as a username or company name.

- **Aging policies should not be enforced.** Users should be able to select if and when a password will be changed, though the system must still be able to force a password change if compromise is detected.

- **Password hints should not be used.** A password hint allows account recovery when the user provides some personal information, such as their primary school or pet's name.

While this guidance may seem counterintuitive, sometimes our best intentions can have an opposite effect. For example, when passwords are required to be very complex and also need to be changed frequently, people may write their passwords down or use poor passwords (like reusing the same password but adding numbers). This is why balance is key when designing a password policy.

 Many organizations find that the most recent NIST recommendations are a bit too aggressive. As an example, you may find organizations that follow all the latest recommendations but still enforce aging policies. Remember that these recommendations from organizations like NIST are just recommendations, and not strict rules.

Enforcement of Password Policies

As with the creation of password policies, it is typically not the DBA's responsibility to enforce them. Both the creation and enforcement of password policies is typically performed in a central account management system, like an IAM system. Although the creation of password policies can be managed within some database servers, this is not recommended in a network where there is an organization-wide set of policies that govern passwords. There is a potential for the varied password policies, if not centrally managed, to become out of sync.

Some database servers will also allow you to configure the database to enforce the password policies created in the network or operating system. In fact, Microsoft SQL Server allows you to specify the enforcement of password policies at the login level, meaning that password policies can be enforced on some logins and not others.

The Login Properties Window in Microsoft SQL Server Management Studio
(Used with permission from Microsoft.)

Double-clicking on a login will display the login properties window, as shown in the screenshot. You can see that the option to "Enforce password policy" is checked, meaning that the database server will enforce the password policies in effect for the system hosting the database.

Review Activity:

Password Policies

Answer the following questions:

1. **What element of a password policy requires a password to contain at least one number?**

2. **True or False: The latest recommendations from NIST suggest that password complexity rules should not be enforced.**

3. **True or False: Global regulations do not factor into the creation of password policies.**

Topic 11D

Work with Service Accounts

EXAM OBJECTIVES COVERED
4.3 Given a scenario, implement policies and best practices related to authentication and authorization.

In most situations, a user will authenticate to a system or application, and they will then be allowed access to necessary resources. But on occasion, persistent applications need their own account, so that they can perform actions on behalf of the users of the application. Service accounts act as proxies for performing automated actions or limited actions for users that have no access to sensitive data and systems.

Service Accounts

A **service account** is a digital identity used by an application or service to interact with other applications or the operating system. Service accounts represent nonhuman users and are intended for scenarios where a scheduled process or application server software, such as a database, needs to access resources or perform actions without end-user involvement. For example, a database server needing to access the file system of the machine it is running on would not require an authenticated user for access. So, the database server would use a service account to access the file system.

A service account differs from a normal user account in that it does not have a password and can't be used for normal sign-ins, such as from a browser or custom application. Windows has several built-in service accounts:

- **The local system account** has the most privileges of any Windows account. It creates the host processes that start Windows before the user logs on. Any process created using the system account will have full privileges over the local computer.

- **The local service account** has the same privileges as the standard user account. It can only access network resources as an anonymous user.

- **The network service account** has the same privileges as the standard user account but can also present the computer's account credentials when accessing network resources.

In the following screenshot, the Services application has been opened to show all the services running in Microsoft Windows. Opening the properties of SQL Server Express displays information about the running service.

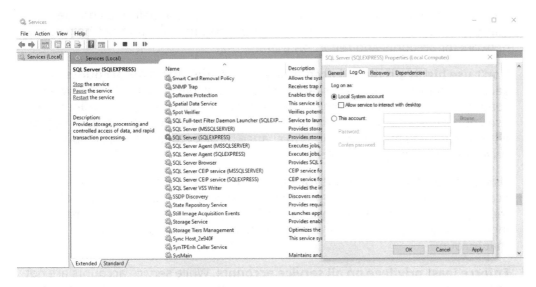

*Local System Account Being Used to Execute the SQL Server Express Service in Microsoft Windows
(Used with permission from Microsoft.)*

The LogOn tab of the service properties window allows for the configuration of the account used to execute the service. We can see that this service is being executed by the local system account.

Linux also uses the concept of service accounts to run noninteractive daemon processes, such as databases. These accounts are usually created by the server application package manager. Users can be prevented from logging into these accounts (often by setting the password to an unknown value and denying shell access).

Traditional Service Accounts

A **traditional service account** is a standard user account that is configured to run a service or application server software. Unlike the service accounts we just discussed, the traditional service account does have a password and can be used for normal sign-ins. If a standard account is manually configured to run a service or application, the password for the service account will effectively be shared by one or more administrators. On occasion, these service account passwords may also be known by multiple development or implementation team members. One of the main reasons we use traditional service accounts is their ability to centrally manage the accounts and the permissions assigned to the accounts using an IAM.

Be aware of the risk of using a personal account when a service account is more appropriate. If you use a personal account and the user changes the password, or the account is disabled for some reason, then the service will fail to run, which can cause serious problems with business applications.

Best Practices for Service Accounts

When working with service accounts, there are some best practices that are helpful to remember:

- **Always keep track of what service accounts you have and what they are used for.** It will not be possible to properly manage service accounts you don't know about. Of course, this might not be an easy task. Service accounts (especially traditional ones) can exist on local workstations, on servers, at the network level, and in commercial IAM solutions, so locating them all manually may not be feasible. However, there are commercial products and tools that can help scan a network for accounts and report on them.

- **Don't use highly privileged accounts, such as administrator accounts, as service accounts.** This might seem obvious at first glance, but it is somewhat common practice for an administrative or other highly privileged account to be used as a service account for the purpose of testing a new application or service. If this occurs, you must remember to change these accounts to one of lower privilege once testing is complete.

- **Use a unique service account for each service.** Using a single service account for multiple services can lead to authorization creep. When one of the applications or services requires additional permissions, this needlessly increases the set of permissions available to all applications or services using that account.

- **Enforce least privilege on all service accounts.** While service accounts are not to be used for standard sign-ins, they still have permissions to access resources. A bad actor could take advantage of a vulnerability in a service or application and get access to any resources the corresponding service account is authorized to access. Minimizing the level of access to just what is necessary for that service or application to function will reduce the resources available to anyone misusing the service account.

- **Disable the ability for a service account to perform a standard sign-in, referred to as an interactive login.** One of the benefits of using a service account is that it protects the credentials of the account. By default, the credentials of a service account are managed by the operating system. If the service account is allowed to perform a standard sign-in, that means the service account credentials have been made available to someone else, and often more than one person, which eliminates this benefit.

- **If using a traditional service account, consider having the operating system maintain the credentials for the account.** This makes password maintenance on the account easier and helps protect the credentials from being exposed to outside parties. Many operating systems support automatic provisioning of credentials for service accounts, reducing the risk of insider threat.

These best practices may not be applicable to all scenarios, but applying as many as possible will increase the effectiveness, manageability, and security of using service accounts.

Service Account Abuse

As we've seen so far, built-in service accounts are a useful tool for running systems and applications without having to manage user credentials. Unfortunately, there are multiple ways in which a bad actor can abuse service accounts:

- **Privilege escalation:** Service accounts often have elevated privileges, which are needed to run services that have access to many machine resources. If an attacker can assume the identity of a service account, they can possibly gain access to more resources than they could through a standard account.

- **Spoofing:** If an attacker can impersonate a service account, then any activity logs that would normally be used to determine what user account performed certain actions would no longer be helpful. The activity logs would simply show that the service account performed the actions, thus obscuring the real identity of the attacker.

- **Non-repudiation:** An attacker can conceal their identity and actions by using a service account to carry out operations on their behalf (which is not always possible to trace back to the bad actor). When this occurs, there is no way to prove that the service account did not perform the action, even though the operation was actually performed by an attacker.

- **Information disclosure:** An attacker can derive information about an organization's infrastructure, applications, or processes simply from the existence of certain service accounts, which are used to execute standard services. As an example, the default service account used to run the IIS6 worker process (W3wp.exe) on a Microsoft Windows web server is Network Service. So if an attacker sees that the Network Service account is active on a machine, the attacker might be able to deduce information about the purpose of that machine.

To prevent or mitigate these kinds of abuses, it is very important to apply the principle of least privilege even to built-in service accounts. Traditional service accounts, which are just standard user accounts, can also be subject to abuse:

- **Information disclosure:** Regular user accounts are often used as service accounts in the name of expediency, which can potentially expose the standard account credentials to bad actors.

- **Privilege escalation:** Standard accounts used as traditional service accounts typically have greater access to resources than would be necessary to perform the purpose of the service or application that is using them. This violates the principle of least privilege.

- **Stale passwords:** The password of any standard account used as a traditional service account will need to periodically be updated, but managing the passwords of hundreds or thousands of service accounts can get complicated very quickly, and changing a service account's password introduces the risk of breaking the applications or services it is used to run. Because of this, many organizations do not require password expiration for traditional service accounts. Thus, these passwords are often never updated—which is not much better than having no password at all.

Review Activity:

Service Accounts

Answer the following questions:

1. What type of account represents nonhuman users?

2. Unlike a standard user account and a traditional service account, a service account does not have a _____.

3. What types of standard user accounts should never be used as service accounts?

4. What are some ways in which built-in service accounts might be abused?

Lesson 11

Summary

After this lesson, you should have a thorough understanding of why and how access to data is secured. You should be able to identify the difference between authentication and authorization and should understand what an IAM system is used for. You should know different factors that can be used for authentication and recognize how they can be combined to create multifactor authentication. You should also understand the importance of following the principle of least privilege, which is important in preventing authorization creep. You should understand how to properly manage change using change management. You should understand password policies, some common elements of password policies, and some ways to enforce them. You should understand that service accounts are special accounts that don't have passwords and are used to execute services and unattended applications. You should also understand that traditional service accounts differ from service accounts, in that they use standard user accounts.

Guidelines for Securing Data Access

Consider these best practices and guidelines when securing data access.

1. **Use an IAM to centralize the management of authentication and authorization.**

2. **Adhere to the principle of least privilege by limiting permissions to the minimum amount required for a user to perform their job duties.**

3. **Use roles to manage groups of permissions granted to users with similar job roles.**

4. **Use schemas to help organize groups of database objects users are authorized to access.**

5. **Implement a change management system to better prepare for changes to a database and the ramifications of those changes.**

6. **Implement common password policies for user accounts, such as complexity and length.**

7. **Use one of the built-in service accounts to run services and unattended applications.**

8. **If using a traditional service account, only use that account with a single service or application to prevent a violation of least privilege.**

Lesson 12

Securing the Database and Server

LESSON INTRODUCTION

In previous lessons, you have seen how to protect the data using encryption or obfuscation techniques. You have also seen how to protect access to the data through authentication and authorization techniques. But what about the physical hardware the database is running on? What about the network the database is connected to? We must protect the database itself from physical loss or unauthorized physical access. We must also protect the database server from improper network, or logical, access.

Lesson Objectives

In this lesson, you will do the following:

- Utilize physical security.

- Utilize logical security.

Topic 12A

Utilize Physical Security

 EXAM OBJECTIVES COVERED
4.4 Explain the purpose of database infrastructure security.

In previous lessons, you've learned why it is important to protect data by encrypting it, obscuring it using multiple masking techniques, and destroying it when it is no longer needed. But none of that matters if an attacker can walk up to the database server and plug in a malicious USB thumb drive.

Physical attacks on database servers do not require a lot of skill and can be accomplished in a number of ways. A malicious USB drive plugged into a server can automatically install malware or be made to act like a USB keyboard, automating a series of commands to access or steal data without authorization. Attackers that have physical access to a server can extract private data while it is in use, as it resides in memory, thereby completely bypassing traditional in-transit and at-rest encryption and protection.

Physical Access Controls

The first thing that must be done to provide physical security for a database server is to control access to the server itself. While this might seem obvious, there are multiple considerations that can affect **physical access controls**. To make matters worse, as the DBA, you are rarely responsible for determining and providing the physical location of the server. But while there will likely be construction and space planning considerations that are outside of your control, you may be able to provide input into the decision-making process.

The database server must be located in a room that is not generally accessible. There must be a way to control who has access to the room, and how accessible the room is to people who don't have access, and thus the server. The extent to which you go to control access to the room will depend on the level of risk involved with your data. For example, if you are working on highly classified research for a government or military project, you will be required to have a much higher level of physical security than if you are storing product information for a company that sells children's toys.

The first thing to consider is the fortification of the room itself. In more risk-tolerant scenarios, a room located in an organization's headquarters might be suitable. In a more risk-adverse scenario, the room might be in a dedicated building with thick cement walls, surrounded by an electric fence with 24-hour guards on duty.

Once the room exists, the points of ingress need to be secured. This process can be thought of as physical authentication. Similar to the factors of authentication (discussed in a previous lesson), physical authentication can utilize one or more factors to control access to the room containing the database. The room may be secured with a simple manual combination lock, a lock and key, or a digital combination lock. Only those authorized to access the room would possess a key or the combination.

Another option would be a digital lock that requires an access card. The benefit of a digital lock is a centralized administration, which makes disabling a user's access much easier, as opposed to changing a combination or retrieving a physical key.

In either case, the door lock would be considered a single factor (either something you have, in the form of a key or access card, or something you know, in the case of a combination). In a scenario that requires enhanced security, multiple factors of authentication may be required. An example of this would be a digital lock requiring an access card alongside a biometric factor, like an iris or fingerprint scan. Going a step further, a third factor could be the additional requirement of a passcode.

 When a database is hosted with a third-party or cloud provider, the responsibility for providing physical access control to the servers is well and truly out of your hands. But it is still important to verify that the proper physical access controls are in place. Third-party hosting providers and cloud providers will provide documentation on their physical access control policies and practices. Before selecting a provider, verify that their physical access control policies meet your requirements.

Surveillance

We've previously talked about how putting data protections in place is only the first step toward protecting private data. We then need to make sure these protections are working as desired. To do this, we audit how data is accessed and who is accessing the data.

In a similar fashion, it is important to monitor the physical access controls put in place and verify who is accessing the room containing the data server. In the case of physical access, this is accomplished using surveillance. The most common form is **video surveillance**, where ingress and egress are under constant monitoring; the interior of the server room may even be monitored. Surveillance may also take the form of notifications when a user gains access to the room using digital locks, which may trigger emails to be sent or certain staff to be notified.

Surveillance video may be monitored in real time by security staff or it may be recorded, or both. However, real-time monitoring is typically only used when the environment requires a high level of security. Surveillance recordings are often kept for some period of time, in case they need to be reviewed for potential breaches of access. These recordings may also be routinely reviewed to confirm access controls are being properly enforced.

Fire Suppression

While protecting the databases in a server room from security threats and unauthorized access should be a top priority for any organization, more tangible threats to those servers cannot be overlooked. Fire is a danger not only to the structure housing the servers, but also to the servers themselves—in fact, it is one of the most significant threats to server equipment. While other threats can cause server downtime, a fire can permanently damage structures, equipment, and subsequently data.

Fires are categorized in classes, typically designated by letters like A, B, C, D, and K. Each letter refers to the type of material that fueled the combustion. The class letters differ by country or geographical region, but the particular letter is not as important as its associated material or fuel. It is important to understand the particular fire risks that affect a server room. In North America, a server room, or datacenter, environment is typically at risk from class A, B, and C fires.

- Class A fires are those in which the fuel source is some solid combustible material like wood, cloth, rubber, or plastic.

- Class B fires involve flammable liquids like oils, greases, and flammable gases.

- Class C fires are initiated by electrical equipment.

Understanding the class of fire a server room is at risk for can help an organization determine what type of **fire suppression** system will be needed. There are two main types: water sprinklers and gaseous agents. Water sprinklers are the traditional choice because they are effective and low-cost. Once sprinklers are activated, they will continue to release water until they are shut off. The caveat of this type of fire suppression is that water can damage electrical equipment. Gaseous agent suppression systems use a newer technology and are effective in suppressing a wider range of fires. The gaseous agent is stored in tanks and piped into overhead nozzles when activated, similar to a water sprinkler system. Gaseous agent suppression systems are ideal for server rooms because they can more effectively suppress fires related to electrical equipment, plus they are less likely to damage electrical equipment upon activation. The downside to many gas suppression systems is that the gas being used might be harmful, or even deadly, to personnel in the room.

Cooling Systems

Fire is not the only tangible threat to a server. Computing equipment generates a lot of heat, but it cannot withstand a lot of heat. Overheating is a serious threat to a data server, as it can cause damage to a server which can, in turn, cause data loss. This threat is even greater if the server room houses multiple servers. Thus, **cooling systems** are an important measure to keep the room or the facility housing the servers cool and to provide good airflow.

Traditional Air Conditioning

A traditional air conditioning solution might suffice for your needs, but there are considerations that must be taken into account before you can determine whether that is your best option. While the building that houses your server room may provide an air conditioner, either built in or portable, server rooms require constant cooling, and most air conditioners are not meant to run 24/7. Running an air conditioner at all times puts a strain on the unit and can increase electric utility expenses. In addition, cooling systems often have the additional responsibility of reducing humidity. An air conditioner may not provide dehumidification, or may not have the capacity to remove the amount of humidity that may exist in a server room or facility. When traditional air conditioning is not sufficient, it should be replaced by a specialized cooling solution.

Other Cooling System Options

There are many options for cooling systems beyond traditional air conditioning. For example, calibrated vectored cooling (CVC) systems, which were designed by IBM specifically for blade server systems, work by passing refrigerated air over the hottest parts of these server systems. This keeps them cool without the need for numerous cooling fans.

Another example of an alternate cooling system is direct-to-chip cooling, which is a method of liquid cooling in which nonflammable, dielectric fluid is directed to the computer chips. The fluid absorbs heat, evaporates into a vapor, and carries heat away from the server equipment.

Close-coupled cooling systems are a special type of air conditioning system that effectively move the air conditioner closer to the equipment rack containing the server or servers. Unlike a traditional air conditioner, which aims to reduce the overall temperature of a room, the close-coupled cooling system directly delivers the cool air to the equipment rack.

These are just a few examples of cooling systems beyond traditional air conditioners. Choosing which solution is the most suitable for a given situation is not arbitrary.

Engaging Professional Help

Most organizations do not have the expertise in-house to properly determine the technical cooling requirements for a server room. However, **heating, ventilation, and air conditioning (HVAC)** professionals utilize calculations accounting for the wattage of the equipment in a room or facility (including lighting and other standard equipment) to determine cooling requirements. A best practice is to engage an HVAC professional who can provide options for cooling that will meet or exceed the calculated need for a particular environment.

Review Activity:

Physical Security

Answer the following questions:

1. How is protecting the door to a server room similar to authenticating a user's access to data?

2. True or False: Surveillance systems should be monitored 24/7 for best results.

3. Why is fire such a serious concern in server rooms or datacenters?

4. Why is providing an adequate cooling solution necessary in a server room or datacenter?

Topic 12B

Utilize Logical Security

EXAM OBJECTIVES COVERED
2.2 Explain database implementation, testing, and deployment phases.
4.4 Explain the purpose of database infrastructure security.

In the previous section, we introduced the importance of preventing unauthorized access to the actual machine. But physical access to the server isn't the only concern; the database server can also be accessed over a network connection. Thus, protection must also be provided for this logical access to the database server. An unauthorized user who gains logical access to a database server can quite easily manipulate, steal, or destroy the data within.

While preventing unauthorized logical access is usually not the responsibility of the DBA, it is still important to understand some of the technology involved, as this will allow you to discuss prevention methods with the IT staff who are responsible for implementation.

Firewalls

The most common logical security measure is a **firewall**. The basic function of a firewall is filtering network traffic according to rules. If the traffic does not conform to a rule that allows it, access is blocked. For example, a rule could be written that prevents network traffic coming from an unauthorized address. Only traffic from authorized addresses would be allowed to access the server. So if someone who is using a machine that is not authorized attempted to gain access to the server over the network, their traffic would be blocked before it even got to the server.

The rules in a firewall can be written not only to filter traffic coming to the server, but also for traffic leaving the server. This can help prevent data from being transmitted to a location that is not authorized. **Data exfiltration**, or stealing data by sending it to a location it should not be sent to, is a common way for bad actors to gain unauthorized access to data. Firewall rules can be written to prevent this unauthorized traffic, which originates on the database server.

While there are many types of firewalls, and many ways of implementing them, a distinction should be made between firewalls that protect a whole network and firewalls that protect a single host/server only. A network firewall is placed inline in the network and inspects all traffic that passes through, in order to protect the whole network. A network firewall blocks unauthorized traffic before it gets to the server. On the other hand, a host firewall is installed on and inspects traffic addressed to a single host/server. A host firewall evaluates traffic once it arrives at the server, blocking unauthorized access at that point.

We would obviously prefer that potentially malicious traffic never arrive at its destination, even if it's blocked once it arrives. For this reason, a network firewall would be the preferred option, although a host firewall is still better than no firewall.

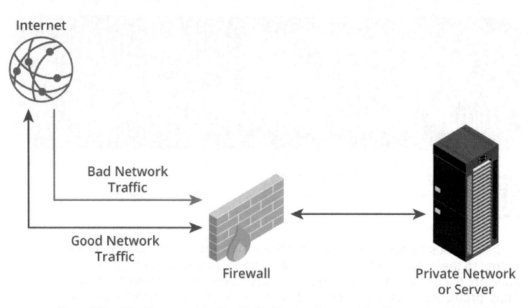

Firewall Blocking Unwanted Traffic While Allowing Expected Traffic on a Network

Perimeter Network

A **perimeter network** is an architectural element that provides logical security, protecting data through secure connectivity between network segments. Perimeter networks enable secure connectivity between your cloud or public networks and your on-premises or physical datacenter networks. A perimeter network is often the final step data takes when traversing a network on its way to the Internet. Conversely, this is the first network encountered by incoming traffic from the Internet. A perimeter network is sometimes called a demilitarized zone or DMZ.

Another use of a perimeter network is to separate one type of network traffic from another. For example, a perimeter network could allow web traffic to an Internet-facing web server but restrict traffic from directly accessing your database server on your private network. Perimeter networks are also still protected from unauthorized, unrecognized, or unexpected traffic via one or more firewalls.

This may be more easily understood with an example. Suppose an individual goes online and accesses the toy company's website, which is being hosted on a web server. A firewall would prevent any traffic other than browser traffic from being transmitted from the Internet to the web server. The web server can, in turn, access the toy company's internal private database. It would do so through another firewall, to make sure that only expected traffic was allowed from the web server to the database server and back. The individual visiting the website would have zero access to the database server, but data from the database server would still be available to the individual through the website. When a network perimeter is in place, an external user only has access to functionality or services in the perimeter network. The following diagram visualizes this process.

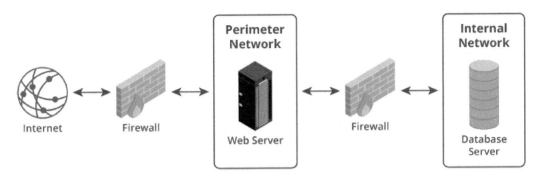

Perimeter Network Isolating the Private
Network from the External Network

A perimeter network enables better control over security, provides more granular access to resources, and can substantially reduce network traffic on a private network, making all other network services work better.

Port Security

To understand what **port security** is, you must first understand what a *port* is. In computer hardware terms, a port is a socket that peripheral hardware can be plugged into, allowing the peripheral to send data to or receive data from the computer hardware. If you plug a USB mouse connector into a USB port on your computer, the mouse can now communicate with the computer. In the context of networking, a port is a virtual point where network connections begin and end. Each of these logical connections is given a unique number and associated with a distinct process or service.

As an example, when you are browsing the Internet using HTTP, the network communication will use the logical port 80. If you are using HTTPS for secure communication, port 443 will be used. As you can imagine, the services provided by database servers must also use ports for network communication. For example, Microsoft SQL Server uses port 1433 by default. One of the Oracle default ports is 1521.

So, what is port security? As we mentioned above, each service running on a server is assigned one or more ports by default. If one of those services has a security vulnerability, by communicating with the server using the port associated to the vulnerable service, an attacker could exploit the vulnerability to gain access to the server. In order to prevent this exploitation, access to ports can be blocked. This would, in effect, turn the port off and prohibit any traffic to that port. But what if the port must be unobstructed in order for legitimate traffic to use it? In that case, the port can be configured to only allow communication with specific machines. This will prevent an attacker's machine from accessing the port while still allowing authorized machines to use the port to communicate with that server.

Review Activity:

Logical Security

Answer the following questions:

1. **What is the difference between physical access and logical access to a database server?**

2. **What is the basic job of a firewall?**

3. **Why is a network firewall preferred over a host firewall?**

4. **What is the basic function of a perimeter network?**

Lesson 12

Summary

After this lesson, you should understand why protecting the physical database server from both unauthorized logical and physical access is so important. You should be able to identify techniques for providing physical security, such as physical authentication systems and video surveillance. You should further be aware that there are more tangible threats to your data servers such as fire and overheating. When it comes to logical security, you should understand the way we use firewalls, perimeter networks, and port security to restrict network access to servers that are securely stored.

Guidelines for Securing the Database and Server

Consider these best practices and guidelines when helping to make sure a database server is secure.

1. **Restrict physical access to the server by securing it in a room or facility with strong locks or access controls.**

2. **Provide surveillance either for the ingress and egress of a server room or facility, or inside the server room or facility.**

3. **Consider implementing fire suppression and cooling systems to protect your servers from fire and overheating.**

4. **Disable ports that are not required for necessary services on a server.**

5. **Firewall rules should block traffic by default, allowing only minimal traffic to known services and applications.**

6. **Consider using a perimeter network to separate one type of network traffic from another, such as web traffic from database traffic.**

7. **Prefer the use of a network firewall over a host firewall when possible.**

Lesson 13

Classifying Types of Attacks

LESSON INTRODUCTION

Cyberattacks can be devastating to an organization. While some cyberattacks are intended to do harm to the operational capability of an organization, many cyberattacks aim to exfiltrate data that can be used for financial gain—either through holding it for ransom or using it to gain access to additional resources. While there are many types of cyberattacks, it is valuable to be familiar with some of the more common types in order to recognize them and, if possible, prevent them.

Lesson Objectives

In this lesson, you will do the following:

- Mitigate the SQL injection attack.

- Mitigate the denial of service (DoS) attack.

- Mitigate the on-path attack.

- Mitigate the brute force attack.

- Mitigate social engineering attacks.

- Mitigate malware.

Topic 13A

Mitigate the SQL Injection Attack

EXAM OBJECTIVES COVERED
4.5 Describe types of attacks and their effects on data systems.

The **Structured Query Language (SQL) injection attack** is one of the oldest, and most common, types of attacks. An SQL injection is not a complex attack to perform, as it only requires a basic understanding of structured query language. This type of attack remains one of our primary concerns when it comes to data breaches and the security of data. SQL injection attacks can be used to destroy data, exfiltrate data, or bypass data restrictions.

Identifying a SQL Injection Attack

A SQL injection attack occurs when an attacker is able to "inject" or insert malicious code into a structured query, so that it is executed by the server. This injection happens through parameters in the structured query which contain unsanitized user input. When we say that user input is unsanitized, we mean that the user input may contain characters or information that is not valid. For example, a user may input the following string: "--something." The "--" is used as the beginning of a comment in structured query language, and if that input is used in a structured query, it will cause an error. The best way to understand SQL injection attacks is to look at some examples.

Bypass Authentication Credentials

Let's say that the developers at our toy store have built a web application for its users, who are required to log in using a username and password. The application does not sanitize the user input, meaning that the user input is used just as the user entered it. When the user enters their username and password into the web application input form, the code sets variables for these values.

```
var userName = Form.Value("username");

var userPassword = Form.Value("password");
```

The application then builds a query to see if an active user exists in the database matching the entered username and the password.

```
"SELECT id FROM UserTable WHERE username='" +
userName + "' AND password='" + userPassword + "'
AND active=1"
```

If an attacker enters `validusername'--` into the username form field, they can enter anything, or nothing, into the password field, as it will no longer matter. The resulting query will be as follows.

```
SELECT id FROM UserTable WHERE
username='validusername'--' AND password='' AND
active=1
```

The query will be executed using the username "validusername," but the remainder of the query will be commented out and will not be executed. So if the attacker can guess a valid username, or acquires the knowledge of a valid username through some other means, then the attacker can use this SQL injection attack to authenticate into the application with only the username.

In a worst-case scenario, suppose the developers of the application have created an administrative user with the username "administrator." The attacker could enter `administrator'--` and gain all the capabilities of an administrator in the application.

Unauthorized Data Destruction

Now suppose the attacker enters the following into the username field:

```
validusername';DELETE * FROM UserTable;--
```

Not only would they be authenticated to the application, but all the users in the UserTable would be deleted, meaning no one else would be able to log into the application.

Unauthorized Data Access

Let's look at another example of SQL injection, in which the attacker is attempting to gain access to data they should not have access to. In our toy store web application, users can search the toy catalog for toys that are available to purchase by entering the name of the toy into a search field, which is stored in a variable called "searchInput/." The information entered by the user is not sanitized.

```
var searchInput = Form.Value("searchproductname");
```

The query that runs is as follows.

```
"SELECT * FROM ProductTable WHERE ProductName='" +
searchInput + "' AND isavailable=1"
```

However, toys that are currently being developed as secret projects are also stored in the toy catalog. The toys that are under development have a value of 0 in the data table column called "isavailable." The search query is written using a `WHERE` clause that will exclude any products where the "isavailable" column is set to 0. So, if an attacker enters the following into the application form field

```
bogusproduct' OR 1=1--
```

the resulting query will be

```
SELECT * FROM ProductTable WHERE
ProductName='bogusproduct' OR 1=1--' AND
isavailable=1
```

When the query is executed, it will return all records in the database table where the productname is "bogusproduct" or 1=1. Since 1 is always equal to 1, all the records in the table will be returned—including those that are not yet available. This would expose data that could potentially give a rival toy company an advantage when coming up with their product strategy.

Mitigating SQL Injection Attacks

As you can see, with a little knowledge of SQL, a malicious actor can use SQL injection attacks to accomplish different goals, all of which will cause concern for the organization being attacked. The good news is there are multiple steps we can take to mitigate these types of attacks.

Methods of Mitigation

- **Limit privileges.** As you will recall from previous lessons, when we follow the principle of least privilege we give a user the fewest privileges necessary to perform their job or function. We can reduce the amount of damage that could be done by a SQL injection attack by limiting the privileges of the user account or accounts being used by any application making queries into the database. When we follow the principle of least privilege, the only data that could be affected if an SQL injection attack were to occur would be only what the user account has access to.

- **Sanitize user input.** Ultimately, user input should never be trusted. All user input should be sanitized before it is used in a query. In fact, user input should be sanitized even before saving that input to the database. Otherwise, that user input could be used in a future query, thus causing a delayed SQL injection attack.

- **Use parameterized queries.** One of the most common methods of mitigating SQL injection, the use of parameterized queries is a technique that separates the SQL query from the input values. The user input values are passed as parameters to the query instead of being concatenated into the query itself. Parameters are checked for data type and length and are treated as literal values instead of executable code.

- **Revoke the permission to perform direct DML commands on the database.** Doing so forces all interactions with the database from an application to use stored procedures. Stored procedures can necessitate the use of parameters, which supports the previous mitigation of using parameterized queries.

Using Parameterized Queries

Let's look at an example of using parameterized queries to mitigate SQL injection vulnerabilities. The following is a snippet of code that is vulnerable to SQL injection because it builds a query by concatenating unsanitized user input directly into the SQL statement.

```
string searchInput = searchproductname.Value;
string connString = "...";
SqlConnection connection = new
SqlConnection(connString);
connection.Open();
SqlCommand command = new SqlCommand("SELECT * FROM
ProductTable WHERE ProductName='" + searchInput +
"' AND isavailable=1", connection);
SqlDataReader reader = command.ExecuteReader();
```

This code can be modified to utilize parameterized queries, in order to mitigate the vulnerability, as follows.

```
string searchInput = searchproductname.Value;

string connString = "...";

SqlConnection connection = new
SqlConnection(connString);

connection.Open();

SqlParameter paramSearch = new
SqlParameter("@ProdName", searchInput);

SqlCommand command = new SqlCommand("SELECT * FROM
ProductTable WHERE ProductName=@ProdName AND
isavailable=1", connection);

command.Parameters.Add(paramSearch);

SqlDataReader reader = command.ExecuteReader();
```

By using a parameter to pass the input data into the SQL query, the input data will be treated as a literal string and will not allow executable code to be executed by the query.

Review Activity:

The SQL Injection Attack

Answer the following questions:

1. What type of damage can an SQL injection attack cause?

2. Modifying an SQL query to use _____ is one way to mitigate an SQL injection attack.

3. True or False: Sanitizing user input before it is used in an SQL query can lead to a SQL injection attack.

4. How can the principle of least privilege help us mitigate SQL injection damage?

Topic 13B

Mitigate the Denial of Service (DoS) Attack

 EXAM OBJECTIVES COVERED
4.5 Describe types of attacks and their effects on data systems.

A **denial of service (DoS) attack** is an attack meant to shut down a machine or network, making it inaccessible to the users it was intended to serve. DoS attacks are accomplished by flooding the target machine or network with traffic—so much traffic that the machine or network is unable to respond to any other requests. DoS attacks can also be accomplished by taking advantage of some vulnerability to trigger the machine or network to crash. Though DoS attacks do not typically result in the theft or loss of significant information or other assets, dealing with them can cost an organization a great deal of time and money.

Identifying a DoS Attack

In order to understand how to mitigate DoS attacks, you need to understand some of the ways DoS attacks can be accomplished. There are two general methods of DoS attacks: flooding services or crashing services.

Flooding Services

A flood attack is very much what it sounds like—when the target system is overwhelmed, or flooded, with too much traffic for the server to process, the server slows down and eventually becomes unresponsive. Your first thought might be of an attacker making so many requests to a server that the server becomes overloaded. But a flood attack is not always caused by a large volume of external traffic; it can also occur when numerous processes (or a single process that consumes a lot of resources) are executed, even if there's a smaller amount of traffic. For example, a single request can trigger the execution of multiple processes used to respond to that request.

For example, consider a shopping website that allows an anonymous user to browse products and add items to a shopping cart. For the purpose of this scenario, the site does not limit the number of items that can be added to your cart and the IDs of the items in the cart are stored in a database table for the anonymous user. Now assume an attacker adds 1,000 items to their cart and then refreshes the cart in the website over and over. The query used to pull the shopping cart items—along with their descriptions, prices, quantity available, and more—will be executed over and over. It is possible that refreshing the cart, an action which would not normally be considered a large amount of traffic, when done rapidly and with so many items could overwhelm the database server. This can lead to the server failing to respond to other requests in a timely fashion. Thus, even though the amount of physical network traffic to the server is not overly large in this scenario, it would still flood the server and achieve the desired result.

Crashing Services

The other general method of executing a DoS attack is to crash services on the machine, or the machine itself. This is most often accomplished by exploiting vulnerabilities in the operating system (or services running on the machine) that cause the system or service to destabilize and ultimately crash, thus rendering it inaccessible or unusable.

Existing examples of service or machine vulnerabilities are difficult to provide, because these types of vulnerabilities are often patched quickly after they have been identified. Yet attackers do a very good job of finding any that have lingered, in addition to discovering new ones, so that they might exploit these vulnerabilities before they are patched by the vendor. For decades, buffer overflows have been one of the main vulnerabilities to be exploited. There have been multiple buffer overflow attacks on Oracle leveraging the PUBLIC privilege that have taken down databases, meaning the vulnerability can be exploited without user credentials. SQL Server has also had similar issues caused by a named pipes vulnerability, and DB2 databases have been taken down by attackers sending specially crafted UDP packets through the network.

Keep in mind that sometimes strengths can be turned into weaknesses. For example, let's say you are trying to prevent an attacker from trying to guess passwords used to log into a database. So you put in place a restriction wherein a user who tries to log in three times with the wrong password will have their account locked for some time period. However, an attacker could attempt to log in as different users, trying random passwords, thus locking all of their accounts and making the database inaccessible to anyone. In this case, what was put in place as a strength to prevent unauthorized access became a vulnerability that could be used in a DoS attack.

 While normally the goal of a DoS attack is to disable a service or machine so that it can no longer function as designed, there are scenarios where the DoS is a cover for additional nefarious activity. Sometimes the attacker will inject and execute arbitrary code while performing a DoS attack, in order to access critical information or execute commands on the server.

DDoS Attacks

An additional type of DoS attack is the **distributed denial of service (DDoS) attack**. A DDoS attack occurs when an attacker utilizes multiple systems to orchestrate a synchronized DoS attack against a single target. The essential difference is that instead of the attack originating from one location, the target is attacked from many locations at once.

Mitigating DoS Attacks

Often, the responsibility for DoS prevention lies with the team responsible for infrastructure and network concerns. While this is typically not the responsibility of a DBA, in some cases, a DBA may be able to assist the infrastructure team with certain mitigations. There are some best practices that can reduce the risk of a DoS attack.

- **Organizations should perform a network vulnerability audit/review.** A network cannot be defended if the weaknesses in the network aren't known. All devices on a network should be reviewed, and the function of each device along with its system information (such as brand, model number, and hardware and software version) should be defined. This information helps organizations identify any known or discovered vulnerabilities that affect the device, which in turn allows them to patch those vulnerabilities as efficiently as possible. A DBA may be asked to provide the database software versions in use so that the infrastructure team can identify any vulnerabilities in those versions.

- **Organizations should utilize networking monitoring and security measures.** To help protect against attacks on vulnerabilities that have not yet been discovered, an organization's network or infrastructure team will often use network monitoring software and network security devices (like firewalls, VPNS, anti-spam systems, and content filtering systems) to detect and block attacks before they are able to overwhelm a vulnerable machine.

- **Organizations should disable unnecessary services.** One of the most effective strategies for defending against DoS attacks, and one where the DBA can be very helpful, is to reduce the size of the **attack surface**, meaning eliminating as many things as possible that can be attacked. Database servers are often set up with many functions and services enabled by default, and in some cases these default functions and services are active but not in use. Turning off, disabling, or uninstalling any services, functionality, or features that are not being used reduces the target for an attacker. If a feature is not enabled, vulnerabilities in that feature cannot be exploited.

Review Activity:

The Denial of Service (DoS) Attack

Answer the following questions:

1. **What are two common methods of performing a DoS attack?**

2. **What is it called when an attacker utilizes multiple systems to orchestrate a synchronized DoS attack against a single target?**

3. **What is one of the most effective strategies a DBA can use to defend against DoS attacks?**

Topic 13C

Mitigate the On-Path Attack

EXAM OBJECTIVES COVERED
4.5 Describe types of attacks and their effects on data systems.

An **on-path attack** occurs when an attacker gains a position between two hosts and transparently captures, monitors, and relays all communication between the hosts. An on-path attack could also be used to covertly modify the traffic. The goal of an on-path attack is for an attacker to covertly insert themselves in the middle of a communication. The word *covertly* is key here, as it pinpoints the idea that the attacker will not be detected. The original data stream will be intercepted by the person in the middle of the conversation, but the information will still be passed on to the destination.

Identifying an On-Path Attack

A typical on-path attack has two steps or phases:

1. The first step is interception, during which the attacker will intercept the online activities of a victim before they reach their intended destination.

2. Once intercepted, the second step, decryption, begins. In this step, the data being communicated is decrypted and stolen or modified.

It's easy to understand why an attacker would want to steal data, but the reason behind modifying the communication is less obvious. An example will help explain this. Suppose an attacker has inserted themself in the communication between a victim and the victim's bank. The victim is attempting to transfer money between two accounts, but the attacker instead modifies the request to have the money transferred into the attacker's account. The attacker could then modify the response to appear as though the transfer was successful to the account the victim intended. Thus, the victim would have unwillingly transferred money to the attacker's account without any indication that the redirect had occurred.

Methods of an On-Path Attack

It is difficult to identify an ongoing on-path attack, since it is a covert operation, but there are a few warning signs that can be observed.

One way an attacker will initiate an on-path attack is to trick you into going to a fake web page. This can be done by sending the victim an email that appears to have come from a legitimate business. However, the URL in the email that supposedly links to that business page is very slightly different from the real website URL. For example, the attacker's URL might be "www.mlntyfreshgum.com" when the real website URL is "www.mintyfreshgum.com" (replacing the "i" with an "l"). The attacker will have built this fake website to look identical to the legitimate website, so this small change might go undetected. Once you are on the attacker's website, you may be prompted to log in using your credentials, which the attacker intercepts and forwards to the real website. The attacker then relays the responses from the real website back to the victim, therefore sitting between the victim and the legitimate website, observing and relaying all the communication. When you receive a fake URL or fake website, this is a warning sign that an on-path attack is being attempted.

Another warning sign of an attempted on-path attack is the presence of intrusive pop-ups. In this scenario, a victim navigates to a website and is presented with a pop-up that contains some urgent message. The pop-up might claim the victim's device is infected with a virus or that their computer needs a critical update, and that the victim should click a link in the pop-up to download a fix immediately. Clicking on this link would download malware.

 Intrusive pop-ups of this nature don't only appear on sketchy websites. You can also experience an on-path attack on a legitimate website, as long as the pop-up was inserted by the attacker as part of the initiation of the attack.

You should also pay close attention if your browser displays a certificate warning when you visit a website. Every legitimate website uses a certificate issued by a certification authority, which proves the identity of the website's owner has been verified. A browser will check for the existence of this certificate when the website is loaded and will warn the user if it's missing, invalid, or expired. If you visit a website and this warning appears, the website might be owned by an attacker attempting to initiate an on-path attack. Recent security measures in browsers have increased the visibility of this warning, so you don't miss it.

Mitigating On-Path Attacks

Because it is so difficult to detect on-path attacks once they have been initiated, the best way to mitigate them is to take a preventative approach by making yourself a less enticing target. Some best practices for preventing on-path attacks are as follows.

- **Only visit secured websites.** One of the warning signs mentioned in the previous section was a website presenting a bad certificate. The easiest preventative measure a user can take is to ensure they only visit websites that have a secure connection and a valid certificate. These sites can be easily identified by the URL, which starts with "https://" and not just "http://." Many browsers will also display a special visual indicator in the URL field as an indicator that the website is secure.

- **Utilize endpoint security features.** If you need to visit websites that do not have a secure connection, you might utilize a software solution called endpoint security software, typically provided by your organization's information technology group. This type of software can check potentially dangerous websites (and even email messages) to help protect a user from falling victim to an on-path attack. Some host firewalls, malware protection software, and antivirus software include endpoint security features.

- **Avoid unsecured public wireless connections.** These types of connections make it very easy for an attacker to initiate an on-path attack. Even public wireless networks that have a password may not be secure if that password is posted or publicly available.

Keep in mind that some devices, like tablets and smartphones, will automatically connect to a wireless connection if the device recognizes the wireless connection name as one it has connected to before. So if an attacker were to set up their own wireless connection and give it the same name as a well-known wireless connection (like those used by popular coffee shops), your device may automatically connect to the attacker's wireless device—without you even taking any action.

- **Use a virtual private network (VPN) when connecting to an unfamiliar network.** A VPN encrypts the data you send while online, which can make it much more difficult for an attacker to initiate an on-path attack. Not all VPN solutions provide adequate protection, so an organization's information technology group should provide a VPN that will meet the security requirements of the organization.

- **Enable multifactor authentication (MFA) for any websites or services that offer it as an option.** While MFA is not a foolproof solution, it can mitigate many attacks because the attacker does not have access to the additional factors required to authenticate. Because MFA requires some other form of identity verification, even if a user was tricked by an on-path attack and entered their login credentials on a fake website, the stolen login credentials alone would not allow the attacker to log in as the user.

- **Educate users on cybersecurity.** Finally, one of the best preventative measures an organization can take to help prevent its users from falling victim to an on-path attack is to put a cybersecurity awareness education program in place. Educating users about the dangers and warning signs of cyberattacks, like on-path attacks, is one of the easiest ways to prevent those users from being victims.

Review Activity:

The On-Path Attack

Answer the following questions:

1. What are the two steps of a typical on-path attack?

2. An attacker may use pop-ups on a legitimate website that present a sense of urgency in order to get a user to do what?

3. True or False: All legitimate websites will have a valid certificate that proves the identity of the owner of the website.

4. If your connection to a website is secure, the URL will start with what?

Topic 13D

Mitigate the Brute Force Attack

EXAM OBJECTIVES COVERED
4.5 Describe types of attacks and their effects on data systems.

A **brute force attack** is a type of attack that relies on trial and error to access passwords, guess login credentials, and discover encryption keys. It's essentially the online equivalent of a would-be thief trying every key on a key ring until they find the one that unlocks the lock, or trying every possible combination on a combination lock until they find the correct code. While this may seem like a daunting task—or at least a time-consuming one—brute force attacks are simple and reliable. An attacker will typically use a computer program to do the guessing. While brute force attacks are most often used to guess user credentials to gain access to a secured resource, they can also be used to find encryption keys and the original value of keys that have been hashed.

Identifying a Brute Force Attack

Brute force attacks can sometimes go completely undiscovered. You may never even know that this type of attack is happening. But once an attack of this type has been discovered, it can be easy to recognize it as brute force, if you know what to look for. It can help to understand how brute force attacks are performed, so you can identify certain signs that a brute force attack may be underway.

Methods of a Brute Force Attack

A normal brute force attack may take place when an attacker knows a user's account name. As an example, many sites that require a user to authenticate use the user's email address as the username. Email addresses can be easily found online in social media profiles and email signatures, to name a few. Once an attacker has a username, a software program can be used to try different passwords until the correct password is found. These software programs are capable of trying a large number of passwords in a short period of time. An attacker may also use a list of commonly used passwords to make the guessing more efficient. These lists, or dictionaries, of passwords are readily available to download from the Internet. When a dictionary of passwords is used, this is a special form of brute force attack called a **dictionary attack**. An attacker may also combine using the passwords in a dictionary with random letters and numbers to create even a larger list of passwords to try.

You may think it sounds implausible that there are enough common passwords in use to necessitate maintaining a dictionary of them. However, in 2022, the five most common passwords globally were "password," "123456," "123456789," "guest," and "qwerty" (according to studies run by multiple organizations in the security industry each year). These dictionaries can actually be very accurate and greatly decrease the amount of time necessary for a brute force attack to succeed.

Another type of brute force attack is called **credential stuffing**. In a credential stuffing attack, credentials acquired in other website data leaks are used to try to authenticate to a different website. What makes this attack successful is the common bad practice of users using the same password on multiple sites.

The methods we've just discussed involve an active attempt to authenticate to a live website. But many times, the brute force attack happens on data that has been exfiltrated in a separate attack. An attacker will obtain data containing credentials that have been hashed, and brute force techniques are then used on that data in order to determine the original password values.

There are even entire dictionaries of hashes of passwords. This type of dictionary is known as a **rainbow table**. The attacker will simply search the dictionary for the hashed value and, if found, will retrieve the original password. If the value is not found, the attacker will brute force the hash until the original password is obtained, and then add that new hash-value pair to the rainbow table so that other hackers benefit. These rainbow tables continue to grow and collect more and more hashed values over time.

Signs of an Active Brute Force Attack

There are some indicators that a brute force attack may be underway, and if you can spot them, you can possibly disrupt the attack.

- A brute force attack will create an unusual pattern of failed login attempts. For example, if an organization detects a large and/or rapid number of failed login attempts for the same account, it could be a brute force attack. Many attackers know that this kind of activity would be noticed, so they may rotate through different accounts, trying passwords for each of them. This, too, can be recognized as a sign of attack. If a large number of failed login attempts occur for multiple accounts originating from the same IP address, this may be a brute force attack. An attacker may try to determine the credentials of multiple users. In this case, if an attacker successfully authenticates with one account, they may switch to try to find the password of another account. This would present itself as a successful login followed by a number of failed login attempts, often from the same originating IP address. Observing this type of behavior may also be indicative of a brute force attack.

- Many applications log user activity in the application. An observation of a successful login attempt followed by unusual behavior may also indicate a successful brute force attack. After successfully identifying a user's password and authenticating as that user, an attacker may begin performing unusual financial transactions or unusual searching through data available to the user. This type of activity could indicate an attacker has gained access to an account that is not their own.

While these symptoms are not absolute proof that a brute force attack is underway, they should at least trigger some investigation to determine if the activity is legitimate or malicious.

Mitigating Brute Force Attacks

Brute force attacks are preventable, although doing so is not the responsibility of a single role or team. There are some best practices that can be put in place by both application development teams and DBAs that can help prevent brute force attacks.

- **Implement industry recommended password policies.** All passwords are susceptible to brute force attacks, but the more complex the password, the longer it will take to "guess" it. Modern hardware is capable of brute forcing an eight-character password using lowercase letters in less than five seconds.

If that same password contains numbers, uppercase letters, and lowercase letters, the amount of time to guess it increases to less than one hour. Increasing the length of the password to just 12 characters will increase the time required to guess that password to 12,000 years.

- **Limit the allowable number of failed login attempts.** Since brute force attacks work by guessing passwords, the login attempt will fail over and over until the correct password is found. Implementing rules that lock a user's account for a specified amount of time after they have exceeded a specific number of failed login attempts is an effective preventative measure against brute force attacks.

- **Use complex encryption.** Just like increasing password complexity can make it more difficult to guess a user's password, increasing the complexity of the hashing and encryption algorithms used to hash and encrypt passwords can increase the amount of time it takes to brute force these passwords.

- **Require multifactor authentication.** Adding this additional layer of authentication security means that even if an attacker were to guess a user's password, they would still not be able to log in due to the required additional factor of authentication.

- **Utilize CAPTCHAs.** A **Completely Automated Public Turing test to tell Computers and Humans Apart (CAPTCHA)** is a program that allows a website to distinguish between humans and computers. A CAPTCHA works by presenting users with a test that is easy for humans to pass but difficult for computers to pass. These tests can conclude with some certainty whether there is a human on the other end. Since brute force attacks are automated using computer programs, CAPTCHAs are a particularly effective preventative measure.

Implementing any one of these measures can help mitigate brute force attacks, but implementing a combination of these will be even more effective.

Review Activity:

The Brute Force Attack

Answer the following questions:

1. What can a user do when creating a password to make brute force attacks less successful?

2. What type of brute force attack involves using a password that was leaked from one website to try to log into other websites?

3. What type of brute force attack uses a list of common passwords as a starting point to guess passwords?

4. What mitigation technique prevents a brute force attack from trying a large number of successive passwords against a user account?

Topic 13E

Mitigate Social Engineering Attacks

EXAM OBJECTIVES COVERED
4.5 Describe types of attacks and their effects on data systems.

Social engineering is a manipulation technique that exploits human behavior and human error in order to gain private information, access, or valuables. People—employees, contractors, suppliers, and customers—represent part of the attack surface of any organization. A person with permissions on a system is a potential target of social engineering. Understanding social engineering techniques will help you avoid falling prey to them and perhaps help you educate others to be more aware.

Describing Social Engineering Principles

Adversaries can use a diverse range of techniques to compromise a security system. A prerequisite of many types of attacks is to obtain information about the network and security system. Social engineering refers to means of either eliciting information from someone or getting them to perform some action for the threat actor. It can also be referred to as "hacking the human." Social engineering might be used to gather intelligence as reconnaissance in preparation for an intrusion, or it might be used to perform an actual intrusion.

Social engineering is one of the most common and successful malicious techniques. Because it exploits basic human trust, social engineering has proven to be a particularly effective way of manipulating people into performing actions that they might not otherwise perform. To be persuasive, social engineering attacks rely on one or more of the following principles.

Familiarity/Liking

Some people have the sort of natural charisma that allows them to persuade others to do as they request. One of the basic tools of a social engineer is simply to be affable and likable, and to present the requests they make as completely reasonable and unobjectionable.

This approach is relatively low risk. Even if the request is refused, it is less likely to cause suspicion, allowing the social engineer to move on to a different target without being detected.

Consensus/Social Proof

The principle of consensus or social proof refers to the fact that without an explicit instruction to behave in a certain way, many people will act just as they think others would act. A social engineering attack can exploit this instinct to coerce the target into acting a certain way. For example, if the victim hesitates to concede to a request, the attacker might suggest that refusing the request would be odd ("That's not something anyone else has ever said no to"). An attacker might also take advantage of someone's polite behavior by slipping into a building while someone holds the door for them.

This type of attack doesn't have to occur in person. For example, an attacker might fool a user into believing that a malicious website is actually legitimate by posting numerous fake reviews and testimonials praising the site. The victim, believing many different people have judged the site to be acceptable, takes this as evidence of the site's legitimacy and places their trust in it.

Authority and Intimidation

Many people find it difficult to refuse a request by someone they perceive as superior in rank or expertise. Thus, social engineers may attempt to intimidate their target by pretending to be a senior executive, police officer, judge, doctor, or any other authority figure. Another technique that falls under this category is using spurious technical arguments and jargon. Few people are willing to admit ignorance and may go along with the request simply to avoid admitting they don't understand it.

Compared to using a familiarity/liking sort of approach, this sort of adversarial tactic might be riskier to the attacker, as there is a greater chance of arousing suspicion and the target reporting the attack attempt.

Scarcity and Urgency

The social engineer may try to pressure their target by creating a false sense of scarcity or urgency, which can disturb people's ordinary decision-making process, and demanding a quick response. For example, they might approach the target with a "limited time" or "invitation-only" trial and request a username and password to sign up the service (hoping that the target will offer a password they have used for other accounts). Fake antivirus products generate a sense of urgency by trying to trick users into thinking that their computer is already infected with malware.

Identifying Phishing Attacks

Phishing is one of the most common types of social engineering. In this type of attack, the attacker persuades or tricks the target into interacting with a malicious resource disguised as a trusted one, traditionally using email as the vector. A phishing message might try to convince the user to perform some action, such as installing disguised malware or allowing a remote access connection by the attacker. Other types of phishing campaigns will imitate a bank, e-commerce site, or some other web resource that should be trusted by the target. The attacker emails users of the genuine website with a hoax alert or alarm (such as informing them that their account must be updated or that their password needs to change due to a breach). The email supplies a disguised link that looks like it leads to the genuine website but actually leads to the fake site. When the user authenticates with the fake site, their login credentials are captured.

Below is an example of a phishing email. On the right, you can see the message in its true form, as the mail client has stripped out the formatting (shown on the left) that is designed to disguise the nature of the links.

Example Phishing Email

There are several phishing variants that you should be aware of: spear phishing, smishing, and vishing.

Spear Phishing

Spear phishing is a phishing scam where the attacker has some information that makes an individual target more likely to be fooled by the attack. In spear phishing, the message is custom tailored to address a specific target user. The attacker might know the name of a document that the target is editing, for instance, and could send a copy that tricks the target, who would not suspect anyone to know the name of the document. The phishing email might contain personal details about the recipient, such as their full name, job title, telephone number, or other details, thereby convincing the target that the communication is genuine. Another technique used in spear phishing is to make the email appear to have come from a co-worker or manager.

Smishing

Smishing is a phishing scam that utilizes text messaging instead of email. Due to the limited capability of text messaging, smishing messages will either provide a link for the user to follow or a phone number for the user to call in order to initiate the attack.

In the smishing message below, the user is told they have made a large purchase and should call the included number to cancel the charge. A false sense of urgency is created by indicating the charge was for a large sum of money, forcing an individual to react without a lot of thought.

Example Smishing Message

Vishing

Vishing is a phishing scam that utilizes voice communication instead of email. In this type of attack, a recorded message typically communicates an urgent situation that requires the individual's immediate response. The individual is given a phone number to call in order to "address the urgent situation." During the call, the individual is manipulated into providing data to or performing a task for the attacker.

Mitigating Social Engineering Attacks

When information technology teams follow security best practices, individuals are less likely to be exposed to social engineering attacks. The use of firewalls, antivirus, antimalware, approved lists, and spam filters will help keep malicious traffic to a minimum. Using endpoint security software can prevent an individual from downloading malicious software or navigating to a site that has been flagged as malicious. Applying patches and keeping your systems up to date can protect the organization from known software and network vulnerabilities.

However, because social engineering attacks exploit human psychology and behavior, mitigation requires more than just a technical solution. Even the most advanced technical techniques cannot completely eliminate the human factor. Therefore, one of the most successful mitigation strategies to help defend against social engineering is education. Every individual within an organization is responsible for avoiding social engineering attacks.

An organization should require all its employees to participate in a comprehensive cybersecurity awareness education program. This type of program serves to make the individuals in an organization more knowledgeable about social engineering as a whole and increase vigilance. Social engineering attacks often rely on catching an individual off guard. An individual who does not pay close attention to their environment and their actions is most vulnerable. Regular training will break the individual's unconscious habits and increase their vigilance for attempted social engineering attacks, which is one of the most powerful tools to combat these types of attacks.

Review Activity:

Social Engineering Attacks

Answer the following questions:

1. In which principle of social engineering does the attacker try to pressure their target by demanding a quick response?

2. What is a red flag that can help identify a message as a phishing attempt?

3. What is the most effective strategy for preventing social engineering attacks?

4. How is spear phishing different than phishing?

Topic 13F

Mitigate Malware

EXAM OBJECTIVES COVERED
4.5 Describe types of attacks and their effects on data systems.

Malware is malicious software that is specifically designed to disrupt, damage, or exploit an endpoint or network. Malware can be used to access private data, steal or destroy data, encrypt information, spy on users, extort money, or take control of a system. Malware can access computers or networks using various methods, including infected email attachments, pop-up and web advertisements, applications, and websites. Many of the intrusion attempts perpetrated against computers and computer networks depend on the use of malware. Malware is usually simply defined as software that does something bad, from the perspective of the system owner, but there are many types of malware that each behave differently.

Identifying Types of Malware

There are many types, or categories, of malware. Malware is not classified in a rigorous way, so some definitions overlap or are blurred. Some malware classifications focus on the vector used by the malware, or the method by which the malware executes on a computer and potentially spreads to other network hosts. Another complicating factor with malware classification is the degree to which its installation is expected or tolerated by the user. The following categories describe some types of malware according to vector:

- **Viruses** are perhaps the most classic form of malware. Viruses function much like their biological namesake. They can infect an endpoint, proliferate throughout the system, and change how it works. They can also multiply and spread from system to system in a network.

- **Worms** behave much like viruses, infecting, multiplying, and spreading through network endpoints. Unlike viruses, they do not need to be attached to a program or activated by a user to be activated. This is an attribute that makes them particularly destructive.

- **Ransomware** is an increasingly popular malware that uses encryption to block legitimate users from being able to access their systems, devices, or information. The attacker will only return control to the rightful users if their demands are met. To add pressure, attackers often threaten to destroy or release the data.

- **Spyware** is malicious software that can steal data and monitor user activity, like specific keystrokes. Spyware can also access computer cameras and microphones. The data gathered using spyware could be valuable or could help instigate further cyberattacks—for example, when login information is stolen and can be used to authenticate as a valid user.

- **Adware** is not as dangerous as the other types of malware on this list, but it can cause a high degree of frustration. Once adware infects a computer, the user's online activity data is compromised and used to force the user to view advertisements, which benefits advertisers financially.

- **Trojans** disguise themselves as something a user wants, like a software update or the latest popular game, to gain access to a system. This can open the gates to additional cyberattacks like ransomware or spyware.

- **Potentially unwanted programs (PUPs) or potentially unwanted applications (PUAs)** are software programs installed alongside a package selected by the user, or perhaps bundled with a new computer system. Unlike a Trojan, the presence of a PUP is not automatically regarded as malicious. It may have been installed without active consent or with consent from a purposefully confusing license agreement. This type of software is sometimes described as grayware rather than malware.

Given the range of malware types, there are many potential indicators that your system is infected. Some types of malware cause obvious changes, such as adjusting browser settings or displaying ransom notices. If the malware is designed to operate covertly, a detailed analysis of processes, file systems, and network behavior will need to be conducted to spot the indicators. These more covert indicators will often take the form of increased system utilization.

For example, in the case of ransomware, the system may exhibit increased CPU utilization and file system utilization due to the modification and encryption of local files. In the case of malware that exfiltrates data, increased outbound network traffic will be present. Some malware will attempt to download additional malware, and in doing so, incoming network traffic will increase. This type of system activity can easily go unnoticed by most casual system users.

Mitigating Malware Attacks

Although malware can affect databases and database servers—and thus, the DBA—the responsibility of preventing malware does not fall solely on the DBA. While an organization's information technology and security teams are responsible for implementing a strategy to combat malware, it is the job of every individual in an organization to defend against malware attacks. Similar to the prevention of social engineering attacks, diligence and awareness practiced by all individuals in an organization will go a long way toward prevention of malware attacks. But there are some additional methods that can be used to prevent malware attacks, or at least keep the damage done by a successful malware attack to a minimum.

- **Use security software.** Security software is an essential part of an organization's defense against malware. Antivirus, antimalware, anti-ransomware, and other constantly evolving technologies help detect threats and protect devices and networks. These tools should protect browsers, endpoints, servers, and an organization's network from compromise.

- **Use strong passwords and secure authentication.** Best practices for password policies, as discussed previously, should be enforced in order to strengthen passwords. Strong passwords can help prevent malware from gaining access to a user's credentials, which could allow further attacks or privilege escalation. Because even the most robust password can be stolen, we also use multifactor authentication to add another layer of security.

- **Use a password manager.** Another best practice is to use a password manager to keep your credentials organized. Password managers promote the creation of unique and strong passwords for each website or application.

- **Educate users.** Every user in your organization plays a vital role in protecting the organization from cyberattack. As mentioned in a previous section, users should be provided cybersecurity awareness training on types of cybersecurity attacks and how to report something they find suspicious. By holding regular training sessions that cover these vital topics, an organization can effectively multiply the size of their security team.

- **Enforce safe emailing and browsing.** Much of the threat malware poses can be avoided by making sure users follow safe browsing practices and keep an eye out for unusual emails or links. Users must diligently and thoroughly scrutinize emails they receive, looking for unusual email addresses, incorrect formatting or spelling in the text, or unusual requests (like asking you to share confidential information). Users should apply equal scrutiny when it comes to Internet use. As discussed in a previous section, users should not connect to public wireless networks or visit any websites that aren't secure and don't have a URL beginning with "https."

- **Maintain up-to-date software.** Information technology teams must install new versions of software, systems, browsers, etc. as quickly as possible. Updates often include new security features and fewer vulnerabilities. Failing to keep systems updated can open a network up to attack. Further, any technologies or software no longer in use should be completely removed, as older software often has numerous vulnerabilities.

Review Activity:

Malware

Answer the following questions:

1. What type of malware uses encryption to block legitimate users from being able to access their systems, devices, or information?

2. What type of malware disguises itself as something a user wants, like a software update or the latest popular game, to gain access to a system?

3. How does implementing best practice password policies help mitigate malware?

4. What practice can help every user in an organization become an effective member of the security team?

Lesson 13

Summary

After this lesson, you should be familiar with some of the more common types of cyberattacks and how they may be mitigated. You should be able to recognize SQL statements that are vulnerable to SQL injection attacks and be able to identify the type of user input that can cause them. You should understand the difference between a denial of service attack and a distributed denial of service attack. You should also understand that attackers use on-path attacks to intercept network traffic and steal data. You should be familiar with the different techniques for brute force attacks. You should know that social engineering attacks take advantage of human behavior and human psychology. You should also be able to recognize a phishing attack or one of its variants. You should recognize the different categories of malware and what they aim to accomplish.

Guidelines for Mitigating Types of Cyberattacks

Consider these best practices and guidelines when mitigating cyberattacks.

1. **Use parameterized SQL statements when incorporating user input as parameters.**

2. **Sanitize all user inputs into an application or system.**

3. **Set applications and databases to lock a user's account after a certain number of failed login attempts.**

4. **Disable all unused services and uninstall all unused features in order to reduce the attack surface.**

5. **Only visit secure websites with "https" in the URL.**

6. **Enable multifactor authentication when available.**

7. **Do not connect to unsecured public networks.**

8. **Take part in regular cybersecurity awareness training.**

9. **Use monitoring software and logging to detect unusual activity concerning authentication that can identify an ongoing brute force attack.**

10. **Scrutinize emails, websites, and links for signs of untrustworthy content.**

Lesson 14

Planning for Disaster Recovery

LESSON INTRODUCTION

Disaster can strike when you least expect it. If an organization is not prepared, it can be devastating. Being prepared does not mean that disastrous and unplanned events won't happen, but it does help minimize the effects of a disaster. An organization that has developed strategies for disaster recovery can continue to operate or quickly resume key operations after an unplanned event occurs.

Lesson Objectives

In this lesson, you will do the following:

- Plan for disaster recovery (DR).

- Conduct DR plan testing.

- Transition/failback to normal operations.

Topic 14A

Plan for Disaster Recovery

 EXAM OBJECTIVES COVERED
3.1 Explain the purpose of monitoring and reporting for database management and performance.
5.1 Explain the importance of disaster recovery and relevant techniques.

The most obvious case for a business-related disaster is a catastrophic event that physically destroys an organization's primary site or location, such as a tornado, fire, or human-made disaster. But less evident events can be equally devastating to the operations of an organization. Corruption or loss of data, security breaches, and service or utility outages can all impact the regular operations of an organization. Even the loss of key personnel can have a major impact on operations. Regardless of the degree of failure an organization may encounter, it must have a plan in place that addresses the necessary steps to restore operations.

Disaster Recovery Documentation

A **disaster recovery (DR) plan** is a formal document created by an organization that contains detailed instructions on how to respond to unplanned incidents. A successful DR plan must address all types of operational disruption, and not just the major natural or human-made disasters that prevent the normal operations of an organization. Keep in mind that even temporary disruptions should be addressed in the DR plan. Some common incidents that a DR plan should be prepared to address include the following:

- Natural disasters, like tornadoes, hurricanes, and earthquakes

- Network access, power, or telephone system outages

- Cyberattacks

- Bomb or other violent threats against a location

- Nondestructive fire or flood

- Failure of heating or cooling system

In order for a DR plan to be effective, it must be created as a team effort. No one individual in an organization typically has the breadth and depth of knowledge to understand the level of detail that is required in a good DR plan. The DBA will often be a member of this team, assigned to address the operational needs and dependencies of database-related tasks. But the team must also include members from the technology and business sectors of an organization. The DR plan is not just technical documentation; it will also include communication protocols, information about alternate work sites, and work arrangements.

Keep in mind that even if every bit of an organization's information technology is outsourced or all of their infrastructure is in the cloud, someone will still need to know who to contact and whose job it is to do so.

DR documentation will supply a detailed roadmap that can be followed by anyone in an organization. In a true disaster situation, there is no guarantee that any particular employee will be available to carry out a particular task. Every missing or incorrect step in the process will result in lost time and require delays while missing information or processes are re-created.

A DR plan should be organized by the type and location of the disaster. In fact, some types of events will warrant their own dedicated document (or set of documents), although they would still be considered part of an organization's overall DR strategy.

A DR plan is a "living document" because an organization's business needs, technology, team structure, and infrastructure are constantly changing or being updated. These changes must be accounted for in the DR plan as they occur. Delays in recognizing these changes, and updating the DR plan accordingly, can mean delays or mistakes made in getting an organization operational again after an event.

Elements of a Disaster Recovery Plan

The material included in a DR plan will vary depending on an organization's structure, type, and operational needs. However, there are certain elements that should be consistent for any organization conducting disaster recovery planning.

Communication and Roles

Two of the most important and necessary elements of a DR plan are as follows:

1. Who will do what

2. How to contact all the necessary people

The roles of team members must be clearly outlined, so we know who to go to for what purpose after a disaster occurs. It is also beneficial to designate primary and backup personnel for certain key roles, in the event that someone cannot be reached in an emergency. Contact information for staff members who are essential to disaster recovery efforts needs to be kept up to date and readily accessible, so they can be immediately contacted following a damaging event. Don't forget that providers and third-party contract staff may be included as essential personnel.

The DR plan should also detail how to establish communication in a reliable way with the entire organization, to communicate changes in status and work arrangements during the recovery process. Another consideration is how to communicate with customers who may be affected by disruptions in operations.

An organization that provides support services to customers will need to prioritize continued access to support staff during the disaster recovery effort. It may be necessary to provide alternative means for customers to contact support staff, such as setting up a call center in an alternate emergency location or routing calls directly to support staff temporarily working from their homes.

Systems and Asset Inventory

A DR plan should include an inventory of systems and assets that must be replaced in the event of a disaster. It's important to note that the DR plan focuses on assets required to return the organization to minimal operation. So while desks and other furniture might be affected by a disaster event, and will surely be important in an insurance claim, these types of assets would not be included in the DR plan. Assets that are often in the DR plan include the following:

- Servers

- Laptop and desktop computers

- Networking equipment

- Phones and printers

In addition to the asset inventory, a DR plan will need to include network and infrastructure diagrams, as well as message and data flow diagrams. All of these diagrams will be essential to an organization attempting to plan and prioritize the tasks necessary for operational recovery.

A company that outsources some or all of their information technology to a hosting or cloud provider will have a smaller list of physical assets. However, companies should be aware of exactly what their agreements with providers and vendors describe when it comes to disaster recovery.

System Dependencies and Prioritization

Similar to the system inventory and data flow diagrams mentioned previously, detailing which systems and applications interact with others is essential to the DR plan. Without understanding these interactions, a dependency of a mission critical system or application might be missed. The plan should identify the systems and applications that are mission critical and thus need to be reestablished and/or restarted first. It should also list all systems and applications whose recovery can be delayed alongside their levels of priority. For example, a point-of-sale payment system and a customer-facing application would likely need to be restored first, and thus would be higher priority.

The aftermath of a disaster is not the time to attempt to remember what systems or applications have what dependencies. If these dependencies and priorities are not identified in the DR plan, mistakes will be made that could lead to delays in getting an organization operational.

Manuals and Build Documentation

It is beneficial to have access to system and operations manuals in the event of a disaster scenario. A system or operational manual will not only provide documentation on the system or application being restored, but will also cut down on the amount of information that must be written into the DR documentation directly. A DR plan can simply refer to the manuals of certain systems and applications in order to provide instruction on initialization and configuration. It is important to note that any manual or build documents that are referenced by a DR plan should be located with the DR plan. (Copies of these documents are acceptable.)

Some applications and software systems will need to be built before they are functional. If the systems and applications manuals don't include the instructions for build out, then it is also important to include this build documentation in the DR plan. Remember that there are no guarantees certain team members will be available during the recovery from a disaster. Thus, we cannot assume technical staff or others who remember all the requirements to build a system will be available. If build documentation is available, it should be included or referenced in the DR plan.

Regulatory Compliance

Most industries have regulatory obligations regarding documenting, reporting on, and identifying future protection against further instances of a disaster. If an organization is subject to regulations that require reporting after an operational outage or breach, this must be included in the DR plan. Examples of regulations that require some, or all, of these are HIPAA, PCI DSS, and ISO 27001.

Business Continuity and System Security

There are two other plans that have their own function but are often associated with DR plans. Some organizations will include these plans in their DR plan, but they can also stand on their own because of their specific areas of focus.

Business Continuity Plans

Some people consider a **business continuity plan (BCP)** and disaster recovery plan to be the same thing. However, while they are very similar, they have different goals. Business continuity focuses on keeping an organization operational *during* a disaster, while disaster recovery focuses on restoring data access and IT infrastructure *after* a disaster. Many organizations need both things to happen at the same time, and thus DR plans will often incorporate a BCP.

Because business continuity is concerned with keeping the day-to-day operations of an organization functioning while the infrastructure of the organization is being rebuilt, a BCP will typically detail alternate physical locations, backup processes, and alternate communication methods. DR strategies, on the other hand, may include other extraordinary needs that would come about due to an extraordinary event, such as purchasing emergency supplies. Combining the two allows a business to place equal focus on maintaining operations and ensuring that employees are safe.

Alternate Location Types

Depending on the needs of an organization, having an alternate physical location (as detailed in the BCP) may be a necessity. There are three terms used to describe the readiness of an alternate location.

A **hot site** is one that contains office space (if necessary), has power, and is populated with all necessary servers, equipment, and infrastructure. Its data and systems are kept up to date constantly. In a disaster scenario, a hot site is ready to take the place of the main location immediately.

A **cold site** is one that contains office space (if necessary) and has power but does not contain any infrastructure or equipment. In the case of a disaster scenario, a cold site would require a large amount of effort from engineering and IT in order to be operational.

A **warm site** is a middle ground between a hot site and a cold site. A warm site contains office space (if necessary), has power, and is populated with all necessary equipment and infrastructure. The difference between a warm site and a hot site is that while a warm site contains the necessary equipment, the systems have not yet been installed and configured, and they do not contain any data. So in a disaster scenario, the latest software will need to be installed and data loaded in order to make the location operational.

System Security Plans

While DR plans do address recovery efforts after a cyberattack, most cybersecurity incidents require a separate **system security plan**. Although DR plans and system security plans are related, their objectives are inherently different and can even sometimes conflict with each other. Disaster recovery is ultimately about business continuity, but security recovery is about protecting information assets.

A security plan provides the high-level structure for an organization's data protection policy and practices, including contingency planning and preventative activities that will take place prior to a security event. A DR plan specifies the steps an organization will follow to rebuild and reestablish its assets after an incident. Further, while DR plans are ideally made available to a response team that is as large as possible, a security plan will most likely require a smaller, more dedicated, and specialized team.

The way an organization responds to a security incident will require a detailed analysis of the root cause of the incident, the collection of evidence throughout a network and its logs, and often a more stealthy response to the event. But disaster recovery efforts are, by nature, very public events. They often require some level of effort from the entire organization and large-scale communications.

Like a DR plan, a system security plan will also need to be a "living document" that is updated when new vulnerabilities are discovered in an organization's assets, changes occur in the security industry as a whole, and updates are made to regulations and compliance requirements affecting the organization.

Replication

While a DR plan provides the steps and activities an organization will follow in order to reestablish normal operations as quickly as possible, there are techniques that can be employed on an ongoing basis that will support that goal in the event of an incident. The first we'll discuss is replication.

Replication can be used to replicate an organization's essential operations and data at a secondary site. This secondary site will become operational when the primary site is rendered unavailable for any reason. Replication of database data utilizes a system called a **distributed database management system (DDBMS)**. The DDBMS ensures that changes, additions, and deletions performed on data at any given location are automatically reflected in the data stored at all other locations. The two main methods of replication are synchronous and asynchronous replication.

Synchronous replication is a technique in which changes to data are copied to a database server called the model server and then replicated to all the replica servers before the original system is notified that the data has been replicated. This takes longer to verify than the asynchronous method, because all replica servers must be updated prior to notifying the original system, but it presents the advantage of knowing that all data was copied before proceeding. Because of its time-intensive nature, an organization may be forced to restrict the geographic distance between sites in order to keep delays lower.

Asynchronous replication is a technique in which changes to data are first copied to a database server called the model, or leader, which responds back to the system where the data change originated and confirms that the data was received. At that point, the data is copied to the replicas at an unspecified or monitored pace. There are no distance limits to where the replica systems can be located, which would be beneficial in the case of a large-scale disaster that could potentially damage an alternate site that is near the primary site.

Since replication of data changes is ongoing, systems that use this data can simply be pointed to one of the alternative sites in the event that a disaster renders the primary site inoperable.

Log Shipping

In a database server, the transaction log records all transactions along with the database modifications made by each transaction. This transaction log is critical for a database server in order to recover from unexpected failures. If a database server fails, not all the data from a transaction might have been committed to the database from the data buffer. This transaction log can be used to complete or roll back transactions against the database that were not committed properly.

Log shipping is the process of automating the backup of transaction log files on a primary database server, and then restoring them onto a standby, or alternate, server. One of the benefits of log shipping is that it has a low cost in regard to human and server resources. Unlike other methods of updating alternate database instances, there is no need for an extra server to facilitate the data synchronization. But there are some disadvantages to log shipping. The alternate database won't be fully available until the log restore process is complete, and there is no possibility of automatically switching to the alternate database in the event of a disaster.

Monitor Servers

Given the criticality of the log actually making it to the alternate server and being restored properly, it only makes sense to monitor this log shipping process. When setting up log shipping, a monitor server may also be set up to monitor the log shipping process and provide alert notifications when any part of the process fails. Without a monitor server, alerts would need to be sent from the primary or the secondary database instances. But if there is an issue on either of these servers, an alert may not be created. So, a monitor server is a remote server that is isolated from both the primary and secondary servers, and thus not affected by problems on those servers.

A monitor server tracks information about the primary and secondary servers involved in log shipping. It also tracks each log shipping operation in order to determine success or failure. For this reason, it is important that a monitor server be set up as part of the initial log shipping setup. If a monitor server is set up after log shipping has been configured and begun, the log shipping will need to be replaced and reconfigured. In this way, the monitor server can be part of the log shipping operation from the beginning.

High Availability

A high availability database is a database system designed to operate continuously with no interruptions in service. **High availability** does not mean the system never encounters errors; it just means the system has enough redundancy to handle errors without causing a wider failure. Database errors and failures must be handled by automatically failing over to redundant nodes. High availability involves the elimination of single points of failure, which enables systems to continue to operate even if one of the components it depends on (such as a server) fails. This is accomplished by having more than one database server that can be used as the primary at any point in time.

When the database that is run on a primary server, or node, fails, database operations can be moved to one or more alternate servers, or nodes, where operation continues. High availability is usually accomplished in one of three ways: active-passive databases, active-active databases, and multi-active databases.

- **Active-passive databases** have an active node that processes requests with a spare that is always running and is ready to go in a disaster. The active-passive availability model works on the two-node concept of one node receiving all requests that it then replicates to its follower.

- **Active-active databases** have at least two active nodes that each store a subset of the data and perform writes to the database. Once the writes have occurred, the written data can be synchronized to the other nodes. But since each node can write data, each node has its own keys for that data. So synchronization between nodes is handled by consensus. Once multiple nodes "agree" on the newly written and synchronized data, the write is committed to all nodes. Active-active availability is evolved from active-passive, enabling databases to scale beyond single machines by letting multiple nodes in a cluster serve reads and writes.

- **Multi-active databases** require that a database has at least three active nodes, each of which can perform reads and writes for any data in the cluster without generating conflicts like the active-active availability mode.

Mirroring

Database mirroring maintains two copies of a single database that must reside on different server instances of SQL Server Database Engine. Typically, these server instances reside on computers in different locations. One server instance serves the database data to clients. This is the principal server. The other instance is the mirror server, which acts as a standby server.

Database mirroring involves redoing every insert, update, and delete operation that occurs on the principal database in the mirror database as quickly as possible. Redoing is accomplished by sending a stream of active transaction log records to the mirror server, which applies log records to the mirror database, in sequence, as quickly as possible. Mirroring is a real-time synchronization of changes, just as the name suggests. In mirroring, database failover is automated.

The key difference between mirroring and replication is what is being copied. Replication is performed on database objects, copying them from one database to another copy of the database. Mirroring is performed on a complete database.

Review Activity:

Disaster Recovery

Answer the following questions:

1. **True or False: A business continuity plan is sufficient to respond to any disastrous event.**

2. **A disaster recovery plan should address any type of disaster that can interrupt what?**

3. **True or False: If an organization's entire infrastructure is outsourced to the cloud, they do not need a disaster recovery plan.**

4. **Why do we refer to a disaster recovery plan as a living document?**

5. **What is the primary difference between log shipping and mirroring?**

6. **High availability implies the elimination of what?**

Topic 14B

Conduct DR Plan Testing

EXAM OBJECTIVES COVERED
5.1 Explain the importance of disaster recovery and relevant techniques.

Most organizations understand the importance of having a DR plan. Those that have gone through the process of creating a DR plan also know the huge amount of effort that is involved with putting a DR plan together. But after going through all of that effort, too many organizations assume that the plan is effective without actually having tested it. The reality is that a DR plan is purely theoretical until it has been put into practice. An organization should not wait until disaster happens to find out if their plan effectively covers all the things it should. At that point, it is too late to make changes and fill in any gaps in the plan.

DR Plan Testing Methods

The only way to truly find out if a DR plan is effective prior to an event requiring its use is to test it. Testing a DR plan will allow an organization to assess the plan's efficacy and make any necessary changes before an actual disaster strikes. A thorough DR plan will actually include a provision for testing the plan. Best practice suggests that a DR plan be tested at least once a year, although changes in an organization might require the plan to be tested more often. There are generally five methods of testing a DR plan: checklist testing, walkthrough testing, simulation testing, parallel testing, and full interruption testing.

Checklist Testing

In checklist testing, all members of the team responsible for developing the plan will review the plan in detail, looking for any inconsistencies or gaps. This form of testing helps to ensure that all of the procedures are fully explained and that all the proper personnel and resources are specified for each step of the process.

Walkthrough Testing

Much like checklist testing, walkthrough testing involves going step-by-step through the DR plan. But walkthrough testing goes a step further, requiring the personnel involved to actually work through all the components of the plan. Not only does this method of testing help identify any gaps in the plan, but it also confirms that each responsible party in the process understands what they are supposed to do in the case of an actual unplanned event.

Simulation Testing

In simulation testing, a particular disaster scenario is selected to test, and all responsible parties in the DR plan role-play through the plan components. This type of testing most closely mimics a real disaster scenario without causing any disruption to regular business operations. A simulation test should incorporate all the components of a DR plan, even going so far as installing software components on local systems (instead of actual production systems), physically changing locations, or making calls to the contact phone numbers in the plan.

Parallel Testing

Parallel testing involves building and using the recovery systems that would be implemented as part of the DR plan in a real interruptive event. These recovery systems built for testing are identical in specification to production systems, but run in parallel. The production systems will still be actively servicing all of the real load of the production environment, but the recovery systems will be tested with real production data in a production-like environment. This type of testing will provide a much deeper analysis of the DR plan, as it's the closest you can get to the real thing.

Full Interruption Testing

As the name suggests, full interruption testing is the most disruptive type of test, in which real production systems and data are used as though a disaster has happened. The only difference is the disaster is purely fictional for purposes of the test. The type of testing will be much more time consuming and will actually disrupt business operations. Therefore, it's typically scheduled for windows of time where a business could withstand an outage. By the time an organization attempts a full interruption test, they should have already successfully performed some of the other test methods in order to identify and correct gaps. While this type of testing may seem extreme, it is the only way to be completely assured that the DR plan is effective.

Recovery Time Objective (RTO)

One metric an organization can use to determine if DR plan testing was successful is the **recovery time objective (RTO)**, which is determined during the creation of an organization's DR plan. The RTO is effectively the time deadline in a disaster recovery situation for any system affected by the disaster. It is the maximum amount of time that a system can be down after a disruption has occurred before an organization's business processes are negatively affected. The RTO can be measured in as little as seconds or as much as days.

Keep in mind that there may be a separate RTO specified for different components of a DR plan. For example, an organization may consider their point-of-sale system to be mission critical, and thus its RTO will be lower than their email system, which may in turn be of lower priority than their employee vacation planning system.

The RTO can also drive the recovery technology used for a system. As an example, the point-of-sale system may have an RTO of 30 minutes in order to maintain the ability to accept orders. This would require database mirroring in order to allow for automatic switchover to a real-time updated recovery database, thus meeting its low RTO. But the vacation planning system might utilize a weekly backup that would take longer to restore after a disruption, because it has a much higher RTO.

Recovery Point Objective (RPO)

Another metric an organization can use to determine if DR plan testing was successful is the **recovery point objective (RPO)**, also determined during the creation of the organization's DR plan.

The RPO is the maximum amount of data loss a business can tolerate after a disruption has occurred before an organization's business processes are negatively affected. An organization's RPO will provide a clear understanding of how data loss would impact their business. While RTO is focused primarily on certain key systems in an organization, like the previous example of a point-of-sale system, RPO focuses more on business processes as a whole, and how loss of data will affect those business processes. Keep in mind that there may be a separate RPO specified for different components of a DR plan. The RPO is measured in terms of time, as little as minutes and as much as hours, that can elapse between the last successful data backup and the point of failure.

For example, an organization that handles financial transactions may specify an RPO of 10–15 minutes because losing financial transactions during recovery would be a critical issue. An extreme example would be a hospital or critical care facility, that might specify an RPO of zero (or very near zero) since losing any data regarding patients in critical health would be unacceptable. A toy manufacturer, on the other hand, might find that an RPO of 24 hours is acceptable.

Review Activity:

DR Plan Testing

Answer the following questions:

1. What disaster recovery testing technique results in the production system as well as the recovery system being active at the same time?

2. What is defined as the amount of time in which an organization's system must be recovered in a disaster recovery operation?

3. What disaster recovery testing technique involves role-playing through the DR plan components?

4. What is defined as the maximum amount of data loss a business can tolerate after a disruption has occurred before an organization's business processes are negatively affected?

Topic 14C

Transition/Failback to Normal Operations

EXAM OBJECTIVES COVERED
5.1 Explain the importance of disaster recovery and relevant techniques.

A solid and tested DR plan will help an organization manage a disastrous event with much more confidence and ease than if they are caught off guard. But what happens after a disaster, once operations have been restored and an organization's systems have been rebuilt or restored? How does an organization return to business as usual? If the organization had to move their operations to an alternate location, they would need to move back to their primary location, and if they had to move to an alternate infrastructure, they would need to move back to their primary infrastructure and systems. Organizations should also reflect on the DR process and ensure they are prepared for any other unintended event.

Disaster Recovery Failback

When disaster strikes, and an organization has to activate its alternate systems in order to restore operations, this is referred to as **failover**. This term is often used as an adjective to describe the alternate systems and locations, and as a verb referring to the act of moving operational processes to these systems. As an example, we might say that an organization will failover to the failover database. **Failback** is the opposite of failover; it involves returning a system that has been restored or recovered after a disaster or outage back to its original location, or back onto its primary infrastructure. Failback activity should be part of a DR plan's development and testing.

It is probably obvious that employees who were displaced and moved to an alternate location need to move back to an organization's primary location once it has been restored and made safe again. But it might be less obvious that applications and data restored to the failover infrastructure need to be moved back to the primary infrastructure once it has been rebuilt or restored to operation. Once these alternate systems are functional, it might seem counter-intuitive to go through another transition to a different system, even if it is the original. But in many cases, the alternate systems used to restore operations to an organization in a disaster do not share the same specifications as the original production systems and are not meant to support a production system in the long term. In fact, they are typically designed specifically to support only a certain percentage of the production capacity. They are a temporary stopgap to be used in the case of an event that disrupts an organization's operations.

After the failback to the primary systems, an organization should again prepare the failover (or alternate) systems for the next time they might be needed.

Disaster Recovery Retrospective

Imagine you've hiked up a challenging mountain, and you are both mentally and physically exhausted by the time you reach the peak. The last thing you're probably thinking about in that moment is "what's next." Going through a disaster of any kind has the same effect on an organization and its employees. An organization that has experienced a disaster, implemented its DR plan, and successfully failed back to its production and primary system and location may be exhausted. But there is one more step that should be taken before the matter can fully be considered settled: performing a post-event **retrospective**. This final step is often not considered when putting together a disaster recovery plan, but it should be.

During a retrospective, each person or group that was involved in the implementation of the DR plan will be allowed to communicate things that they thought went well and things they thought did not. Everyone's opinion must be given equal weight, and no opinion should be considered unimportant or irrelevant. No plan is perfect. A well-run retrospective will help an organization identify the things that went well and should be continued in future events, as well as any difficulties faced that may necessitate changes to the DR plan. It is never pleasant to consider that an organization might experience multiple disasters. But if the organization that has experienced a disaster takes the opportunity to learn from it, navigating any future events will be less difficult.

It is common for a retrospective to result in changes to the DR plan. Changes should be made to the DR plan to address any improvements to processes, documentation, personnel, and more that were identified during the retrospective activity.

Review Activity:

Transition/Failback to Normal Operations

Answer the following questions:

1. **Failback can only happen after _____.**

2. **A retrospective allows an organization to determine what about the implementation of a disaster recovery plan?**

3. **True or False: The specifications of failover systems are typically designed to support 100% of the typical production load.**

Lesson 14

Summary

After this lesson, you should understand why it is important to create and maintain a disaster recovery (DR) plan and be able to identify its components. You should understand the techniques involved when designing systems in preparation for disaster recovery. You should further understand the various methods used to test a disaster recovery plan and be able to explain the purpose that each method serves. You should understand how RTO and RPO can be used to measure the success of disaster recovery testing and why they are important in a disaster recovery scenario. You should also understand what it means to failback to a production, or primary, system or location. Finally, you should understand the importance of performing a retrospective post disaster recovery.

Guidelines for Disaster Recovery Planning

Consider these best practices and guidelines when creating and implementing a disaster recovery plan.

1. **A disaster recovery plan should be considered a living document and kept up to date as changes in an organization necessitate it.**

2. **Review the disaster recovery plan to verify it contains all the elements necessary to successfully recover from a disaster.**

3. **Testing of a disaster recovery plan should occur at least once a year and more frequently if major changes are made to the plan.**

4. **Whether it is a walkthrough test or a full interruption test, perform the highest method of testing that the organization will tolerate.**

5. **Determine, or help a larger team determine, an RTO and RPO based on an organization's requirements during the creation of a disaster recovery plan.**

6. **Once primary systems have been restored after a disaster, perform a failback to those systems and off the alternate systems.**

7. **Perform a retrospective post disaster recovery and update the disaster recovery plan based on the outcome.**

Lesson 15

Implementing Backup and Restore Best Practices

LESSON INTRODUCTION

Preparing for the possibility of media or hardware failure and restoring databases from valid backups after a disaster does occur are important responsibilities of the DBA. Backup and restore activities are a crucial part of business continuity, and essential in meeting the RTO and RPO defined in an organization's disaster recovery plan. There are multiple types of backups, and each type has a particular use case. A DBA should know which type of backup best fits what situation. It is also important that backups are tested regularly and stored properly in order to be available in the situations where they are needed.

Lesson Objectives

In this lesson, you will do the following:

- Identify types of backups.

- Implement a backup strategy.

- Store and purge backups.

Topic 15A

Identify Types of Backups

 EXAM OBJECTIVES COVERED
5.2 Explain backup and restore best practices and processes.

Databases support several types of backup operations. The most common backup types are a full backup, incremental backup, and differential backup. Less common types of backup operations are synthetic full backup and database dumping. Each has its own advantages and disadvantages. Further, not all databases support all backup types. You must consider all of these factors when considering which type of backup is right for your purposes.

Full Backup

A **full backup** is the most basic and complete type of backup operation, in which all the data is copied to a storage device or cloud storage location. Because of this, the full backup also serves as a base for other types of backups.

The primary advantage of performing a full backup during every operation is that a complete copy of all data is available with a single set of media. Because all the data is copied, a full backup offers the best protection and requires the least amount of time to restore the data. The main disadvantage of a full backup is that it takes longer to perform than other types of backups—sometimes significantly longer. It also requires more storage space.

Because of these factors, full backups are not typically run on a daily basis. It is more likely that a periodic full backup will be combined with other backup types in order to provide the necessary level of protection. That being said, there are some cases where performing a daily full backup is justified, such as when you're protecting a critical business application.

Incremental Backup

Unlike a full backup, an **incremental backup** does not copy all of the data in the database, but instead only backs up the data that has changed since the previous backup. The previous backup can be a full backup or another incremental backup.

Because incremental backups only back up what has changed, they require less time and storage space to run. While this seems ideal, there are some disadvantages, the biggest being that incremental backups can be time consuming to restore. Incremental backups only contain what has changed since the last backup. So if you're performing an incremental backup daily, and you need to restore data from the last week, you can't just restore from the most recent backup—you would need to restore the incremental backup from yesterday, and the day before that, and so on.

This process highlights another drawback, which is that you will be unable to restore all of your data if any of the incremental backups are lost. (This could happen, for example, if each incremental backup is stored on a separate disk and one of the disks is lost.)

To combat these disadvantages, it is best practice to perform full backups on a periodic basis alongside more frequent incremental backups. Each full backup creates a new starting point for the smaller incremental backups, preventing a large number of incremental backups from accumulating and minimizing that longer recovery time.

Differential Backup

Like an incremental backup, a **differential backup** also contains only changes in the data. But unlike an incremental backup, which backs up changes made since the last full or incremental backup, a differential backup will contain all changes made after the most recent full backup. What this effectively means is that each differential backup could replace the previous differential backup, instead of augmenting it. For example, suppose a full backup is created on Monday. A differential backup performed on Tuesday will contain all changes made since the full backup on Monday, and so will the differential backup performed on Wednesday, and Thursday, and so on until the next full backup is performed.

The biggest benefit of differential backups is that the recovery time is shorter, since only two backups are ever needed—the full backup and the latest differential backup. This is particularly advantageous in a disaster recovery scenario where the RTO is small and thus the speed at which data can be recovered is crucial.

However, as with most things, there are always trade-offs. Because differential backups contain all data since the last full backup, they can become quite large in size. Thus, it is best practice to perform full backups on a periodic basis to create new starting points for smaller differential backups. Even so, size is still a consideration when deciding which backup type to perform. Incrementals are the smallest option and might be your only choice if you're storing backups somewhere with limited space. Further, some database systems don't offer differential backups (or incremental, for that matter). All else equal, most DBAs would choose differential backups over incremental backups.

Synthetic Full Backup

A **synthetic full backup** is a variation of an incremental backup. When using an incremental backup strategy, a full backup is performed first, followed by one or more incremental backups. Similarly, using a synthetic full backup also starts with a full backup followed by one or more incremental backups. The difference is in what happens to the incremental backup and the resulting backup file. Unlike the incremental backup strategy, in the synthetic full backup strategy, each incremental backup after the initial full backup creates a new full backup file.

When using a synthetic full backup, the incremental backup is combined with the previous full backup to create a new full backup. The next incremental backup uses this new full backup as the starting point for its backup. The result is a new full backup which will be used as the starting point for the next incremental backup, and this cycle continues. The resulting full backup produced after each incremental backup when performing a synthetic full backup is the same as a full backup created normally.

The advantage of the synthetic backup is the speed of recovery that can be attained. A full backup can take a long time to create. If you're working with a very short RPO, you likely will need to make multiple backups throughout the day. Full backups wouldn't be fast enough, but you also don't want to have 30 backup files to restore (if it comes to that). A synthetic backup gives you the result of a full backup, with the speed of an incremental backup. Thus, synthetic backups are the best of both worlds.

The disadvantage of a synthetic full backup is that it overwrites the existing backup when it creates the new backup. This might seem like an advantage, as it saves storage space, but it does not allow you to maintain multiple versions of the backup. The resulting new backup will be the only version available, replacing the previous versions.

Database Dumping

A database dump is a logical backup of a database that generates a file called a **dump file**. This dump file contains all of the SQL statements that can be executed to re-create the original database and all of its contents. This includes both the DDL statements used to create the database schema, like all the database tables, as well as the DML statements used to add data into these tables.

Dump files are helpful when you need to restore a database without a traditional backup. The main disadvantage of the database dump is the time it takes to perform the restore process, as executing all of the SQL statements for a sizeable database can take a very long time.

A dump file can be created for a single table (or multiple tables) instead of the entire database. Thus, a database dump can also function as a way to simply export a single table that needs to be imported, or restored, to another database.

Review Activity:

Types of Backups

Answer the following questions:

1. **What type of backup produces smaller files but requires a longer restoration time?**

2. **Synthetic full backups combine the benefits of what two backup types?**

3. **A differential backup requires what type of backup to have been run prior?**

4. **What is a best practice when utilizing differential backups?**

Topic 15B

Implement a Backup Strategy

 EXAM OBJECTIVES COVERED
5.2 Explain backup and restore best practices and processes.

After you have identified the type of backup you need, the next step will be determining the overall strategy you will use to manage your backup. Your choice should take scheduling, testing, and validation into consideration. Each alternative strategy involves making trade-offs among backup and restore performance, the amount of data that is retained, data protection levels, and cost.

Scheduling Backups

Backups are essential to disaster recovery. The ability to recover data and databases quickly, and in compliance with an organization's RTOs and RPOs, requires the presence of reliable and timely backups. In order to ensure your backups are ready and available in the event of an interruption, you should schedule regular backups to occur at consistent times.

Although scheduling backups might seem like a simple task, there are several questions to ask yourself when creating a schedule strategy. Your answers to these questions will factor into how and when you schedule your backups.

- **What needs to be backed up?** Not all data, and not all databases, need to be backed up. For example, it might be possible to re-create a development database from a restored production database, thus eliminating the need to back up both. You don't want to back up more than you need, as this adds to the time it takes to back up and restore databases (and requires more storage resources).

- **What business requirements impact the timing of the schedule?** An organization may have business requirements that dictate when backups can be scheduled. For example, if an organization has identified a certain database as critical, it might need to be backed up hourly in order to meet the RPO for that data. This in turn may affect the type of backup that is scheduled, as you would most likely not want to perform a full backup hourly. On the other hand, if a full backup is required, you would typically schedule it outside of normal business operations, such as during the night or on weekends.

- **Are there any other processes that affect the timing of your backup?** Backing up a database will require memory, processing power, and storage availability. If other processes are running at the same time that a backup is scheduled, the backup may fail due to a lack of resources. In addition, it is important to make sure that backing up a database does not interfere in normal production activities. A backup should never consume resources necessary to keep a production system operating properly and at peak performance. For example, if your organization performs regular nightly data import tasks, the database backup should not interfere with these processes. Thus, you would need to schedule your backups around these other tasks.

- **What business requirements impact how often it should be scheduled?**
  How often a backup should be scheduled is largely driven by the organization's RPO for that data. If the RPO is an hour, then backups must be scheduled often enough to allow for no more than one hour of data loss. The priority level of the data is also a factor—critical data will need to be backed up more often than less critical data. Three of the most common backup schedules from a frequency standpoint are the following:

  a) Nightly full backups

  b) Weekly full backups followed by nightly differential backups

  c) Weekly full backups followed by nightly incremental backups

- **Is automation an option?** While an organization's DBA can, and sometimes does, manually perform backups, automation is the preferred option when available. Automation ensures that the backup is performed when it is supposed to be, regardless of the day or time. Scheduling software is typically used to automate backups. This type of software can be configured to send notifications when the backup has started and when it is complete (whether it was a success or failure).

Every organization will have unique needs, and thus there is no single solution to properly scheduling backups. You will need to evaluate the factors at play in your organization in order to determine the schedule that is the most appropriate for your needs.

Testing Backups

Database backups need to be tested to ensure their reliability, just like any other plan or activity we undertake. There are multiple methods of testing a database backup, and while any one can be used on its own, using all of the methods together is a best practice. This provides the most reliability, as backing up data is such a crucial process.

The first step when validating a database backup is to make sure that the backup was created successfully. While this may seem obvious, it may be overlooked if database backups are scheduled to occur automatically and there is no mechanism to receive notifications upon completion. How would you know if a backup failed? It is possible that a database backup might actually not exist. Utilizing notifications to report when a backup has succeeded or failed is a best practice that can increase your confidence in the backup being available when you need it.

The next step when validating your backup is confirming that it can actually be restored when the need arises. Many databases provide tools to validate that a backup is valid and can be restored. While these tools differ from database to database, the concept is the same. For example, Oracle databases use the recovery manager (RMAN), while SQL Server uses the recovery option flag VERIFYONLY. In either case, the tool will confirm that the backup file can be restored.

However, no matter how many tools are used or how many checks and balances are put in place, there is no substitute for the real thing. The best and most complete way to test a backup is to actually restore it. Best practice would be to periodically restore the most recent backup to a non-production database and validate that the restore succeeds and the data is available.

Validating Backup Hash

Testing a backup involves more than just making sure that the backup can be restored. It is also important to make sure that the data in the backup is not corrupted.

When a backup file is created, optionally a **checksum** hash can be created as well. A checksum feature, when used during a backup operation, can not only verify any existing checksums that exist at a data page level, but also generate a checksum for the entire database backup file. Each page is read from a disk when the backup operation starts, and a checksum is added to each page when it is added to the backup. Finally, a checksum for the whole backup file is calculated and compared with the sum of the checksums of each page.

A damaged backup can be identified by recalculating the checksum and comparing it against the checksum that is stored with the backup. If they don't match, there has been a corruption in the data. If a bad checksum is found while creating the backup, the backup process will be stopped. While there is no guarantee that this process will identify all corruption in the database, it is certainly a start.

Review Activity:

A Backup Strategy

Answer the following questions:

1. **Why is it important to consider storage location when creating a backup strategy?**

2. **When testing a backup, which method offers the most thorough validation?**

3. **When creating a scheduling strategy, what consideration is largely driven by RPO?**

4. **What can be utilized to ensure that a backup is performed when it is supposed to, regardless of the day or time?**

Topic 15C

Store and Purge Backups

EXAM OBJECTIVES COVERED
5.2 Explain backup and restore best practices and processes.

In a previous lesson, we discussed data retention policies, which define how inactive data is stored and disposed of. Backup retention policies serve the same purpose, but apply specifically to data backups. A backup retention policy determines what data an organization keeps, where the data is stored (off-site, on-site, or both), how long the data is retained, and how it is disposed of. The storage location of a database backup can impact both cost and the ability to quickly restore a backup, should the need arise. Before any decisions are made about where to store backup files, it's important to understand the different types of storage, the trade-offs involved in each, and the different ways they might be utilized. These storage decisions will also help drive the purging and archiving cycles that an organization abides by.

On-Site Storage

When backup files are stored on a local disc, drive, server, or other media, this is known as **on-site storage**, or on-premise storage. With on-site storage, backup files are stored at the organization's physical location.

The biggest advantage when using on-site storage for backups is that it is a simple and straightforward process to retrieve the backup files when they are needed. The organization maintains complete control over these files, which is especially important when working with sensitive and private data. However, there are a few disadvantages to on-site storage.

- When the backup files are stored locally, it is likely that a disaster affecting the organization's location and infrastructure will also affect the backup files; damaged or destroyed backup files will not be helpful in restoration and recovery after a disaster.

- On-site storage space is limited, and it can be expensive to continue to increase the space over time as backups get larger.

- The responsibility for securing any backup files that contain sensitive or private data falls on the organization.

Off-Site Storage

When backup files are stored on a remote server or on media that is transported off-site, this is known as **off-site storage**. There are a few forms of off-site storage that are frequently utilized for backups.

- A traditionally hosted server, or a server located at an alternate location for the organization

- A cloud storage server

- Physical media that is then shipped to a remote location where it is stored and secured

There are a few advantages to storing backup files off-site. The main benefit is that it is typically a less expensive solution, as most cloud-based storage providers allow an organization to pay only for what they need. An additional benefit is that cloud-based storage providers and professional remote storage providers leverage state-of-the-art security to protect their storage systems, which means the organization can be confident that any sensitive and private data is well guarded.

When you utilize off-site storage, you typically only pay for the amount of storage space you need. So while the initial cost might be low, as the amount of data you're backing up grows, so too will the cost. Thus, it is important to consider what data actually needs to be backed up in order to keep the demands on storage as low as possible.

The main disadvantage of off-site storage is that timely access to the backup files can be challenging. Files that are located in a remote location will take time to physically retrieve. Even in a cloud-based scenario, where an organization has 24-hour real-time access to the files, they would still take time to download. Depending on an organization's RTO, the time to retrieve files from any remote storage location might be restrictive.

Rotating Both On-Site and Off-Site

While we've talked about the advantages and disadvantages of on-site and off-site storage, it might not be necessary to choose between them. In fact, the best choice may be both. Some organizations use a combination of on-site and off-site storage, rotating backup files between the two storage locations.

To decide how this rotation occurs, we use what's known as the **3-2-1 backup rule**. This best practice states that an organization should have *three* copies of the data stored on *two* different types of media, with *one* copy of the media stored off-site. The two copies of the backup data that are stored locally can be quickly accessed. The copies are stored on two different types of media to protect against one particular type of media being rendered unusable. For example, if one of the media is a storage server, and that server is corrupted, the second media may still be viable. The off-site copy of the backup is the copy that will be used in the event of a disaster, ransomware attack, or other incident at the organization's primary location. If a disaster affecting the local site destroys the two local copies, the organization will be able to recover by retrieving the off-site backup from the cloud or remote storage location. So while the local backup copies offer quicker access, the off-site backup serves as a critical safety net. This off-site copy is rotated out with an updated backup on a periodic basis, although the frequency of the rotation depends on an organization's RPO.

Combining on- and off-site storage is the ideal storage solution, as it's the only way to provide full coverage in the event of an accident or disaster. However, cost can be prohibitive for some organizations.

 Don't forget that an organization may also be required to abide by regulations that dictate how backups must be stored. Thus, you should consider both the trade-offs and the regulatory aspect when deciding where backup files that you schedule will be stored.

Purging and Archiving Data

An important function of a data retention policy is defining how data should be archived when it is no longer actively in use and how data should be destroyed, or purged, when it will no longer need to be accessed in the future. Usually this means the data will be stored on-site, off-site, or rotated between the two.

Archiving data is the process of moving data that is not currently in use to a separate storage device or location for long-term retention. Archived data most often consists of backups of older data that is important to retain because it may be needed in the future, even if it is not currently being referenced. Archived data may also include data that is required to be retained for regulatory compliance.

The location to which data is archived will depend on how accessible the data needs to be while it is archived. For example, if the archived data needs to be available for historical reporting, it might make sense to archive that data to a live database (just not the main production database) that is used for reporting only. On the other hand, if the data only needs to be accessible for legal reasons, it might make more sense, and be less costly, to archive the data to on-site storage. If the data is only being retained for compliance purposes, off-site storage may be more appropriate.

Purging data is the process of completely removing, or deleting, data that is no longer required—not now, and not in the future. Factors that play into the decision to purge data include the age, type, and confidentiality of the data. The data destruction techniques discussed in a previous lesson also apply to backups. Depending on the type of data, purging backups can be as simple as using a delete process or as complex as shredding a physical storage drive.

The archive and purge processes can extensively affect storage, network, and memory resources, which means running these processes can negatively affect users in a production system. A best practice, where possible, is to automate the archival and purging of data. If the criteria for when data should be archived and purged are well defined, then these processes can be automated and scheduled to run during a time where the impact to production systems will be minimized. This automation may also transfer any archived data to either an additional on-site location or an off-site, cloud-accessible location.

Review Activity:

Store and Purge Backups

Answer the following questions:

1. **Which type of storage provides a more rapid recovery time?**

2. **Which type of storage typically provides a more secure storage environment?**

3. **Which type of storage provides extra protection against disasters?**

4. **What best practice ensures backups are available in the event that a disaster destroys an organization's primary location?**

5. **True or False: Purge cycles only affect data that has been archived.**

6. **How can purging or archiving data negatively affect production systems?**

Lesson 15

Summary

After this lesson, you should understand why backup and restore processes are key in planning for disaster recovery. You should understand the different types of backups and how each is used. You should also understand the benefits and drawbacks of each type of backup. You should be able to implement various means of testing to validate that the backups will serve their intended purpose as recovery in the event of a disaster. You should understand the implications of storing backups on-site and off-site and why it is necessary to archive and purge data.

Guidelines for Implementing and Restoring Backups

Consider these best practices and guidelines when planning backup and restoration practices.

1. **Use an organization's RPO and RTO to aid in backup type decisions.**

2. **Automate and schedule backups to make sure they happen at the most appropriate time, when systems and resources will be least affected.**

3. **Test backup files regularly using multiple testing methods.**

4. **Validate backup files to ensure data has not been corrupted.**

5. **Rotate on-site and off-site storage of backups to ensure both rapid availability and disaster preparedness.**

6. **Automate purge cycles and, if necessary, archive cycles to minimize the impact on data system users.**

Appendix A

Mapping Course Content to CompTIA DataSys+ (Exam DS0-001) Objectives

Achieving CompTIA DataSys+ certification requires candidates to pass Exam DS0-001. This table describes where the exam objectives for Exam DS0-001 are covered in this course.

1.0 Database Fundamentals	
1.1 Compare and contrast database structure types.	**Covered in**
Relational vs. non-relational databases	Lesson 1, Topic A
Linear vs. non-linear format	Lesson 1, Topic B
NoSQL types	Lesson 1, Topic B
Document databases	
Key-value stores	
Column-oriented databases	
Graph databases	
Tools	Lesson 1, Topic B
Cassandra	
MongoDB	
Neo4j	
Amazon DynamoDB	
Cosmos	

1.2 Given a scenario, develop, modify, and run SQL code.	Covered in
Data definition language (DDL)	Lesson 3, Topic A
Data manipulation language (DML)	Lesson 3, Topic B
Set-based logic	Lesson 4, Topic C
Transaction control languages (TCLs)	Lesson 3, Topic C
Atomicity, consistency, isolation, durability (ACID) principles	Lesson 2, Topic A
American National Standards Institute (ANSI) Structured Query Language (SQL)	Lesson 2, Topic A
Programming with SQL	Lesson 4, Topic C
Triggers	Lesson 4, Topic D
Stored procedures	
Functions	
Views	

1.3 Compare and contrast scripting methods and scripting environments.	Covered in
Script purpose and runtime location	Lesson 7, Topic A
Server side	
Client side	
Languages	Lesson 2, Topic B
PowerShell	
Python	
Command line scripting	Lesson 2, Topic B
Linux	
Windows	

1.4 Compare and contrast scripting methods and scripting environments.	Covered in
Object-relational mapping (ORM)	Lesson 4, Topic B
Hibernate	
Entity Framework	
Ebean	
Process to gauge impact	Lesson 4, Topic B
Review SQL code generated by ORM	
Confirm validity of code	
Determine impact to database server	
Provide solutions/alternate approach, as needed	

2.0 Database Deployment	
2.1 Compare and contrast aspects of database planning and design.	**Covered in**
Requirements gathering	Lesson 5, Topic B
Number of users	
Storage capacity	
Size	
Speed	
Type	
Database objectives	
Use cases/purposes	

2.1 Compare and contrast aspects of database planning and design.	Covered in
Database architecture factors	Lesson 1, Topic C
Inventory of needed assets	Lesson 5, Topic A
Gap analysis	Lesson 5, Topic B
Cloud-based vs. on-premises	Lesson 5, Topic C
Types of cloud-hosted environments	
Platform as a service (PaaS)	
Software as a service (SaaS)	
Infrastructure as a service (IaaS)	
Database schema	
Logical	
Physical	
View	
Data sources	
System specifications	
Design documentation	Lesson 1, Topic C
Data dictionary	Lesson 5, Topic C
Entity relationships	
Data cardinality	
System requirements documentation	

2.2 Explain database implementation, testing, and deployment phases.	Covered in
Acquisition of assets	Lesson 6, Topic A
Phases of deployment	Lesson 6, Topic A
Installation and configuration	Lesson 6, Topic C
Database prerequisites	
Provisioning	
Upgrading	
Modifying	
Importing	
Database connectivity	Lesson 7, Topic A
Database server location	
Networking concepts	
Domain name service (DNS)	
Client/server architecture	
Firewall and perimeter network considerations	
Static and dynamic Internet protocol (IP) addressing	
Ports/protocols	

2.2 Explain database implementation, testing, and deployment phases.	Covered in
Testing	Lesson 6, Topic B
Database quality check (columns, tables, fields)	
Code execution	
Schema meets original requirements	
Syntax errors	
Stress testing	
Stored procedures stress test	
Application stress test	
Notification triggers and alerts	
Version control testing	
Regression testing	
Negative testing	
Validate	Lesson 6, Topic C
Index analysis	Lesson 8, Topic B
Data mapping	
Data values	
Queries	
Referential integrity/integrity validation	
Scalability validation	

3.0 Database Management and Maintenance	
3.1 Explain the purpose of monitoring and reporting for database management and performance.	**Covered in**
System alerts/notifications	Lesson 6, Topic A
Growth in size/storage limits	Lesson 7, Topic B
Daily usage	Lesson 14, Topic A
Throughput	
Resource utilization	
Central processing unit (CPU) usage	
Memory	
Disk space	
Operating system (OS) performance	
Baseline configuration/trending	
Monitoring job completion/failure	
Replication	
Database backup alerts	
Transaction log files	Lesson 7, Topic B
System log files	Lesson 7, Topic B
Deadlock monitoring	Lesson 7, Topic C
Connections and sessions	Lesson 7, Topic B
Concurrent connections	
Failed/attempted connections	

3.2 Explain common database maintenance processes.	Covered in
Query optimization	Lesson 8, Topic B
Index optimization	Lesson 8, Topic B
Patch management	Lesson 8, Topic A
Updates	
Security and maintenance patches	
Database integrity checks	Lesson 8, Topic C
Table locking techniques	
Data corruption checks	Lesson 8, Topic C
Periodic review of audit logs	Lesson 10, Topic D
Performance tuning	Lesson 8, Topic B
Transaction volumes	
Load balancing	Lesson 8, Topic B
Change management	Lesson 10, Topic E
Release schedules	
Capacity planning	
Upgrades	
Vulnerability remediation	
Change approval	
Communication	
Database refresh	

3.3 Given a scenario, produce documentation and use relevant tools.	Covered in
Data dictionaries	Lesson 5, Topic C
Entity relationship diagram (ERD)	Lesson 1, Topic C
Maintenance documentation	Lesson 5, Topic C
Standard operating procedure (SOP) documentation	Lesson 5, Topic C
Organizational compliance documentation	
Third-party compliance documentation	
Tools	Lesson 5, Topic C
Unified modeling language (UML) editors	
Word processors	
Spreadsheet tools	

3.4 Given a scenario, implement data management tasks.	Covered in
Data management	Lesson 1, Topic C
Modify data	Lesson 3, Topic A
Define data	Lesson 3, Topic B
Append columns	Lesson 3, Topic D
Create new data sets	Lesson 4, Topic A
Views/materialized views	
Index creation	
Create data tables	
Create data relationships	
Data redundancy	Lesson 1, Topic C
Data sharing	Lesson 9, Topic E

4.0 Data and Database Security	
4.1 Explain data security concepts.	**Covered in**
Encryption	Lesson 10, Topic A
Data in transit	
Client-side encryption	
In-transit encryption	
Server-side encryption	
Data at rest	
Data masking	Lesson 10, Topic B
Data discovery	
Data destruction techniques	Lesson 10, Topic C
Data security audit	Lesson 10, Topic D
Expired accounts	
Connection requests	
Code auditing	Lesson 10, Topic E
SQL code	
Credential storage checks	

4.2 Explain the purpose of governance and regulatory compliance.	Covered in
Data loss prevention	Lesson 9, Topic A
Data retention policies	Lesson 9, Topic B
Data classification	Lesson 9, Topic C
Personally identifiable information (PII)/personal health information (PHI)	
Payment Card Industry Data Security Standard (PCI DSS)	
Global regulations	Lesson 9, Topic D
General Data Protection Regulation (GDPR)	
Regional regulations	Lesson 9, Topic D

4.3 Given a scenario, implement policies and best practices related to authentication and authorization.	Covered in
Access controls Rights and privileges Least privilege	Lesson 11, Topic B
Password policies	Lesson 11, Topic C
Service accounts	Lesson 11, Topic D
Identity and access management	Lesson 11, Topic A

4.4 Explain the purpose of database infrastructure security.	Covered in
Physical Access control Biometrics Surveillance Fire suppression Cooling system	Lesson 12, Topic A
Logical Firewall Perimeter network Port security	Lesson 12, Topic B

4.5 Describe types of attacks and their effects on data systems.	Covered in
SQL injection	Lesson 13, Topic A
Denial of service (DoS) attacks	Lesson 13, Topic B
On-path attacks	Lesson 13, Topic C
Brute-force attacks	Lesson 13, Topic D
Phishing	Lesson 13, Topic E
Malware Ransomware	Lesson 13, Topic F

5.0 Business Continuity	
5.1 Explain the importance of disaster recovery and relevant techniques.	**Covered in**
Disaster recovery (DR) planning	Lesson 14, Topic A
DR documentation	
Manuals	
System security plan	
Continuity of operations plan	
Build documentation	
DR techniques	
Replication	
Log shipping	
High availability	
Mirroring	
DR plan testing	Lesson 14, Topic B
Recovery point objective (RPO)	
Recovery time objective (RTO)	
Transition/failback to normal operations	Lesson 14, Topic C

5.2 Explain backup and restore best practices and processes.	**Covered in**
Full backup vs. incremental	Lesson 15, Topic A
Differential	
Database dumping	Lesson 15, Topic A
Schedule and automate backups	Lesson 15, Topic B
Test backups	Lesson 15, Topic B
Validate backup hash	Lesson 15, Topic B
Storage location	Lesson 15, Topic C
On-site vs. off-site	
Retention policy	Lesson 15, Topic C
Purge vs. archive cycles	

Solutions

Review Activity: Relational and Non-Relational Databases

1. **A relational database uses _____ to establish relationships that control how certain data relates to data in other tables.**

primary keys and foreign keys

2. **A non-relational database is often referred to as what?**

NoSQL

3. **What are the four basic categories of non-relational databases?**

Document-oriented databases, key-value stores, column-oriented databases, and graph databases

4. **Which category of non-relational database tends to run alongside a relational database?**

Graph database

5. **What type of software maintains relational databases?**

A relational database management system (RDBMS)

Review Activity: Different Types of NoSQL Databases and Tools

1. **In a document-oriented database, what is a group of documents with content that would be considered similar in nature called?**

A collection

2. **Where is data stored in key-value stores?**

In memory

3. **When navigating a key-value store, what challenge will you likely encounter, and how is it resolved?**

You are unable to directly search for a specific value in key-value stores. To get around this disadvantage, you must search for the keys to then gain the values.

4. **What type of data is not compatible with column-oriented databases?**

Online transactional processing

5.   In graph databases, data is stored in what form?

Nodes and connections

Review Activity: Relational Database Design

1.   What are the three types of entity relationship models?

Conceptual data model, logical data model, and physical data model

2.   What is the objective of an entity relationship model?

To visualize the database schema

3.   What are the two types of key fields used to join tables?

Primary key and foreign key

4.   What must be set in a database design in order to establish relationships between records?

Referential integrity

5.   When dealing with a many-to-many relationship, what serves as a bridge?

Another table that uses the associated keys from each table that's related

Review Activity: Other Data Systems

1.   Data warehouses can leverage which technology to make data processing more effective?

Online analytical processing (OLAP)

2.   What characteristic of both data warehouses and data marts allows reporting without requiring access to every single source system?

They are both structured.

3.   True or false: A data lake is a subset of a data warehouse.

False. A data mart is a subset of a data warehouse, not a data lake.

4.   Which data system stores data that has been collected but is not yet ready for cleaning or analysis?

A data lake

Review Activity: Standards and Principles

1. **When a data system is an ANSI-compliant database, this means that it conforms to what standard for the SQL language?**

ANSI

2. **Which organization publishes standards for an international audience?**

ISO

3. **Which principles exist to guide us in developing data systems that create complete transactions?**

ACID principles

4. **Which principle takes the "all or nothing" approach to records being entered into a data system?**

Atomicity

5. **What are some benefits of the ACID principles?**

Answers may vary: Ensures that all requirements of a record have been completed before the record is saved; in the event of system failure, a transaction won't be partially saved.

Review Activity: Operating Systems and Command Line Scripting

1. **Which two operating systems are most commonly used?**

Windows and Linux

2. **What program layer executes the commands that you input?**

The shell

3. **Which command program allows for multiple commands to be executed at once?**

PowerShell

4. **Which program is the Linux equivalent to PowerShell?**

Bash scripts

5. **Which popular programming language has packages that allow DBAs to use the language to interact with their data systems?**

Python

6. **What language is used to create scripts and statements that allow you to query and retrieve data from databases?**

SQL

Review Activity: Data Definition Language

Answer the following questions:

1.   True or False: DDL is a separate language from SQL.

False. DDL is the commands within SQL, and not a separate language.

2.   A database and its contents are referred to as what?

Objects

3.   When creating a table, what must be paired with the column name?

Data type

4.   Which clause would be used to change columns in a table: `ALTER` or `TRUNCATE`?

`ALTER`

5.   What clause is used to remove a table entirely?

`DROP TABLE`

Review Activity: Data Manipulation Language

1.   Which clause is most commonly used to query data?

`SELECT`

2.   When adding new records into a new table with the values of the original table, which clause should be used?

`INSERT`

3.   A business rule has been set that all fields containing a price of 5.00 be changed from 5.00 to 7.00. Which clauses should be used to change the values from 5.00 to 7.00?

`UPDATE` and `WHERE`; you need the `WHERE` clause to filter to the products with a price of 5.00 and the `UPDATE` clause to change the price for those products.

4.   To remove a specific value from a table or view, what three clauses are needed?

`DELETE`, `FROM`, and `WHERE`

5.   What clause is used when working with aggregate functions?

`GROUP BY`

6.   When working with `GROUP BY`, which clause is used when data needs to be filtered?

`HAVING`

Review Activity: Transactions

1. **When a user has a transaction open, what limitation is applied to other users?**

Those records are locked and cannot be edited.

2. **Which command can set the data to the previous set of changes?**

ROLLBACK

3. **Which command is used to open a transaction?**

BEGIN TRANSACTION

4. **Which command is used to mark the end of a transaction?**

COMMIT

5. **When you are not opening transactions to perform changes, but instead using DML to perform and execute changes, what type of commit is this?**

AUTO COMMIT

Review Activity: Data Management Tasks

1. **When a data type is designed as text or string but you need it for calculation like sum or average in your query, what do you do to prepare it for calculation?**

Convert it to the correct data type in the query that's using it.

2. **Where are data types for fields designed for the database?**

They are designed in the table for each field typically during the design process.

3. **What SQL clause do you use to append tables/queries into a single data set?**

UNION

4. **What type of table can you design that is only temporarily available and can be used to create a smaller subset of data for use?**

Temporary tables

5. **Which type of fields are automatically indexed when designed?**

Primary keys

6. **DBAs will often share data with others in the organization. What is the primary reason for this?**

DBAs will often have more access to the data systems than employees, and often have higher permissions than most in the organization.

Review Activity: Views

1. A read-only query of data at a specific point in time is known as what?

A snapshot

2. A read-only query that typically updates with the source data is known as what?

A materialized view

3. When a data set is needed by multiple people who may not know how to query data, you can save the script as what type of object?

Views

4. What are some of the benefits of creating views?

Answers may vary: Views can be made available to others who do not have access to the data otherwise, can be used by other applications for reporting, and provide data to others without requiring them to perform or even know how to query.

Review Activity: Object-Relational Mapping

1. A company website has a java front end and an SQL back end. What should we use to enable communication between these two different applications/systems?

Object-relational mapping software

2. Which type of ORM is used with .NET?

Entity Framework

3. What is the point of ORM?

To map data between different front-end and back-end systems, so developers can create and maintain data-oriented applications with less code

Review Activity: Program with SQL

1. Using the GROUP BY **command in an SQL query performs the grouping and provides a total. What type of logic is this an example of?**

Set-based logic

2. **Unlike a view, a _____ can be used for steps that regularly need to occur and in a certain order.**

stored procedure

3. **A discount table has a date field for expiration and a Boolean field for active or inactive status. When the date passes on the discount, and we want to make the status "inactive," what function would be helpful?**

A trigger

4. **What consideration should be made for using a trigger that runs automatically?**

Whether or not it slows the processing down

Review Activity: Functions

1. **When you need to use a function that is not already available as a system function, what type of function would you build?**

User-defined function

2. **Which type of user-defined function is often used to perform complex calculations on the input values or perform some special formatting on the returned value?**

Scalar functions

3. **Pre-built functions are also know as what?**

System functions

4. **What type of function would you use to calculate the total number of days between when an order was shipped and when it was delivered?**

A date function, which is a type of built-in function. If you are being more specific, in SQL Server the date function is known as Date Diff.

5. `CASE WHEN Color = 1 THEN 'RED' ELSE 'Gray'` **is an example of a(n) _____ function.**

logical

Review Activity: Types of Architecture

1. **A database hosted on-site is known as what?**

On-premise

2. **What are the three database storage solutions?**

On-premise database, cloud database, and hybrid

3. **An organization will typically utilize a _____ solution when they require an infrastructure for various types of technical projects.**

platform as a service (PaaS)

4. **True or False: Software as a service (SaaS) is only consumed by IT users.**

False. It is also consumed by the public, such as for streaming services and online shopping.

5. **What main responsibilities exist for a DBA using an infrastructure as a service (IaaS) solution?**

Answers may vary: Gathering technical requirements; assessing the infrastructure needs; managing data, backup, and recovery; evaluating the processing power necessary for your database systems

Review Activity: Data System Requirements

1. **What is the first critical step when gathering requirements?**

Determine the objective of the database.

2. **If an employee database is being developed, what additional user-related information might be needed?**

Answers may vary: Permissions, read-write access, system user requirements, number of users, user groups

3. **Two companies are merging, and a new database is being created to accommodate historical data. The objective, users, and data sources have been outlined. What other consideration must be taken?**

Storage requirements

4. **When moving a legacy system to a new system, which requirement is critical for populating the data?**

Gathering data sources

Review Activity: Documentation Requirements

1. **What type of documentation ensures consistency in the execution of processes by those across an organization?**

Standard operating procedures (SOPs)

2. **What information might be contained within a data dictionary?**

Answers may vary: Table design, relationships, key fields, views, data types, data properties

3. **What process is used to ensure minimum system requirements are met before implementation can occur?**

Inventory and gap analysis

4. **What is Unified Modeling Language (UML)?**

A general development and modeling language in software and database engineering

Review Activity: Deployment

1. **What is the default server authentication?**

Windows Authentication

2. **A recently restored database would not have which property value?**

Last backup date

3. **When an organization acquires a new company, what will the DBA spend time reviewing to prepare for a merge?**

The system specifications and requirements for the systems that the acquired organization is using

4. **What types of deployments might you work with as a DBA?**

New data systems and upgrading data systems

5. **When configuring a database, you will spend time reviewing what options?**

Database properties

Review Activity: Testing and Other Quality Measures

1. **What quality checks are performed to ensure a database meets the original requirements?**

Answers may vary: Checking that tables and views are defined, tables and views have appropriate settings to the logical design, tables and views have appropriate attributes, the views execute the expected results, necessary functions and store procedures are available

2. **Using a** WHERE **clause in a** GROUP BY **is an example of what type of error?**

A syntax error

3. **The CustomerID field should only contain numbers. A test is performed on the Product table to see if a value of 'Betty' will be accepted into the CustomerID field. Which type of testing is this considered?**

Negative testing

4. **A product is being deployed that is expected to result in an increase in sales. What type of testing should be performed before deployment?**

Stress testing

5. **A company that has introduced an internship program uses a stored procedure to update the Employees table. Which type of testing should be performed to ensure the Employees table remains up to date?**

Regression testing

6. **What is the primary benefit of version control?**

Tracking changes

Review Activity: Validation Techniques and Methods

1. **Which data quality constraint follows business rules on naming conventions for a field?**

Data consistency

2. **A subtotal field set as a text type would likely lead to which data quality issue?**

Data accuracy

3. **Data validation is the process of confirming _____.**

the type, structure, and accurate representation of the data

4. **Which process entails confirming the type, structure, and accurate representation of the data?**

Verification

5. **Confirming the record count for data before and after a data transfer is a step in which process?**

Data verification

6. **A confirmation email is sent when a new user signs up for a newsletter. This is an example of which process?**

Automated validation

Review Activity: Database Connectivity Needs

1. **What type of architecture is the roadmap for how the server communicates with the client?**

Client -server architecture

2. **Suppose visitors to the toy company's website can sign up for an account and save their wish-listed items. Which side of the architecture would this website represent?**

Client-side

3. **A database is stored in what type of server?**

Database server

4. **The toy company has created a new website. What service will convert it to an IP address?**

Domain name service (DNS)

Review Activity: Monitor the Database

1. **What information is available through the Log File Viewer?**

Answers may vary: Events and errors, log files, messages

2. **True or False. A connection cannot have multiple sessions.**

False. A connection will have at least one session, and every query or other connection (like Power BI) that uses the connection will also generate a session.

3. **A sales team of 50 people connects to a report with data sourced from SQL Server that is accessible on their company desktops, tablets, and mobile devices. In order to accommodate the possibility of each user connecting on each of their devices, what should the minimum for concurrent connections be set at?**

150

4. **What is a drawback of automatic size increase settings?**

Answers may vary: Cost, timeout on transactions, unnecessary data being retained, performance issues

5. **SQL Server Management Studio's Performance Dashboard report focuses primarily on which performance metrics?**

CPU utilization for all databases on the server

6. **A database has a sales table that is updated each night through a scheduled job. You check this process and determine that it has failed. Which SQL application is responsible for managing this job?**

SQL Server Agent

Review Activity: Deadlocks

1. **A _____ causes processes to be blocked, slows performance of the data system, and creates rollbacks in the data.**

deadlock

2. **When experiencing a deadlock, or any lock for that matter, where might you begin to identify the cause of the issue?**

Reviewing active transactions

3.   What is the most typical cause of deadlocking?

Deadlocking typically occurs when the locking of two or more co-dependent tasks causes them to block each other.

4.   Why is it important to address deadlocks?

They must be addressed so the data system can continue to operate and perform as expected.

Review Activity: Patch Management

1.   What process involves installing an update to fix an issue that has been discovered?

Patch management

2.   What critical type of patch should be implemented immediately?

Security patch

3.   True or False: Only operating systems receive patches.

False. Systems designed with any software can receive updates and patches.

Review Activity: Database Performance

1.   What are issues that can lead to poor database performance?

Answers may vary: Poor database design, too many or too few indexes, using sorts in large data sets, a complicated stored procedure that is slowing down performance

2.   Which process is used to determine how an application or data system performs with a large number of users?

Scalability validation

3.   True or False: You can have many clustered indexes in a table.

False. You can have many non-clustered indexes, but each table will have only one clustered index, and traditionally it's the primary key.

4.   What can you include when you execute a query to determine if and where it is slow?

Adding the actual execution plan

5.   What is the process of optimizing performance also known as?

Performance tuning

Review Activity: Database Integrity

1. We would establish a _____ to ensure that a record has a unique identifier.

primary key

2. True or False: Creating a relationship between two tables allows us to add records to one of the tables without needing a primary key in the other table.

False. When a relationship is established, it ensures that a record with the associated primary key field exists in one table before it will allow you to add the record to the other table.

3. What prevents a table from being dropped or altered while in use by another person?

Table locking

4. Which Database Console Command for SQL Server can be used to check for corruption?

DBCC CHECKDB

Review Activity: The Importance of Protecting Data and Preventing Data Loss

1. What is the first step that must be taken in order to determine how to properly protect data?

Identifying the location and type of data, and classifying what data is considered private data

2. What are two states of data that must be considered when determining how to protect data?

Data at rest and data in transit

3. Data in which state is vulnerable to an on-path attack?

Data in transit

4. Why are traditional perimeter security measures no longer sufficient for protecting network endpoints?

Modern networks consist of endpoint devices that are often outside of the boundaries of perimeter security. Devices such as smartphones, tablets, and equipment with network-enabled sensors all become endpoints that might be outside the traditional network perimeter.

5. What is often the biggest threat to data security?

Employees

Review Activity: Data Retention Policies

1.   What does the data destruction part of the data retention policy specify?

How to destroy or properly dispose of data when it is no longer necessary.

2.   Why should a data retention policy be reviewed periodically?

Changes to regulations or laws may require data to be treated differently, and changes will be necessary to the policies to reflect these required changes.

3.   What does the retention period dictate?

How long inactive data must be kept before being destroyed or disposed of.

4.   True or False: A data retention policy only applies to digital data.

False. A data retention policy applies to all private data, whether it is digitally stored or physically stored in the form of printed reports, forms, and emails.

5.   What are the ramifications of violating a data retention policy?

Heavy fines can be imposed on the violating company, and individuals may be fired.

Review Activity: Data Classification

1.   What is one of the major variables that affects whether data needs to be protected and how it must be protected?

The classification of the data

2.   Data that is not generally known and should be considered secret is generally categorized as what?

Confidential data

3.   What is the primary law that oversees the use of, access to, and disclosure of PHI in the United States?

HIPAA

4.   What regulation defines how credit and debit card data must be stored, transmitted, and destroyed?

PCI DSS

5.   What is data that can be used to identify a unique individual?

Personally identifiable information (PII)

Review Activity: Global Jurisdiction and Regional Regulations

1. **True or False: Regulations only affect companies located in the regions in which the regulations are defined.**

False. Companies outside the region where the regulation is defined might be affected by the regulation if that company does business with individuals in the region.

2. **Why do many organizations find identifying the privacy laws that affect their business challenging?**

Many organizations do business on the Internet, which means they can reach customers all across the globe and thus may be affected by one or more regulations that exist in the regions those customers reside in.

3. **How do we know that the importance of privacy and data protection is increasingly being recognized by local, regional, and global organizations and governments?**

Many of the world's countries (over 70%) are putting legislation in place to address data privacy and protection.

Review Activity: Third-Party Agreements and Release Approvals

1. **What type of agreement exists between an organization and another party that requires both parties to avoid disclosing information to any other party?**

A nondisclosure agreement (NDA)

2. **What type of agreement exists between two parties that specifies what data will be exchanged and how that data can be used?**

A data use agreement

3. **What type of nonbinding agreement establishes the rules of engagement between two parties, defining roles and expectations?**

A memorandum of understanding (MOU)

4. **True or False: It's a best practice to share your insights with everyone as you discover them.**

False. There are several reasons for this. One reason is that not everyone has the same access to information. Also, in many cases release approvals are required before any information can be released outside the team.

Review Activity: Data Encryption

Answer the following questions:

1. What is data in transit?

Data in transit is data that is actively moving from one location to another.

2. If a storage drive containing data is being transferred to an off-site archive facility, is that data considered data at rest or data in motion?

Data at rest; while the storage media might physically be moving from one place to another, the data itself is stationary on that device and must be protected as data at rest.

3. What protocols are used to establish secure communication to protect data in transit?

IPSec or TLS protocols are used to encrypt data while it is being transferred between locations.

4. What type of cryptography is used to protect data at rest, usually chosen for speed and responsiveness?

Symmetric cryptography, which uses a single key for both encryption and decryption.

Review Activity: Data Masking

1. As an alternative to encryption, what de-identification method can be used to protect data that is currently in use?

Data masking

2. Between pseudonymization and anonymization, which data masking technique is reversible?

Pseudonymization

3. Which data masking technique has been used if the original user data is not recoverable from the masked value?

Anonymization, because the data is truly randomized and cannot be reversed.

Review Activity: Data Destruction Techniques

1. What data destruction technique sanitizes the data but leaves the storage media usable for future storage?

Logical destruction leaves the physical storage media usable while destroying the data on the media.

2.   True or False: Deleting a file completely removes the data from the storage media.

False. When you delete a file, the only thing removed is the master file table reference, which tells the operating system where the file was located.

3.   In what scenario is logical data destruction absolutely not an option?

When the storage device is unusable and not able to be written to. Logical destruction requires the device to be usable in order to destroy the data.

4.   Why shouldn't most companies attempt physical device destruction themselves?

Most organizations do not have the specialized equipment needed to perform physical destruction techniques. Further, some techniques (like incineration and chemical destruction) may produce environment, health, and safety hazards.

5.   What organization is responsible for creating the most widely known and globally recognized standards for data destruction?

The National Institute of Standards and Technology (NIST)

Review Activity: Data Access Auditing

1.   Auditing _____ will identify accounts that have more permissions than is necessary.

account authorization

2.   In what scenario might you leave an expired account found during an audit as-is?

The account has expired during its user's prolonged inactivity (such as during an extended leave of absence), yet that user is expected to return to work at some point

3.   An attacker attempting to gain access to your database performs attacks very early in the morning, hoping to go unnoticed. What type of audit activity could help catch this?

Auditing connection requests, as this identifies connection attempts occurring at times that are out of the ordinary

4.   True or False: When an audit identifies an anomaly, it means that illicit activity was occurring.

False. There are times when an anomaly identified in an audit is completely benign and can be explained.

Review Activity: Code Auditing and Change Management

1.   What is considered best practice when identifying the number of people that can make changes to database code?

Best practice is to keep the number of people that can make changes to the database to a minimum.

2. **Besides restricting the number of people who can make changes to database code, what else can be done to help prevent code changes from inadvertently exposing private data?**

Put in place a process where the DBA can review code changes prior to them being deployed to the database.

3. **How does a database identify itself to another database or system it integrates with?**

Stored credentials are used by a database to identify itself to other systems or databases.

4. **What is the main goal of change management?**

Change management provides a process to better control and monitor the changes made to a database, its configuration, and its code.

Review Activity: Identity and Access Management

1. **What type of authentication factor is a user's fingerprint?**

Something you are/do authentication, also called a biometric factor

2. **What is the difference between authentication and authorization?**

Authentication is the process of determining whether someone is who they say they are.

Authorization is the process of giving a user permission to access a specific resource or function.

3. **Which security policy requires more than one factor to be used during user authentication?**

Multifactor authentication (MFA)

4. **What are the four main processes of an identity and access management (AIM) system?**

Identification, authentication, authorization, and accounting

Review Activity: Access Controls

1. **True or False: Permissions can contain one or more roles that allow a user to perform certain actions in a database.**

False. Roles contain permissions, or privileges, that allow a user to perform certain actions.

2. **What is occurring when a user acquires more and more rights over time, either directly or by being added to security groups and roles?**

Authorization creep

3. **What activity involves planning what privileges should be assigned to a user prior to adding them to a database?**

Change management

4. **When following the principle of _____, a user is granted sufficient rights to perform their job and no more.**

least privilege

Review Activity: Password Policies

1. **What element of a password policy requires a password to contain at least one number?**

Password complexity

2. **True or False: The latest recommendations from NIST suggest that password complexity rules should not be enforced.**

True. This is because when complex passwords are required, people tend to write their passwords down or use poor passwords.

3. **True or False: Global regulations do not factor into the creation of password policies.**

False. As an example, PCI DSS requires certain minimum password policies.

Review Activity: Service Accounts

1. **What type of account represents nonhuman users?**

The service account

2. **Unlike a standard user account and a traditional service account, a service account does not have a _____.**

password

3. **What types of standard user accounts should never be used as service accounts?**

Administrative accounts and highly privileged accounts

4. **What are some ways in which built-in service accounts might be abused?**

Answers may vary: Privilege escalation, spoofing, non-repudiation, information disclosure

Review Activity: Physical Security

1. **How is protecting the door to a server room similar to authenticating a user's access to data?**

In both cases, a user will be required to provide one or more factors to prove they are who they say they are, in order to prove that the user is authorized to access the room or data.

2.   True or False: Surveillance systems should be monitored 24/7 for best results.

False. It is not always necessary for surveillance systems to be monitored at all times. Surveillance events can be recorded and reviewed regularly, or as needed.

3.   Why is fire such a serious concern in server rooms or datacenters?

If a fire breaks out in a server room or datacenter, the equipment (and data contained within) could be destroyed, or even the facility itself. The data may be lost completely or may take a lengthy amount of time to recover.

4.   Why is providing an adequate cooling solution necessary in a server room or datacenter?

Servers and other electrical equipment are susceptible to overheating, which can damage or destroy the equipment and the data contained within.

Review Activity: Logical Security

1.   What is the difference between physical access and logical access to a database server?

Physical access requires a person to be in the same physical vicinity of the server. Logical access involves accessing the server across a network.

2.   What is the basic job of a firewall?

Filter incoming and outgoing network traffic

3.   Why is a network firewall preferred over a host firewall?

A network firewall blocks traffic before it ever gets to the server, while a host firewall requires the communication to arrive at the server before it can be blocked.

4.   What is the basic function of a perimeter network?

To enable secure connectivity between a cloud or public network and your on-premise or private network

Review Activity: The SQL Injection Attack

1.   What type of damage can an SQL injection attack cause?

SQL injection attacks can be used to destroy data, exfiltrate data, or bypass data restrictions.

2.   Modifying an SQL query to use _____ is one way to mitigate an SQL injection attack.

parameterized queries

3.   True or False: Sanitizing user input before it is used in an SQL query can lead to a SQL injection attack.

False. Unsanitized user input can lead to an SQL injection attack, and sanitizing the user input before it is used in a query can help mitigate an attack.

4.   **How can the principle of least privilege help us mitigate SQL injection damage?**

Answers may vary: If the user account has a restricted set of permissions, the attacker will be limited to acting only on that set of data or functions if an SQL injection attack does occur.

Review Activity: The Denial of Service (DoS) Attack

1.   **What are two common methods of performing a DoS attack?**

Flooding services or crashing services

2.   **What is it called when an attacker utilizes multiple systems to orchestrate a synchronized DoS attack against a single target?**

A distributed denial of service (DDoS)

3.   **What is one of the most effective strategies a DBA can use to defend against DoS attacks?**

Reducing the attack surface

Review Activity: The On-Path Attack

1.   **What are the two steps of a typical on-path attack?**

Interception and decryption

2.   **An attacker may use pop-ups on a legitimate website that present a sense of urgency in order to get a user to do what?**

Click a link to download malware

3.   **True or False: All legitimate websites will have a valid certificate that proves the identity of the owner of the website.**

True. A certificate proves that the identity of the website's owner has been verified by a certificate authority.

4.   **If your connection to a website is secure, the URL will start with what?**

https://

Review Activity: The Brute Force Attack

1.   **What can a user do when creating a password to make brute force attacks less successful?**

Create a more complex password using recommended industry standard password policies (like using numbers, uppercase and lowercase letters, symbols, and increased length).

2.   **What type of brute force attack involves using a password that was leaked from one website to try to log into other websites?**

Credential stuffing

3.   **What type of brute force attack uses a list of common passwords as a starting point to guess passwords?**

Dictionary attack

4.   **What mitigation technique prevents a brute force attack from trying a large number of successive passwords against a user account?**

Locking an account after a certain number of failed login attempts

Review Activity: Social Engineering Attacks

1.   **In which principle of social engineering does the attacker try to pressure their target by demanding a quick response?**

Scarcity and urgency

2.   **What is a red flag that can help identify a message as a phishing attempt?**

Answers may vary: Some red flags include links that are disguised to appear as though they lead to a secure location, but the URL does not match the correct site; asking you to call some number for urgent action; creating a sense of urgency by requiring you to take action in a short period of time, such as within 24 hours; spelling or grammar mistakes; containing unexpected attachments, especially HTML files, executable files, and old Microsoft Office document formats.

3.   **What is the most effective strategy for preventing social engineering attacks?**

Regular cybersecurity awareness education programs

4.   **How is spear phishing different than phishing?**

A spear phishing message is tailored to address a specific target user by including information that demonstrates more familiar knowledge of that user.

Review Activity: Malware

1.   **What type of malware uses encryption to block legitimate users from being able to access their systems, devices, or information?**

Ransomware

2.   **What type of malware disguises itself as something a user wants, like a software update or the latest popular game, to gain access to a system?**

Trojans

3. **How does implementing best practice password policies help mitigate malware?**

Strong passwords prevent further attacks using stolen credentials or privilege escalation.

4. **What practice can help every user in an organization become an effective member of the security team?**

Regular cybersecurity awareness training, which helps users recognize unusual behavior in emails, websites, and links.

Review Activity: Disaster Recovery

1. **True or False: A business continuity plan is sufficient to respond to any disastrous event.**

False. The business continuity plan focuses on operational continuity, while a disaster recovery plan focuses on infrastructure and technical system restoration. It is ideal for an organization to have both.

2. **A disaster recovery plan should address any type of disaster that can interrupt what?**

Normal business operations

3. **True or False: If an organization's entire infrastructure is outsourced to the cloud, they do not need a disaster recovery plan.**

False. An organization still needs a disaster recovery plan in order to define how to communicate with the cloud provider during the recovery process, as well as to define the business continuity plan.

4. **Why do we refer to a disaster recovery plan as a living document?**

A disaster recovery plan is a living document because it must be regularly updated with any major change in an organization's infrastructure, team structure, business needs, technology, and more.

5. **What is the primary difference between log shipping and mirroring?**

Mirroring allows for automatic failover to an alternate database, while log shipping must be manually failed over.

6. **High availability implies the elimination of what?**

Single points of failure

Review Activity: DR Plan Testing

1. **What disaster recovery testing technique results in the production system as well as the recovery system being active at the same time?**

Parallel testing

2. **What is defined as the amount of time in which an organization's system must be recovered in a disaster recovery operation?**

Recovery time objective (RTO)

3. **What disaster recovery testing technique involves role-playing through the DR plan components?**

Simulation testing

4. **What is defined as the maximum amount of data loss a business can tolerate after a disruption has occurred before an organization's business processes are negatively affected?**

Recovery point objective (RPO)

Review Activity: Transition/Failback to Normal Operations

1. **Failback can only happen after _____.**

failover

2. **A retrospective allows an organization to determine what about the implementation of a disaster recovery plan?**

What worked well and what did not, thus identifying areas of the DR plan that could use improvement

3. **True or False: The specifications of failover systems are typically designed to support 100% of the typical production load.**

False. Failover systems are typically specified to support some percentage less than 100% of the typical production load and are intended to be temporary solutions.

Review Activity: Types of Backups

1. **What type of backup produces smaller files but requires a longer restoration time?**

Incremental backups produce smaller files, but since many backup files may need to be restored, the restoration time is longer.

2. **Synthetic full backups combine the benefits of what two backup types?**

Full backup and incremental backups

3. **A differential backup requires what type of backup to have been run prior?**

A full backup

4. **What is a best practice when utilizing differential backups?**

It is best practice to periodically run full backups in order to create new starting points for future differential backups.

Review Activity: A Backup Strategy

1. **Why is it important to consider storage location when creating a backup strategy?**

Where your backup is being stored can affect cost and also the time it takes to retrieve the backup, which means the storage location may influence the type of backup you run, or how often you run it.

2. **When testing a backup, which method offers the most thorough validation?**

Restoring the backup to a test database

3. **When creating a scheduling strategy, what consideration is largely driven by RPO?**

How often a database backup should be performed/scheduled

4. **What can be utilized to ensure that a backup is performed when it is supposed to, regardless of the day or time?**

Automation

Review Activity: Store and Purge Backups

1. **Which type of storage provides a more rapid recovery time?**

On-site storage

2. **Which type of storage typically provides a more secure storage environment?**

Off-site storage

3. **Which type of storage provides extra protection against disasters?**

Off-site storage provides a safe location for the backup data if an organization's primary location is destroyed.

4. **What best practice ensures backups are available in the event that a disaster destroys an organization's primary location?**

Storing at least one backup off-site, and rotating off-site and on-site stored backups

5. **True or False: Purge cycles only affect data that has been archived.**

False. Some organizations may purge certain production data without archiving it first.

6. **How can purging or archiving data negatively affect production systems?**

Purging and archiving data can consume a larger than normal amount of resources, thus negatively impacting production systems.

Glossary

3-2-1 backup rule A best practice maxim stating that at any given time there should be at least three copies of data stored on two media types, with one copy held off-site.

acceptable use agreement An agreement that describes not only how data can be used, but also for what purpose.

actual execution plan The actual process used to execute a query.

aggregate functions Functions that are written for all or a group of records, as opposed to a single record.

American National Standards Institute (ANSI) A private, non-profit organization that administers and coordinates the U.S. voluntary standards and conformity assessment system.

archiving The long-term storage of data that must be retained but is rarely accessed.

Atomicity, Consistency, Isolation, Durability (ACID) Principles that exist to provide guidance for developing data systems that create complete transactions and reject partial transactions from being recorded.

attack surface The points at which a network or application receive external connections or inputs/outputs that are potential vectors to be exploited by a threat actor.

authentication A method of validating a particular entity's or individual's unique credentials.

authorization The process of determining what rights and privileges a particular entity has.

authorization creep Occurs when individuals acquire and retain more than the bare minimum privilege required to do their job, usually as a result of their job role changing.

automated validation Using the power of software to ensure data achieves a validated result.

block erase A method of data destruction that uses device-specific commands to wipe flash-memory-based storage media.

bring your own device (BYOD) The practice of allowing the employees of an organization to use their own computers, smartphones, or other devices for work purposes.

brute force attack A type of password attack where an attacker uses an application to exhaustively try every possible alphanumeric combination to crack encrypted passwords.

business continuity plan (BCP) Documentation that identifies how business processes should deal with both minor and disaster-level disruption by ensuring that there is processing redundancy supporting the workflow.

capacity planning The process of determining the production capacity needed by a database to meet the demands of changes being implemented.

cardinality How many possible occurrences of one entity can be associated with the number of occurrences in another.

change management The process through which changes to the configuration of information systems are implemented as part of the organization's overall configuration management efforts.

checksum The output of a hash function.

client-server An administration paradigm where some host machines are designated as providing server and services and other machines are designated as client devices that only consume server services.

client-side In a web application, input data that is executed or validated as part of a script or process running on the client.

cloud database A database hosted by a cloud computing vendor who installs, configures, and manages server and system infrastructure.

cold site A predetermined alternate location where a network can be rebuilt after a disaster.

collection A group of documents with contents that would be considered similar in nature.

command prompt A basic shell interpreter for Windows.

Completely Automated Public Turing test to tell Computers and Humans Apart (CAPTCHA) A type of challenge-response system that is difficult for a computer to respond to successfully. CAPTCHAs and reCAPTCHAs are used for purposes such as preventing bots from creating accounts on web forums and social media sites to spam them.

confidential data Data that is material to the operations of a business or government organization, which cannot be learned outside of that business or government organization.

connection The physical connection/communication to the database server.

cooling systems Mechanical systems that typically use air or liquid to maintain a temperature that is lower than the ambient temperature.

credential stuffing A brute force attack in which stolen user account names and passwords are tested against multiple websites.

crytographic erase A method of data destruction in which the media encryption key (MEK) for the encrypted target data is destroyed, making recovery of the decrypted target data infeasible.

data anonymization The process of removing personally identifiable information from data sets, so that the individuals the data describes remain anonymous.

data at rest Information that is primarily stored on specific media, rather than moving from one medium to another.

data corruption Errors that occur during writing, reading, storage, transmission, or processing which can produce damaged data, data loss, or corrupted data systems.

data definition language (DDL) SQL commands that are used to create, alter, and remove database objects.

data dictionary A document that serves as the authority on all definitions that have been agreed upon for the organization, as well as key metrics.

data exfiltration The process by which an attacker takes data that is stored inside of a private network and moves it to an external network.

data governance The overall management of the availability, usability, and security of the information used in an organization.

data in transit Information that is being transmitted between two hosts, such as over a private network or the Internet. Also known as data in motion.

data lake A technology for storing large amounts of structured and unstructured types of information in their original format.

data lakehouse A data management system that combines the best of both data warehousing and data lakes.

data leakage The unauthorized transfer of data from inside an organization to a destination outside its secured boundary.

data loss prevention (DLP) A software solution that detects and prevents sensitive information from being stored on unauthorized systems or transmitted over unauthorized networks.

data manipulation language (DML) Commands within the SQL language used for manipulating objects in a database.

data mart A subset of the data warehouse that is dedicated to a specific department or group.

data masking A de-identification method where generic or placeholder labels are substituted for real data while preserving the structure or format of the original data. Also known as data obfuscation.

data pseudonymization A data masking method that allows you to switch the original data set (for example, an email or a name) with an alias or pseudonym.

data retention The process an organization uses to maintain the existence of and control over certain data in order to comply with business policies and/or applicable laws and regulations.

data sovereignty In data protection, the principle that countries and states may impose individual requirements on data collected or stored within their jurisdiction.

data use agreement An agreement between two parties about the exchange of data that specifies what data will be shared and how that data can be used.

data validation The process of confirming the type, structure, and accurate representation of the data.

data verification The process of confirming that the data is accurate or true.

data warehouse A technology that is dedicated to the storage of company data from a wide range of sources for reporting and decision-making purposes.

database as a service (DBaaS) A cloud service that provides a database infrastructure to the customer. DBaaS is considered a type of platform as a service deployment.

database mirroring A database replication technique in which a secondary database is kept in sync with a primary database by transferring all changes in the primary database directly to the secondary database, so it is always up to date and available in case the primary database fails.

database refresh Updating a database from the testing environment to the production environment.

database schema The structure and design of a database.

database transactions Statements of one or more DML commands that perform a change or update to record(s).

deadlocking A situation that occurs when two or more transactions prevent each other from continuing because each of the two transactions has locked a resource the other needs to continue.

degaussing The process of decreasing or eliminating a remnant magnetic field.

denial of service (DoS) attack Any type of physical, application, or network attack that affects the availability of a managed resource.

dictionary attack A type of brute force attack where an attacker attempts to crack a password-protected security system with a "dictionary list" of common words and phrases used by businesses and individuals.

differential backup A job type in which all selected files that have changed since the last full backup are backed up.

disaster recovery (DR) plan A documented and resourced plan showing actions and responsibilities to be used in response to critical incidents.

distributed database management system (DDBMS) A system that manages a collection of multiple logically interrelated databases, which may be physically located in various locations (even across the world) in a manner that makes it appear as a single database to users.

distributed denial of service (DDoS) attack An attack that involves the use of infected Internet-connected computers and devices to disrupt the normal flow of traffic of a server or service by overwhelming the target with traffic.

domain name service (DNS) A service that maps fully qualified domain name labels to IP addresses on most TCP/IP networks, including the Internet.

dump file A list of SQL statements containing a record of the table structure and the data from a database.

entity relationship diagram (ERD) The pictorial representation of a database model.

estimated execution plan The estimated requirements for executing a query.

failback The return of service to a previously failed asset, making it an active node once more.

failover A technique that ensures a redundant component, device, or application can quickly and efficiently take over the functionality of an asset that has failed.

fire suppression Fire detection and suppression systems are mandatory in most public and private commercial premises. Water-based fire suppression is a risk to computer systems, both in the event of fire and through the risk of flood. Alternatives include dry pipe and gas-based systems.

firewall Software or a hardware device that protects a network segment or individual host by filtering packets to an access control list.

foreign key A field or fields that are primary in another table.

full backup A job type in which all selected files, regardless of prior state, are backed up.

functions Blocks of code that can be reused to perform a specific task.

gap analysis An analysis that measures the difference between the current and desired states in order to help assess the scope of work included in a project.

General Data Protection Regulation (GDPR) A regulation in EU law that imposes data privacy obligations onto organizations anywhere, so long as they target or collect data related to people in the EU.

Health Insurance Portability and Accountability Act (HIPAA) U.S. federal law that protects the storage, reading, modification, and transmission of personal health care data.

heating, ventilation, and air conditioning (HVAC) Control systems that maintain an optimum heating, cooling, and humidity level working environment for different parts of the building.

high availability A metric that defines how closely systems approach the goal of providing data availability 100% of the time while maintaining a high level of system performance.

hot site A fully configured alternate processing site that can be brought online either instantly or very quickly after a disaster.

identity and access management (IAM) A security process that provides identification, authentication, and authorization mechanisms for users, computers, and other entities to work with organizational assets like networks, operating systems, and applications.

incremental backup A job type in which all selected files that have changed since the last full or incremental backup (whichever was most recent) are backed up.

index analysis The process of analyzing indexes for performance.

indexing A field property setting that tells the database that a field needs to be used to create an index.

infrastructure as a service (IaaS) A cloud service model that provisions virtual machines and network infrastructure.

International Organization for Standardization (ISO) An organization that supports worldwide standards for a large range of activities and which companies can certify they have obtained.

joins A join line between fields in a query.

jurisdiction The official power to make legal decisions and judgments.

key-value pairs A type of non-relational structure that establishes a unique identifier or key field and maps it to a value.

key-value store A set of key-value pairs.

latency Time taken for a signal to reach the recipient, measured in milliseconds. Latency is a particular problem for two-way applications, such as VoIP (telephone) and online conferencing.

least privilege A basic principle of security stating that something should be allocated the minimum necessary rights, privileges, or information to perform its role.

load balancer A type of switch, router, or software that distributes client requests between different resources, such as communications links or similarly configured servers. This provides fault tolerance and improves throughput.

load balancing The technique of distributing network traffic or computing workload among multiple devices in a network.

log shipping The process of automating the backup of transaction log files on a primary database server and then restoring them onto a standby, or alternate, server.

logical destruction The destruction of data only, but not the physical storage media on which it is stored.

malware Software that serves a malicious purpose, typically installed without the user's consent (or knowledge).

many-to-many relationship Many records in a table are associated to many other records in other tables.

memorandum of understanding An acceptable use agreement that establishes the rules of engagement between two parties and defines roles and expectations.

mixed authentication mode An authentication mode that enables logging into the database with both Windows and SQL Server authentication methods. Also known as mixed mode.

multifactor authentication (MFA) An authentication scheme that requires the user to present at least two different factors as credentials; for example, something you know, something you have, something you are, something you do, and somewhere you are. Specifying two factors is known as "2FA."

National Institute of Standards and Technology (NIST) A nonregulatory government agency that develops technology, metrics, and standards to drive innovation and economic competitiveness at U.S.-based organizations in the science and technology industry.

negative testing A testing process for unexpected use of a program or data for a data system.

nondisclosure agreement (NDA) An agreement that defines the conditions under which an entity cannot disclose information to outside parties.

non-relational database A database system that stores data without the use of relational database models.

normalized data Data that is structured for optimal storage and use within a program.

object-relational mapping (ORM) A programming technique for converting data between a relational database and the storage used by an object-oriented programming language.

off-site storage A physical location outside of the main site that stores copies of data. Also known as off-site backup.

one-to-many relationship One record in a table is associated with multiple records in another table or tables.

one-to-one relationship One record in a table is associated with only one record in another table.

online analytical processing (OLAP) A class of software that allows complex analysis to be conducted on large databases without negatively affecting transactional systems.

online transactional processing (OLTP) A class of software that allows large numbers of database transactions in real time, typically over the Internet.

on-path attack An attack where the threat actor makes an independent connection between two victims and is able to read and possibly modify traffic. Also known as a Man-in-the-Middle (MitM) attack.

on-premise database A database hosted on an organization's own server.

on-site storage Storage owned, operated, and maintained by an organization and located on the organization's property.

open source Computer code that embodies the principles of both the free software movement and the open source software (OSS) movement.

password policy A security policy that promotes user selection of strong passwords by specifying a minimum password length, requiring complex passwords, requiring periodic password changes, and placing limits on the reuse of passwords.

patch A small unit of supplemental code meant to address either a security problem or a functionality flaw in a software package or operating system.

patch management Identifying, testing, and deploying OS and application updates. Patches are often classified as critical, security-critical, recommended, and optional.

Payment Card Industry Data Security Standard (PCI DSS) An information security standard for organizations that process credit or bank card payments.

performance tuning The process of increasing the performance of a data system by ensuring queries are performing at optimal levels.

perimeter network A segment isolated from the rest of a private network by one or more firewalls that accepts connections from the Internet over designated ports.

personal health information (PHI) Data that can be used to identify an individual and includes information about past, present, or future health as well as related payments and data used in the operation of a healthcare business.

personally identifiable information (PII) Data that can be used to identify or contact an individual (or, in the case of identity theft, to impersonate them).

phishing An email-based social engineering attack in which the attacker sends email from a supposedly reputable source, such as a bank, to try to elicit private information from the victim.

physical access controls Controls that restrict, detect, and monitor access to specific physical areas or assets through measures such as physical barriers, physical tokens, or biometric access controls.

physical destruction Using drilling, shredding, incineration, or degaussing of storage media before recycling or repurposing to minimize the risk of leaving persistent data remnants.

physical media destruction The process of rendering a device completely unusable.

platform as a service (PaaS) A cloud service model that provisions application and database services as a platform for development of apps.

port security A security feature that prevents a device attached to a switch port from communicating on the network unless it matches a given MAC address or other protection profile.

PowerShell A command shell and scripting language built on the .NET Framework that use cmdlets for Windows automation.

primary account number (PAN) A 14-, 15-, 16-, or even up to 19-digit number generated as a unique identifier designated for a primary account. Also called payment card numbers, as they are found on payment cards like credit and debit cards.

primary key A unique identifier for a record that cannot contain duplicates and is used to reference a record.

private data Any personal, personally identifiable, financial, sensitive, or regulated information (including credit or debt card information, bank account information, or usernames and passwords).

production database A database available to end users for normal, day-to-day use.

purging The process of completely removing, or deleting, data that is no longer required.

Python A high-level programming language that is widely used for automation.

quality data Data that has integrity and is accurate, complete, and consistent.

query execution plan The order of steps in which a query is processed.

rainbow table A tool for speeding up attacks against passwords by precomputing possible hashes.

recovery point objective (RPO) The longest period that an organization can tolerate lost data being unrecoverable.

recovery time objective (RTO) The maximum time allowed to restore a system after a failure event.

referential integrity Established to maintain that records are not orphaned by ensuring the proper table has the key field.

regression testing The process of testing an application after changes are made to see if these changes have triggered problems in older areas of code.

relational database A structured database in which information is stored in tables where columns represent typed data fields and rows represent records. Tables can have relationships, established by linking a unique primary key field in one table with the same value in a foreign key field in another table. The overall structure of a particular database and its relations is called a schema.

relational database management system (RDBMS) Software that maintains relational databases.

release schedule Defines the features or changes that will be released in future updates.

replication Automatically copying data between two processing systems either simultaneously on both systems (synchronous) or from a primary to a secondary location (asynchronous).

retention policy A policy that dictates for how long information needs to be kept available on backup and archive

systems, and how it must be disposed of. This may be subject to legislative requirements.

retrospective A process improvement session where an agile team reflects on the previous sprint and identifies ways that the team can improve how they work together.

scalability The property by which a computing environment is able to gracefully fulfill its ever-increasing resource needs.

schema A named container for database objects, which allows you to group objects into logical collections.

server-side In a web application, input data that is executed or validated as part of a script or process running on the server.

service account A host or network account that is designed to run a background service, rather than to log on interactively.

session The authenticated interaction with the database server for the exchange of information.

set-based logic SQL operations that are performed on a complete set of rows, returning a subset of the rows that are affected, or a single result.

shell A program that can be used to execute commands usually through a command line interface.

smishing A form of phishing that uses SMS text messages to trick a victim into revealing information.

snapshot A read-only copy of the data that was queried.

social engineering An activity where the goal is to use deception and trickery to convince unsuspecting users to provide sensitive data or to violate security guidelines.

software as a service (SaaS) A cloud service model that provisions fully developed application services to users.

software development lifecycle A process used by software development teams to design, develop, and test high quality software.

spear phishing An email-based or web-based form of phishing that targets specific individuals.

specifications Descriptions of the work to be done or the service or product to be provided; they define the requirements that must be met in exacting detail.

standard operating procedures (SOPs) Documentation of best practices and work instructions used to perform a common administrative task.

stored procedures A set of pre-compiled database statements that can be used to validate input to a database.

stress test A software testing method that evaluates how software performs under extreme load.

structured query language (SQL) Programming and query language common to many relational database management systems.

Structured Query Language (SQL) injection attack An attack that injects a database query into the input data directed at a server by accessing the client side of the application. Also known as SQL injection.

symmetric cryptography A two-way encryption algorithm where encryption and decryption are performed by a single key, shared between the system performing the encryption and the system performing the decryption. Also known as symmetric encryption.

synthetic full backup A job type that combines incremental backup jobs to synthesize a full backup job.

system requirements The minimum specifications for CPU speed, memory, and disk capacity for installing an OS or app.

system security plan A formal document that provides an overview of the security requirements for an information system and describes the security controls in place or planned for meeting those requirements. Also known as a security recovery plan.

temporary table A table that is stored on the database server until the user disconnects from the server, existing only during the session in which it was created.

throughput The amount of data transfer supported by a link in typical conditions. This can be measured in various ways with different software applications.

traditional service account A standard user account that is configured to run a service or application server software.

transaction control language (TCL) Commands used to help a user manage all the transactions taking place in a database.

trigger A type of stored procedure that will automatically run when a specified event triggers the action to occur.

two-factor authentication (2FA) A strong authentication mechanism that requires a user to submit two different types of credentials, such as a fingerprint scan plus PIN. Often, the second credential is transmitted via a second trusted device or account. This is also referred to as 2-step verification.

Unified Modeling Language (UML) A general development and modeling language in software and database engineering. Also known as source control.

version control The practice of ensuring that the assets that make up a project are closely managed when it comes time to make changes.

video surveillance A physical security control that uses cameras and recording devices to visually monitor the activity in a certain area.

vishing A social engineering attack where the threat actor extracts information while speaking over the phone or leveraging IP-based voice messaging services (VoIP).

vulnerability remediation A plan that includes the discovery, prioritization, elimination, and monitoring of a vulnerability to ensure a successful long-term fix.

warm site An alternate processing location that is dormant or performs noncritical functions under normal conditions, but which can be rapidly converted to a key operations site if needed.

Index